Christ's Prophetic Plans

A Futuristic Premillennial Primer

CHRIST'S PROPHETIC PLANS

General Editors

JOHN MACARTHUR

&

RICHARD MAYHUE

Moody Publishers
Chicago

Editor: Christopher Reese
Interior design: Ragont Design
Cover design: Kirk DouPonce, DogEared Design
Cover image: iStockPhoto/CG Textures

Library of Congress Cataloging-in-Publication Data

Christ's prophetic plans : a futuristic premillennial primer / John MacArthur and Richard Mayhue, general editors.
p. cm.
Includes bibliographical references and index.
ISBN 978-0-8024-0161-8
1. Millennialism. I. MacArthur, John II. Mayhue, Richard.

BT892.C47 2012
236'.9--dc23

2011031866

We hope you enjoy this book from Moody Publishers. Our goal is to provide high-quality, thought-provoking books and products that connect truth to your real needs and challenges. For more information on other books and products written and produced from a biblical perspective, go to www.moodypublishers.com or write to:

Moody Publishers
820 N. LaSalle Boulevard
Chicago, IL 60610

1 3 5 7 9 10 8 6 4 2

Printed in the United States of America

CONTRIBUTORS

John MacArthur, D.D., President, The Master's College and Seminary. General Editor.

Dr. MacArthur is pastor-teacher of Grace Community Church in Sun Valley, California, author, conference speaker, and featured teacher with *Grace to You*. He is best known for the MacArthur New Testament Commentary series and the *MacArthur Study Bible.* John and his wife, Patricia, have four grown children. They also enjoy the enthusiastic company of their fifteen grandchildren.

Richard Mayhue, Th.D., Executive Vice President and Dean, The Master's Seminary. General Editor.

Dr. Mayhue has authored, contributed to, and/or edited twenty-five books, including *How to Study the Bible* and *1 & 2 Thessalonians: Triumphs and Trials of a Consecrated Church*, plus numerous periodical and journal articles. He is active in Bible conference ministries. Dick and his wife, "B," have two grown children and two grandsons.

Michael Vlach, Ph.D., Associate Professor of Theology, The Master's Seminary.

Dr. Vlach has authored several books, including *Has the Church Replaced Israel?* Mike and his wife, Holly, have four young children.

Nathan Busenitz, Th.M., Instructor of Theology, The Master's Seminary.

Nathan serves on the pastoral staff at Grace Community Church. He has written several books, including *Reasons We Believe* and *Men of the Word*. He is currently pursuing his Th.D. in historical theology. Nathan and his wife, Beth, have four young children.

Matthew Waymeyer, Th.M., Instructor of Bible Exposition, The Master's Seminary.

Matt served as senior pastor of Community Bible Church in Vista, California, for seven years before returning to The Master's Seminary to teach full time in 2011. He is the author of *Revelation 20 and the Millennial Debate* and *A Biblical Critique of Infant Baptism*. He is currently pursuing his Th.D. in systematic theology at TMS. Matt and his wife, Julie, have five young children.

CONTENTS

Preface 9
John MacArthur

Futuristic Premillennialism Chart 12
Richard Mayhue

Introduction – Why Study Prophecy? 13
Richard Mayhue

1. What Is Dispensationalism? 19
Michael Vlach

2. What Is Dispensationalism Not? 39
Michael Vlach

3. Why Futuristic Premillennialism? 59
Richard Mayhue

4. Why a Pretribulation Rapture? 85
Richard Mayhue

5. What about Israel? 103
Michael Vlach

6. What about Revelation 20? 123
Matthew Waymeyer
7. Does Calvinism Lead to Futuristic Premillennialism? 141
John MacArthur
8. Does the New Testament Reject Futuristic Premillennialism? 161
John MacArthur
9. Did the Early Church Believe in a Literal Millennial Kingdom? 177
Nathan Busenitz
10. How Certain Is Futuristic Premillennialism? 197
John MacArthur

Recommended Resources 205
Glossary 207
Scripture Index 211

PREFACE

John MacArthur

Imagine this hypothetical dialogue about the millennium between two well-meaning Christians. One proudly announces, "I am 'Promillennial'—whatever it involves, although we cannot really know for certain, I am for it!" The other responds, "Well, I am 'Panmillennial' —while prophecy is not that important for Christians to know, I am sure it will all 'pan out' in the end." The first Christian concludes that one cannot know for sure what Scripture says about prophetic issues and the second declares that it is not important to know. Both are sincere, but woefully ignorant that Scripture abounds with information on future things. Biblically minded Christians do not have to settle for such a muddled approach to eschatology.

This *primer* (basic, introductory book) intends to provide a clear and convincing biblical explanation for the interpretive approach to Scripture that results in a knowable *futuristic* view of Christ's *millennial* reign on earth, the certain validity of God's promises to future Israel, and the crucial differences between Israel (as a people and a nation) and the NT church. Dispensationalism, a broader term than "Futuristic Premillennialism" (see chart on p.12), distinctively sees a major contrast between God's past and future dealings with national Israel and His dealings with the church.

Futuristic Premillennialism serves as a more focused term than dispensationalism when addressing prophetic issues. Futuristic Premillennialism stands in contrast to Historic (or Covenant) Premillennialism, which is one of three major prophetic options associated with Covenant theology, along with Amillennialism and Postmillennialism.

Many people do not understand the term "dispensationalism." But, it does not have to be this way. Dispensationalism basically results from:

1. Interpreting Scripture normally just as one would any other piece of literature, resulting in . . .
2. Understanding the restoration promises to Israel in the Old Testament and the events of John's Revelation as future, which necessitates . . .
3. Distinguishing decisively between Israel and the church.

As a result, dispensationalists teach that Israel was the primary focus of God's redemptive plan in one dispensation. The church, consisting of redeemed people including Jews and Gentiles, is the focus in another. All dispensationalists believe at least one dispensation is still future—the one thousand-year reign of Christ on earth, known as the millennium, in which Israel will once again take a central role and during which Jesus Christ will reign on earth from His throne in Jerusalem as King of kings and Lord of lords.

Dispensations are not merely periods of time, but different administrations in the outworking of God's redemptive purpose. It is essential to understand that the way of salvation—by God's grace alone through faith alone in Jesus Christ—remains the same in each dispensation. God's redemptive plan never changes, but the way He administers it has varied from one dispensation to another. And succeeding generations from Moses' time understood this truth in more detail as God's revelation progressed, especially with the New Testament.

Dispensationalists expect that all of God's future covenant

promises (Abrahamic, Davidic, and New) to Israel will be literally fulfilled—including promises of earthly blessings and an earthly messianic kingdom. God promised Israel that they would possess the Promised Land for an extended time and that their descendants would flourish (Gen. 13:14–17; Ex. 32:13). Scripture foretells that Messiah will rule over the kingdoms on earth for one thousand years from Jerusalem (Zech. 14:9–11; Rev. 20:1–6). Old Testament prophecy explains that all Israel will one day be returned to the Promised Land (Amos 9:14–15), the temple will be rebuilt (Ezek. 40:1–48:35), and the people of Israel will be redeemed (Jer. 23:6; Rom. 11:26–27).

Futuristic Premillennialism results from understanding and applying prophetic Scripture in a way that is most consistent with the normal or literal[1] approach for interpreting Scripture. If one is careful not to presume a certain prophetic outcome before interpreting the Bible and employs a consistent, normal approach to understanding Scripture, then Futuristic Premillennialism will be embraced as God's true prophetic plan of the ages. The chapters that follow define and discuss the biblical approach that leads to Futuristic Premillennialism, starting with why a Christian should study biblical prophecy and concluding with convincing reasons for the certainty of Christ's future, earthly return.

Notes

1. E. R. Craven, ed., "The Revelation of John," in *Lange's Commentary on the Holy Scriptures* (1874; repr., Grand Rapids: Zondervan, 1968), 12:98. "The *Literalist* (so called) is not one who denies that *figurative* language, that *symbols*, are used in prophecy, nor does he deny that great *spiritual* truths are set forth therein; his position is, simply, that the prophecies are to be *normally* interpreted (i.e., according to the received laws of language) as any other utterances are interpreted—that which is manifestly literal being regarded as literal, that which is manifestly figurative being so regarded."

FUTURISTIC PREMILLENNIALISM

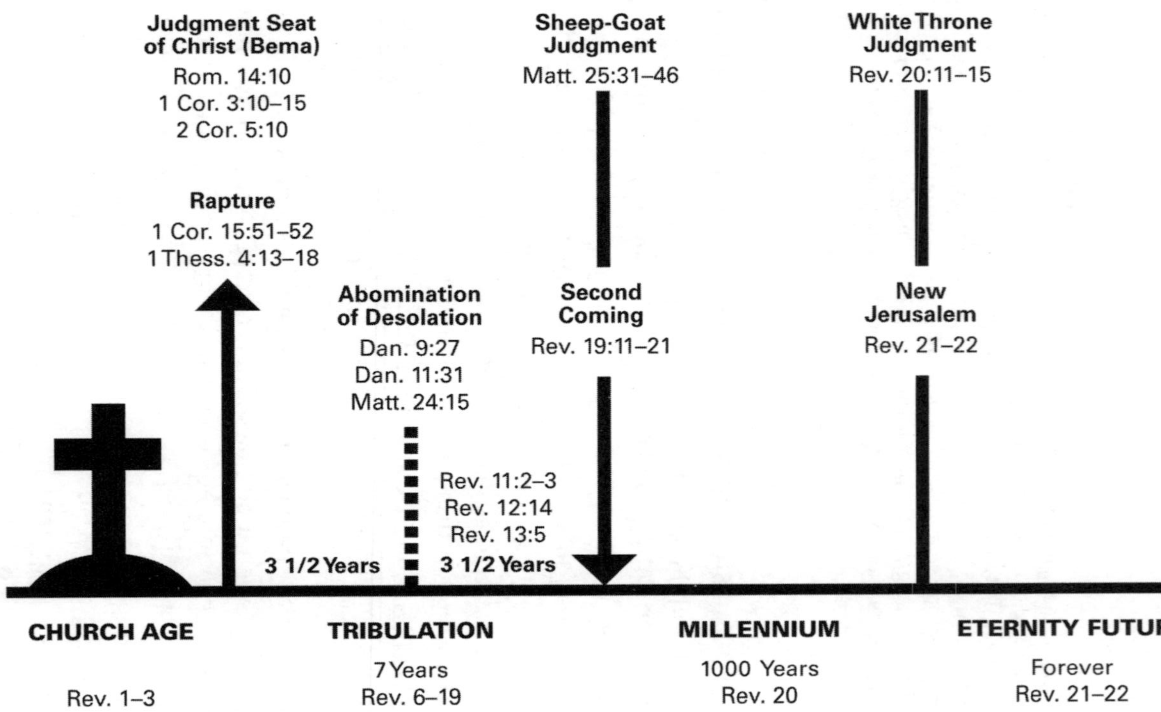

Taken from Richard Mayhue, *First and Second Thessalonians*, Christian Focus, 1999.

Introduction

WHY STUDY PROPHECY?

Richard Mayhue

I have heard on more than one occasion, as I am sure that you have also, people who declare with confidence that the study of biblical prophecy is a secondary matter or even optional when contrasted with pursuing supposedly weightier doctrines like that of Christ or of salvation.

Now it is true that a person does not enter into a redemptive relationship with God by believing in any particular prophetic scenario, but rather by placing one's faith in the person, cross work, and resurrection of the Lord Jesus Christ (Rom. 10:9–10; Eph. 2:8–10). Further, a true believer does not necessarily mature in the Christian faith by embracing a certain eschatological scheme (2 Pet. 3:14–18).

However, the Bible does exhort believers to interpret the Bible with precision (2 Tim. 2:15). Scripture teaches that God's Word is profitable for teaching, reproof, correction, and instruction in righteousness (2 Tim. 3:16–17). God even promises His blessing on those who know and obey the things of biblical prophecy (Rev. 1:3; 22:7). On the other hand, nowhere does either the Old Testament or New Testament even hint that prophetic portions are exempted from careful, detailed knowing and understanding.

Think about this for a moment—who planned, revealed, and then executes God's prophetic intentions? Is it not God alone who planned the end from the beginning (Is. 46:9–11)? Did God reveal in Scripture anything that is so unimportant or trivial that it could be considered optional for Christians (Acts 20:20, 25, 27)? Where in the Bible does one find the slightest hint that prophetic matters should be avoided because they might be controversial or hard to understand?

So let's compare the assertion that the study of biblical prophecy is secondary at best with Scripture in order to discover God's perspective on the matter. Why should Christians study prophetic Scriptures?

Scriptural Content

Scripture teems with prophetic material.[1] Not even one slight indication exists that prophetic materials are to be ignored, be set aside, or be marginalized. Consider the following facts about eschatological information in the Bible, especially Christ's second coming.

- In Scripture, 62 (94 percent) out of 66 books contain predictive information (Ruth, Song of Solomon, Philemon, and 3 John are the exceptions).
- In the Bible, 27 percent (8352) of all verses (31,124) refer to prophetic issues.
- In God's Word, 22 percent (1845) of all prophetic verses (8352) refer to Christ's second coming.
- All nine authors of the NT mention Christ's second coming.
- Next to the subject of faith/salvation, the theme of Christ's second coming is most prominent in the NT.
- Only three out of 27 NT books do not mention Christ's second advent (Philemon, 2 John, and 3 John).
- Of the approximately 333 specific biblical prophecies dealing with Christ's two advents, one-third deal with His first coming and two-thirds deal with His second coming.

Scriptural Commands and Commendations

Throughout the Bible, God commands and commends the thorough study of all Scripture. This theme appears in the teaching of Christ, the preaching of the apostles, plus the writings of Paul and Peter.

Matthew 28:19–20
"Go therefore and make disciples of all the nations, baptizing them in the name of the Father and the Son and the Holy Spirit, *teaching them to observe all* that I commanded you; and lo, I am with you always, even to the end of the age."

Acts 2:42
"They were continually devoting themselves to *the apostles' teaching* and to fellowship, to the breaking of bread and to prayer."

Acts 5:20
"Go, stand and speak to the people in the temple *the whole message of this Life.*"

Acts 20:27
"For I did not shrink from declaring to you *the whole purpose of God.*"

2 Timothy 2:15
"Be diligent to present yourself approved to God as a workman who does not need to be ashamed, *accurately handling the word of truth.*"

1 Peter 1:10–11
"As to this salvation, the prophets who prophesied of the grace that would come to you *made careful searches and inquiries, seeking to know* what person or time the Spirit of Christ within

them was indicating as He predicted the sufferings of Christ and the glories to follow." (All emphases added.)

Scriptural Consequences

The life benefits and spiritual blessings from knowing and obeying prophetic Scripture enriches every committed Christian. The following ten positive outcomes representatively illustrate how and why the Bible extols studying biblical prophecy.

- Fulfilled prophecy proves that the Bible is true and inspires confidence in Scripture (Acts 13:32–35 with 42–44).
- The study of prophecy promotes obedience and provides the gateway to God's blessing (Rev. 1:3; 22:7).
- Prophetic material equips the saints to refute those who mock the Christian hope (2 Pet. 3:1–13).
- Prophecy provides answers to theological questions that are found nowhere else, such as the relationship between the resurrection and the rapture (1 Thess. 4:13–18).
- Prophecy gives motivation for holy living today (1 Thess. 5:6–9; Titus 2:11–14; 2 Pet. 3:11–13).
- Prophetic expectation purifies (1 John 3:2–3).
- Prophecy provides a biblical basis for prayer (cf. Dan. 9:1–19 with Jer. 25:11–12).
- Prophecy is a source of hope, comfort, and encouragement for the Christian (1 Thess. 4:18; 5:11; Titus 2:13).
- The study of prophecy encourages patient endurance in the midst of suffering and trials (James 5:7–11).
- Prophecy assures that unjust persecution of the righteous will be avenged by God (2 Thess. 1:5–10).

Scriptural Confidence

What will be the ultimate fruit from studying God's Word, including those portions explaining Christ's second coming? The prophet

Isaiah crafted the answer with these infallible words given originally to Israel, but which continue to be true today.

> For as the rain and the snow come down from heaven, and do not return there without watering the earth and making it bear and sprout, and furnishing seed to the sower and bread to the eater; so will My word be which goes forth from My mouth; it will not return to Me empty, without accomplishing what I desire, and without succeeding in the matter for which I sent it. (Is. 55:10–11)

Notes

1. J. Barton Payne, *Encyclopedia of Biblical Prophecy* (Grand Rapids: Baker, 1973). Pages 674–75 provide extensive biblical statistics.

Chapter One

What Is Dispensationalism?

Michael Vlach

Nine-year-old Danny came bursting out of Sunday school like a wild stallion. His eyes were darting in every direction as he tried to locate either mom or dad. Finally, after a quick search, he grabbed his daddy by the leg and yelled, "Man, that story of Moses and all those people crossing the Red Sea was great!" His father looked down, smiled, and asked the boy to tell him all about it.

"Well, the Israelites got out of Egypt, but Pharaoh and his army chased after them. So the Jews ran as fast as they could until they got to the Red Sea. The Egyptian Army was getting closer and closer. So Moses got on his walkie-talkie and told the Israeli Air Force to bomb the Egyptians. While that was happening the Israeli Navy built a pontoon bridge so the people could cross over. They made it!"

By now old dad was shocked. "Is *that* the way they taught you the story?"

"Well, no, not exactly," Danny admitted, "but if I told it to you the way they told it to us, you'd *never* believe it, Dad."

That is the way that many believe dispensationalists treat prophetic Scripture. They have to jazz it up to make it believable. But nothing could be further from the truth. With a few fringe exceptions, dispensationalists want to say no more and no less than what the Bible reports. The design of this chapter is to set the record straight about dispensationalism.

Much has been written about dispensationalism in general and Futuristic Premillennialism in particular. In order to accurately understand dispensationalism, one must have a proper perspective on what this theological approach actually involves. So, this chapter will set forth dispensationalism's essential or foundational characteristics. These beliefs define the heart of dispensational theology—perspectives that differentiate dispensationalism from other systems of theology, especially Covenant theology. In order to accomplish this, we will survey how leading representatives of dispensationalism have defined dispensational theology, followed by a list of unique features that comprise the core beliefs of dispensationalism.

Recent Background to Dispensationalism

In his 1965 book *Dispensationalism Today*, Charles Ryrie offered three points that he considered to be the essentials or *sine qua non* of dispensationalism: (1) a distinction between Israel and the church, (2) an approach to hermeneutics called literal interpretation, and (3) the belief that the underlying purpose of God in the world is God's glory.[1] Ryrie's *sine qua non* was well received by most dispensationalists and was often used as a starting point for explaining dispensationalism. Opponents also grappled with Ryrie's findings and used them as starting points for critiquing dispensational theology.

In his 1988 article "Systems of Discontinuity," John Feinberg presented six "essentials of dispensationalism": (1) belief that the Bible refers to multiple senses of terms like "Jew" and "seed of Abraham"; (2) an approach to hermeneutics that emphasizes that the Old Testament be taken on its own terms and not reinterpreted in light of the New Testament; (3) belief that Old Testament promises will be fulfilled with national Israel; (4) belief in a distinctive future for ethnic Israel; (5) belief that the church is a distinctive organism; and (6) a philosophy of history that emphasizes not just soteriology and spiritual issues but social, economic, and political issues as well.[2]

Although not giving a list of "essentials," Craig Blaising and Darrell Bock offered a list of "common features" of dispensationalism in their 1993 book *Progressive Dispensationalism*. These features included: (1) the authority of Scripture; (2) dispensations; (3) uniqueness of the church; (4) practical significance of the universal church; (5) significance of biblical prophecy; (6) Futurist Premillennialism; (7) imminent return of Christ; and (8) a national future for Israel.[3]

Not all the characteristics mentioned in the above lists, particularly those of Blaising and Bock, are unique to dispensationalism. Many nondispensationalists, for instance, believe in the authority of Scripture, dispensations, and the significance of biblical prophecy. Some nondispensationalists also believe in Premillennialism—holding that a future millennial kingdom will be established with the second coming of Christ. George Ladd, for instance, held to Historic Premillennialism while also arguing against Futuristic Premillennialism. Thus, being a Premillennialist does not necessarily make one a dispensationalist.

Ryrie's claim that a defining mark of dispensationalism is belief that the underlying purpose of God in the world is God's glory has been controversial. When properly understood, Ryrie correctly pointed out that dispensationalists have a broader understanding of God's purposes in the world than nondispensationalists who often focus mostly on the doctrine of salvation. But the wording Ryrie offered was not helpful. Many nondispensationalists take the glory of God seriously, and to them Ryrie seemed to claim that dispensationalists valued the glory of God more than nondispensationalists. But telling a Covenant theologian that he did not emphasize the glory of God as much as a dispensationalist was not received well. So while there was a sense in which Ryrie was correct, his wording was not as clear as it could have been. John Feinberg was more precise when he pointed out that dispensationalists promote a philosophy of history that emphasizes the *spiritual* and *physical* implications of God's purposes more so than their nondispensational counterparts. Dispensationalists emphasize the fulfillment of both the spiritual and physical promises of the biblical covenants.[4] In this sense, dispensationalists are more holistic in their understanding of God's kingdom purposes than many nondispensationalists.

When examined closely, however, the lists of Ryrie, Feinberg, and Blaising and Bock reveal three important marks of dispensationalism. First, all mention the uniqueness of the church as a characteristic of dispensationalism. Though disagreement may exist on some details of this distinction, dispensationalists are agreed that the church began at Pentecost (see Acts 2) and is not to be identified as Israel.[5] Thus, all dispensationalists reject "replacement theology" or "supersessionism" in which the church is said to have permanently *replaced* or *superseded* the nation Israel as the people of God.

Second, Ryrie, Feinberg, and Blaising and Bock point out that dispensationalists believe in a future for the nation Israel. Dispensationalists assert that Old Testament promises and covenants made with Israel will be fulfilled in the future. Though dispensationalists may disagree as to how much the church also participates in the Old Testament promises and covenants, they are agreed that Israel will experience a future salvation and restoration.

Both Ryrie and Feinberg mention a third area—a dispensational approach to hermeneutics—as somehow being distinctive to dispensationalism. For Ryrie, dispensationalists interpret the Bible in a consistently literal (i.e., normal) manner while non-dispensationalists do not.[6]

Feinberg claims that Ryrie was "too simplistic" in stating the matter this way.[7] According to Feinberg, the issue of hermeneutics "is not an easy issue," and he points out that many nondispensational theologians claim to interpret the Bible literally. Their literalism, though, differs at points from the literal approach of dispensationalists. Thus, for Feinberg, "The difference is not literalism v. non-literalism, but different understandings of what constitutes literal hermeneutics."[8]

According to Feinberg, the difference between dispensational and non-dispensational hermeneutics is found in three areas: (1) the relation of the progress of revelation to the priority of one testament over the other; (2) the understanding and implications of the New Testament's use of the Old Testament; and (3) the understanding and implications of typology.[9] In sum, the main difference rests in how dispensationalists and nondispensationalists view the relationship between the testaments.

Feinberg's analysis is accurate. The main difference between dispensationalists and nondispensationalists on the matter of hermeneutics is not simply "literal" versus "spiritual" interpretation, but how each camp views the relationship between the testaments. As Herbert Bateman puts it, the central issue is "testament priority."[10] Testament priority is "a presuppositional preference of one testament over the other that determines a person's literal historical-grammatical hermeneutical starting point."[11]

An interpreter's testament-priority assumptions are especially significant when interpreting how New Testament authors use the Old Testament. Dispensationalists want to maintain a reference point for meaning in the Old Testament. They desire to give justice to the original authorial intent of the Old Testament writers as discovered by historical-grammatical hermeneutics. Nondispensationalists, on the other hand, emphasize the New Testament as their reference point for understanding the Old Testament. In other words, they start with the New Testament to understand the Old Testament. Feinberg explains the difference:

> Nondispensationalists begin with NT teaching as having priority and then go back to the OT. Dispensationalists often begin with the OT, but wherever they begin they demand that the OT be taken on its own terms rather than reinterpreted in the light of the NT.[12]

Thus, nondispensationalists start with the New Testament to understand Old Testament prophetic passages. And the New Testament is the lens for viewing the Old Testament. This is what often leads to a "non-literal" understanding of Old Testament texts since nondispensationalists believe the New Testament sanctions less than literal understandings of Old Testament passages, especially prophetic texts about Israel. In other words, for nondispensationalists, a literal interpretation of the New Testament sanctions a non-literal understanding of some Old Testament passages, especially those regarding Israel.

Six Essential Beliefs of Dispensationalism

This section presents the essential beliefs of dispensationalism. By "essential" I mean foundational beliefs that are central and unique to the system, beliefs upon which the system stands or falls. These are also beliefs that if denied would probably make one a nondispensationalist. This list takes into consideration the contributions of Ryrie, Feinberg, and Blaising and Bock, but also offers my own distinctions that hopefully add clarity.

1. Progressive revelation from the New Testament does not interpret Old Testament passages in a way that cancels the original authorial intent of the Old Testament writers as determined by historical-grammatical hermeneutics.

This first point, a hermeneutical issue, is the most foundational of all the points. All dispensationalists affirm that the *starting point* for understanding Old Testament passages are the original Old Testament passages themselves. The meaning of Old Testament texts is not primarily found in New Testament interpretations. The New Testament may, with progressive revelation, shine light on Old Testament passages, offer commentary, or add additional applications or referents, but the New Testament does not override the original intent of the Old Testament writers. In the progress of revelation, the New Testament writers may provide more in the way of application or fulfillment of Old Testament passages, but they do not nullify or transfer the meaning of Old Testament passages in a way that goes against what the Old Testament writers originally intended. Thus, as Paul D. Feinberg states, "The sense of any OT prediction must be determined through the application of historical-grammatical hermeneutics to that text."[13] Bruce A. Ware applies this principle to promises made to Israel:

> There can be no question that the prophets meant to communicate the promise of a national return of Israel to its land. To the extent that our hermeneutics are regulated by the principle of authorial intent, we are given ample reason to accept this literal rendering of what God, through the prophets, originally promised to his people Israel.[14]

Let's look at one key passage as an example. Hebrews 8:8–12, which quotes the original new covenant passage of Jeremiah 31:31–34, certainly includes the church in the spiritual blessings of the new covenant, but since the new covenant was originally promised to Israel, the full fulfillment of the covenant must involve national Israel. The author of Hebrews includes the church in the blessings of the new covenant, but he does not exclude national Israel from the covenant. Thus, the new covenant has a "both/and" element to it—both Israel and the church. The church is related to the new covenant (Heb. 8:8–13), and Israel will be related to the new covenant at the second coming of Christ (see Rom. 11:25–27). Bock is right when he states, "The additional inclusion of some in the promise does not mean the original recipients are thereby excluded. *The expansion of promise need not mean the cancellation of earlier commitments God has made.* The realization of new covenant hope today for Gentiles does not mean that the promise made to Israel in Jeremiah 31 has been jettisoned."[15]

This approach is different from that of nondispensationalists who often view the new covenant as being entirely fulfilled with the church in such a way that does not include national Israel. With this approach, the physical and material blessings of the new covenant are believed to find a more spiritual or less literal fulfillment with the church, which is now viewed as the new or true Israel.[16] Thus, one should not look for a future inclusion of national Israel into the covenant.

The dispensational principle of maintaining the original authorial intent of Old Testament texts has great importance for understanding the eternal and unconditional covenants given to Israel in the Old Testament (Abrahamic, Davidic, New). John Feinberg points out that

God's unconditional covenants with Israel guarantee that the New Testament would never introduce the idea that God would not fulfill His covenants and promises with Israel, the people with whom the original promises were made. To do so, God would have to contradict Himself, and that is not possible. If an Old Testament promise is made unconditionally with a specific group such as Israel, then that promise must be fulfilled with that group. Progress of revelation cannot cancel unconditional promises to Israel. Feinberg states:

> If an OT prophecy or promise is made unconditionally to a given people and is still unfulfilled to them even in the NT era, then the prophecy must still be fulfilled to them. While a prophecy given unconditionally to Israel has a fulfillment for the church if the NT *applies* it to the church, it must also be fulfilled to Israel. Progress of revelation cannot cancel unconditional promises.[17]

David L. Turner points out that "covenant theologians and dispensationalists disagree on the nature of progressive revelation."[18] He writes, "Each group accuses the other of misinterpreting the NT due to alien presuppositions."[19] Turner states that dispensationalists deny that the New Testament reinterprets Old Testament promises to Israel: "It is their contention that the NT supplies no 'reinterpretation' of OT prophecy which would cancel the OT promises to Israel of a future historical kingdom. In their view the NT use of the OT does not radically modify the OT promises to Israel."[20] Turner contends that the nondispensational understanding brings into question God's faithfulness to Israel: "If NT reinterpretation reverses, cancels, or seriously modifies OT promises to Israel, one wonders how to define the word 'progressive' [in progressive revelation]. God's faithfulness to His promises to Israel must also be explained."[21]

Ryrie, too, asserts that the New Testament does not contradict the meaning of Old Testament texts. He states, "New revelation cannot mean contradictory revelation. Later revelation on a subject does not make the earlier revelation mean something different."[22] "If this were so," says Ryrie, "God would have to be conceived of as deceiving the Old Testament prophets when He revealed to them a nationalistic kingdom, since He would have known all the time that He would completely reverse the concept in later revelation."[23] For Ryrie, the concept of progressive revelation can be likened to a building in progress: "The superstructure does not replace the foundation."[24] Thus, maintaining the original authorial intent of Old Testament passages is an essential of dispensationalism.

2. Types exist, but national Israel is not a type that is superseded by the church.

The issue of typology has significant implications for eschatology. Nondispensationalists hold that national Israel functioned as a type of the New Testament church. Once the greater antitype (the "fulfillment" of the type), the church, was revealed, Israel's place as the people of God was transcended and superseded by the church.[25]

Dispensationalists, too, believe in types. However, they take a different approach to understanding Israel in relation to typology. John Feinberg, for instance, points out that the nature of the unconditional promises to Israel has implications for understanding Israel's relationship to typology. While acknowledging the existence of Old Testament types that prefigure New Testament realities, the people with whom the promises were made are not types:

> The unconditionality of the promises to Israel guarantees that the NT does not even implicitly remove those promises from Israel. OT civil and ceremonial laws and institutions are shadows and are explicitly removed in the NT. But unconditional promises are not shadows, nor are the peoples to whom they are given.[26]

Paul Feinberg, too, while acknowledging the existence of types, does not view Israel as a symbol of the church: "While historical-grammatical interpretation allows for symbols, types, and analogies, I see no evidence that Israel is a symbol for the church, Palestine for the new

Jerusalem, et al."[27] Caution should be used when determining when the New Testament cancels an Old Testament type. As John Feinberg declares, "If the NT antitype cancels the meaning of the OT type, the NT must tell us so."[28]

Are dispensationalists asserting that there is no typological connection whatsoever between Israel and the church? Not necessarily. Saucy, for example, argues that the nation Israel is not a type in the sense that Israel has been transcended by a greater spiritual reality, the church. Yet, he also believes there is a historical and theological correspondence between Israel and the church that may have typological implications. As he explains, "If a type is understood as shadow pointing forward to the reality of an antitype, then it is questionable whether Israel is a type."[29] On the other hand, if a type is viewed in terms of a correspondence between two groups, then a typological connection between Israel and the church may exist:

> If a type is defined as a general historical and theological correspondence, then the many analogies between Old Testament Israel and the New Testament people of God may well be explained by seeing Israel as a type of the church. But the correspondence with God's actions among Old Testament Israel would not in this understanding of typology deny the continued existence of that nation in the future.[30]

Thus, there may be a typological connection between Israel and the church, but this connection is not that of the church superseding national Israel. Instead, the typological connection is that of a historical and theological correspondence that reveals a close relationship between Israel and the church.

This typological connection between the Old and New Testaments, however, does not alter the original sense of the Old Testament promises to Israel. As David L. Turner explains, "Genuine typology and analogy between OT and NT should not be viewed as destructive to the literal fulfillment of the OT promises to Israel, but rather an indication of a greater continuity between Israel and the church."[31] Thus, whatever typological relationship exists between Israel and the church, this cannot be taken to mean that Israel's significance has been transcended and superseded by the church.

3. Israel and the church are distinct, thus the church cannot be identified as the new or true Israel.

As the lists from Ryrie, Feinberg, and Blaising and Bock indicate, all dispensationalists are united in holding that one cannot equate the New Testament church with a "new" or "true" "Israel." There may be differences of opinion when it comes to the specifics of the relationship between the church and Israel or the exact relationship of the church to the biblical covenants, but all dispensationalists reject a "replacement theology" or "supersessionism" in which the New Testament church is viewed as the replacement or fulfillment of the nation Israel as the people of God.[32]

Traditional and progressive dispensationalists have differences on how they view the church. Traditional dispensationalists tend to view the church as a distinct anthropological group, while progressive dispensationalists are more apt to view the church as a soteriological or new covenant community starting with the events of Acts 2.[33] But both sides agree that there is no biblical evidence to indicate that the church is the new or true Israel that forever supersedes national Israel.

Dispensationalists do acknowledge that believing Gentiles have been brought near to the covenants of Israel (see Eph. 2:11–22), but they also point out that the New Testament distinguishes Israel and the church in such a way that rules out the idea that the church is now identified as Israel or that the church entirely inherits Israel's promises and covenants to the exclusion of the nation Israel.

Arnold Fruchtenbaum, for example, points out that the title *Israel* is used a total of seventy-three times in the New Testament, but is always used of ethnic Jews: "Of these seventy-three citations, the vast majority refer to national, ethnic Israel. A few refer specifically to Jewish believers who still are ethnic Jews."[34] Saucy confirms this point when he says, "The NT evidence reveals that outside of a few disputed references . . . the name Israel is related to the 'national' covenant people of the OT."[35] For dispensationalists, it is significant that the New Testament still consistently refers to the nation Israel as "Israel" even after the establishment of the church. Israel is addressed as a nation in contrast to Gentiles after the church was established at Pentecost (Acts 3:12; 4:8, 10; 5:21, 31, 35; 21:28). As Ryrie observes, "In Paul's prayer for national Israel (Romans 10:1) there is a clear reference to Israel as a national people distinct from and outside the church."[36]

Ryrie argues that Paul's linking of national Israel to the covenants and promises of the Old Testament, even while in a state of unbelief, is further proof that the church has not absorbed Israel's blessings:

> Paul, obviously referring to natural Israel as his "kinsmen according to the flesh," ascribes to them the covenants and the promises (Romans 9:3–4). That these words were written after the beginning of the church is proof that the church does not rob Israel of her blessings. The term Israel continues to be used for the natural (not spiritual) descendants of Abraham after the church was instituted, and it is not equated with the church.[37]

Dispensationalists also claim that the book of Acts maintains a distinction between Israel and the church. In the book of Acts, both Israel and the church exist simultaneously, but the term *Israel* is used twenty times and *ekklēsia* (church) nineteen times. Yet the two groups are always kept distinct.[38] Thus, the continued use of the term "Israel" for the physical descendants of Jacob is evidence that the church is not Israel. As Saucy explains, "The church is not . . . identified with 'Israel.' They share a similar identity as the people of God enjoying equally the blessings of the promised eschatological salvation. But this commonality does not eliminate all distinctions between them."[39] In sum, the Israel/church distinction continues to be a defining characteristic of dispensationalism.

4. There is both spiritual unity in salvation between Jews and Gentiles and a future role for Israel as a nation.

One of the main arguments made against dispensationalism is that it does not do justice to the unity that Jews and Gentiles experience in Christ. The emphasis on "one new man" (Eph. 2:15) and "one body" (Eph. 2:16) in the New Testament is taken to mean there can be no future role for Israel since unity in Christ supposedly rules this out. In reference to Ephesians 2, Anthony Hoekema declares, "All thought of a separate purpose for believing Jews is here excluded."[40] In regard to Ephesians 2:11–15, Raymond Zorn argues, "Through Christ's fulfilling of the law an end has come to the exclusivity of Israel as a holy nation and a holy people."[41] Wayne Grudem says that Ephesians 2 "gives no indication of any distinctive plan for Jewish people ever to be saved apart from inclusion in the one body of Christ, the church."[42] According to nondispensationalists, it appears unlikely that God would bring Jews and Gentiles together only to make a distinction between the two groups in the future. To do so appears to be going backward. Hoekema declares that this is like putting the scaffolding back on a finished building:

> To suggest that God has in mind a separate future for Israel, in distinction from the future he has planned for Gentiles, actually goes contrary to God's purpose. It is like putting the scaffolding back up after the building has been finished. It is like turning the clock of history back to Old Testament times. It is imposing Old Testament separateness upon the New Testament, and ignoring the progress of revelation.[43]

An essential belief of dispensationalism, though, is that spiritual unity between believing Jews and Gentiles does not cancel their God-ordained functional distinctions. To be sure, in the realm of salvation and status before God, believing Gentiles are equal with believing Jews. However, salvific unity between Jews and Gentiles does not erase all ethnic or functional distinctions between the two groups. As Carl Hoch states:

> Paul's comments in Ephesians . . . exclude any salvific priority for Israel in the ecclesiological structure of the new man. . . . However, while there is no longer *salvific* advantage, there is still an *ethnic* distinction between Jews and Gentiles. Paul continues to speak of Jews and Gentiles as distinct ethnic groups in his letters (Romans 1:16; 9:24; 1 Corinthians 1:24; 12:13; Galatians 2:14, 15).[44]

This dispensational belief that salvific equality does not rule out functional distinctions among groups is seen in other examples in Scripture. For example, according to Galatians 3:28 men and women share equally in salvation blessings but the Bible still teaches that men and women have different roles (see 1 Tim. 2:9–15). Thus, in the case of men and women, salvific unity does not nullify functional distinctions. The same is true for elders and non-elders in a church. Both are equal in essence and share the same spiritual blessings, but elders have a distinct role in the plan of God (see Heb. 13:17). The same distinction could be made between parents and children or even within the Trinity itself in which there is equality of essence among the three members of the Godhead yet functional distinctions within this oneness. Hence, equality in essence and spiritual blessings does not nullify functional distinctions. As Saucy writes:

> The union of Jew and Gentile in the church does not rule out the possibility of *functional* distinctions between Israel and the other nations in the future—in the same way that there are functional distinctions among believers in the church today amid spiritual equality.[45]

Thus, when it comes to the issue of salvific unity between believing Jews and Gentiles *and* a future role for Israel in a millennial kingdom, the dispensationalist says, "Yes, it is a both/and situation."

5. The nation Israel will be saved, restored with a unique identity, and function in a future millennial kingdom upon the earth.

Dispensationalists have often not explained this point well, but it is extremely important.[46] Often dispensationalists state that belief in "a future for Israel" or "the salvation of Israel" is a distinguishing characteristic of dispensationalism. But these statements are not specific enough. Many nondispensationalists also affirm the above two claims. In fact, a fair number of nondispensationalists, including many Postmillennialists and some Amillennialists, believe in a literal salvation of Israel based on Paul's words in Romans 11:26 that "all Israel will be saved." This view was held by many of the theologians of the patristic era. More recently, this understanding of Romans 11:26 has been promoted by Handley C. G. Moule, John Murray, Leon Morris, F. F. Bruce, and Wayne Grudem.[47] So it is not accurate to claim that belief in a future salvation of Israel is a uniquely dispensational view.

What distinguishes all dispensationalists, however, is that they believe not only in a *salvation* of Israel but also in a *restoration* of Israel. The concept of "restoration" certainly includes the idea of salvation, but it goes beyond that. "Restoration" involves the idea of Israel being reinstalled as a nation, in her land, with a specific identity and role of service to the nations. In other words, in a literal, earthly kingdom—a millennium—the nation Israel will perform a functional role of service to the nations. This point is something all dispensationalists affirm while all nondispensationalists deny. Even Historic Premillennialists, who agree with dispensationalists on the issues of a national salvation of Israel and a future millennial kingdom, will disagree with the dispensational idea that Israel will be restored with a unique identity and function that is distinct from the church. Thus, there is a distinction between saying the nation Israel will be saved into the church, and saying that the nation Israel will be saved and restored with a unique identity and role in an earthly millennium. Dispensationalists affirm the latter.

6. There are multiple senses of "seed of Abraham"; thus, the church's identification as "seed of Abraham" does not cancel God's promises to the believing Jewish "seed of Abraham."

Galatians 3:7 states that those who exercise faith are "sons of Abraham." Galatians 3:29 also declares that those who belong to Christ are "Abraham's descendants" and "heirs according to promise." Non-dispensationalists have argued that since Gentiles are "sons" and "descendants" (or "seed") of Abraham, they must also be spiritual Jews.[48] Dispensationalists, however, have contested this understanding. They have done so by challenging the idea that being a "son" or "seed" of Abraham automatically makes one a Jew. Saucy, for example, asserts that Abraham's fatherhood goes beyond being the father of ethnic Israel since he trusted God before he was recognized as a Hebrew:

> If Abraham were merely the father of Israel, we would have to conclude that the Gentiles who are now a part of this seed are therefore a part of Israel. But according to the New Testament, Abraham is more than that; he is portrayed as the father of both the people of Israel and of the Gentiles. On the grounds that Abraham was a believer before he was circumcised—that is, before he was recognized as a Hebrew—the Apostle Paul declared him to be "the father of all who believe but have not been circumcised . . . and . . . also the father of the circumcised" (Romans 4:9–12; cf. v. 16).[49]

As a result, "The fact that the true seed of Abraham includes both Jews and Gentiles does not rule out a continuing distinction for Israel in the New Testament. Nor should the calling of the Gentiles as the seed of Abraham be construed as the formation of a 'new spiritual Israel' that supersedes the Old Testament nation of Israel."[50]

Dispensationalists have argued that the concept of "seed of Abraham" is used in several different ways in the New Testament.

Fruchtenbaum, for example, lists four senses of "seed of Abraham." First, he says it can refer to those who are biological descendants of Abraham. Second, it can refer to the Messiah, who is the unique individual seed of Abraham. Third, it can indicate the righteous remnant of Israel (cf. Is. 41:8 with Rom. 9:6). Fourth, it can be used in a spiritual sense for believing Jews and Gentiles (Gal. 3:29).[51] It is in this last sense—the spiritual sense—that believing Gentiles are the seed of Abraham. John Feinberg also distinguishes between a physical sense and a spiritual sense of being a seed of Abraham. According to him, nonsupersessionists hold that "no sense (spiritual especially) is more important than any other, and that no sense cancels out the meaning and implications of the other senses."[52] Consequently, the application of the titles "sons of Abraham" or "seed of Abraham" to believing Gentiles does not mean that believing Gentiles are spiritual Jews or part of Israel.[53]

Together, these six points comprise the foundation of dispensational theology. It is upon these six points that dispensationalism stands or falls.

Notes

1. Charles C. Ryrie, *Dispensationalism Today* (Chicago: Moody, 1965), 43–47. Cf. Charles C. Ryrie, *Dispensationalism* (Chicago: Moody, 1995), 38–41.
2. John S. Feinberg, "Systems of Discontinuity," in *Continuity and Discontinuity: Perspectives on the Relationship Between the Old and New Testaments*, ed. John S. Feinberg (Wheaton, IL: Crossway, 1988), 67–85.
3. Craig A. Blaising and Darrell L. Bock, *Progressive Dispensationalism: An Up-To-Date Handbook of Contemporary Dispensational Thought* (Wheaton, IL: Bridgepoint, 1993), 13–21.
4. More recent Amillennialists like Anthony Hoekema have emphasized the fulfillment of physical blessings in the coming eternal state.
5. According to Blaising and Bock, "One of the striking differences between progressive and earlier dispensationalists, is that progressives do not view the church as an anthropological category in the same class as terms like Israel, Gentile Nations, Jews, and Gentile people. . . . The church is precisely redeemed humanity itself (both Jews and Gentiles) as it exists in this dispensation prior to the coming of Christ." *Progressive Dispensationalism*, 49.
6. Ryrie, *Dispensationalism*, 84.
7. John Feinberg, "Systems of Discontinuity," 73.

8. Ibid., 74. Saucy makes the same point: "An analysis of non-dispensational systems, however, reveals that their less-than-literal approach to Israel in the Old Testament prophecies does not really arise from an a priori spiritualistic or metaphorical hermeneutic. Rather, it is the result of their interpretation of the New Testament using the same grammatico-historical hermeneutic as that of dispensationalists." Robert L. Saucy, *The Case for Progressive Dispensationalism: The Interface between Dispensational & Nondispensational Theology* (Grand Rapids: Zondervan, 1993), 20.

9. John Feinberg, "Systems of Discontinuity," 73–74.

10. Herbert W. Bateman IV, "Dispensationalism Yesterday and Today," in *Three Central Issues in Contemporary Dispensationalism: A Comparison of Traditional and Progressive Views*, ed. Herbert W. Bateman IV (Grand Rapids: Kregel, 1999), 38.

11. Ibid.

12. John Feinberg, "Systems of Discontinuity," 75. Feinberg's view is supported by the nondispensationalist George Ladd: "Here is the basic watershed between a dispensational and a nondispensational theology. Dispensationalism forms its eschatology by a literal interpretation of the Old Testament and then fits the New Testament into it. A nondispensational eschatology forms its theology from the explicit teaching of the New Testament." George Eldon Ladd, "Historic Premillennialism," *The Meaning of the Millennium: Four Views*, ed. Robert G. Clouse (Downers Grove, IL: IVP, 1977), 28.

13. Paul Feinberg, "Hermeneutics of Discontinuity," in *Continuity and Discontinuity*, 123.

14. Bruce A. Ware, "The New Covenant and the People(s) of God," in *Dispensationalism, Israel and the Church: The Search for Definition*, eds. Craig A. Blaising and Darrell L. Bock (Grand Rapids: Zondervan, 1992), 93.

15. Blaising and Bock, *Progressive Dispensationalism*, 103–4. Emphasis in original.

16. Those who believe that Heb. 8:8–13 indicates that the church fully inherits the new covenant include: Bruce K. Waltke, "Kingdom Promises as Spiritual," in *Continuity and Discontinuity*, 281; Wayne Grudem, *Systematic Theology: An Introduction to Biblical Doctrine* (Grand Rapids: Zondervan, 1994), 862; O. Palmer Robertson, *The Christ of the Covenants* (Phillipsburg, NJ: P&R, 1980), 289; Hans K. LaRondelle, *The Israel of God in Prophecy: Principles of Prophetic Interpretation* (Berrien Springs, MI: Andrews University Press, 1983), 116–18; John Bright, *The Kingdom of God: The Biblical Concept and Its Meaning for the Church* (Nashville: Abingdon, 1953), 228–29; Willem A. VanGemeren, "A Response," in *Dispensationalism, Israel and the Church*, 337.

17. John Feinberg, "Systems of Discontinuity," 76. Emphasis in original.

18. David L. Turner, "The Continuity of Scripture and Eschatology: Key Hermeneutical Issues," *Grace Theological Journal* 6:2 (1985): 280.

19. Ibid., 280–81.

20. Ibid., 279.

21. Ibid., 281.

22. Ryrie, *Dispensationalism*, 84.

23. Ibid. George N. H. Peters concurs, "If no restoration was intended; if all was to be understood typically, or spiritually, or conditionally, then surely the language was most eminently calculated to deceive the hearers. . . ." George N. H. Peters, *The Theocratic Kingdom of Our Lord Jesus: The Christ as Covenanted in the Old Testament*, vol. 2 (1884; repr., Grand Rapids: Kregel, 1988), 51.
24. Ryrie, *Dispensationalism*, 84.
25. See LaRondelle, *The Israel of God in Prophecy*, 45.
26. John Feinberg, "Systems of Discontinuity," 76.
27. Paul Feinberg, "Hermeneutics of Discontinuity," 124.
28. John Feinberg, "Systems of Discontinuity," 79.
29. Saucy, *The Case for Progressive Dispensationalism*, 32.
30. Ibid., 31–32. See also W. Edward Glenny, "The Israelite Imagery of 1 Peter 2," in *Dispensationalism, Israel and the Church*, 180.
31. Turner, "The Continuity of Scripture," 282. See also Howard Taylor, "The Continuity of the People of God in Old and New Testaments," *Scottish Bulletin of Theology* 3 (1985): 14–15.
32. For a case against supersessionism from a dispensational perspective, see Craig A. Blaising, "The Future of Israel as a Theological Question," *Journal of the Evangelical Theological Society* 44:3 (2001): 435–50.
33. For more on this distinction see Blaising and Bock, *Progressive Dispensationalism*, 49–51.
34. Arnold G. Fruchtenbaum, "Israel and the Church," in *Issues in Dispensationalism*, eds. Wesley R. Willis and John R. Master (Chicago: Moody, 1994), 120.
35. Robert L. Saucy, "Israel and the Church: A Case for Discontinuity," in *Continuity and Discontinuity*, 244–45.
36. Ryrie, *Dispensationalism*, 127.
37. Ibid.
38. Fruchtenbaum, "Israel and the Church," 118.
39. Saucy, *The Case for Progressive Dispensationalism*, 210. For Saucy "It is the lack of national characteristics that distinguishes the church from Israel" (210).
40. Anthony A. Hoekema, *The Bible and the Future* (Grand Rapids: Eerdmans, 1979), 200.
41. Raymond O. Zorn, *Christ Triumphant* (Carlisle, PA: Banner of Truth, 1997), 190.
42. Grudem, *Systematic Theology*, 862.
43. Hoekema, *The Bible and the Future*, 201.
44. Carl B. Hoch Jr., "The New Man of Ephesians 2," in *Dispensationalism, Israel and the Church*, 118. Emphases in original.
45. Saucy, *The Case for Progressive Dispensationalism*, 167. Emphasis in original.
46. Arnold Fruchtenbaum would be one notable exception.
47. F. F. Bruce, *The Letter of Paul to the Romans: An Introduction and Commentary*, TNTC, vol. 6 (Grand Rapids: Eerdmans, 1985; repr., 1990), 209; Grudem,

Systematic Theology, 861 n. 17; Leon Morris, *The Epistle to the Romans* (Grand Rapids: Eerdmans, 1988), 421; Handley C. G. Moule, *The Epistle of St. Paul to the Romans* (New York: A. C. Armstrong & Son, 1899), 311–12; John Murray, *The Epistle to the Romans*, 2 vols. (Grand Rapids: Eerdmans, 1997), 2:99.

48. The following authors assert that Gal. 3:7, 29 teaches that believing Gentiles are considered spiritual Jews: Ladd, "Historic Premillennialism," 24; Hoekema, *The Bible and the Future*, 198–99; William Neil, *The Letter of Paul to the Galatians* (Cambridge: Cambridge University Press, 1967), 62; Robert B. Strimple, "Amillennialism," in *Three Views on the Millennium and Beyond*, ed. Darrell L. Bock (Grand Rapids: Zondervan, 1999), 88–89; LaRondelle, *The Israel of God in Prophecy*, 108; Bright, *The Kingdom of God*, 227; Bruce K. Waltke, "Kingdom Promises as Spiritual," in *Continuity and Discontinuity*, 267.

49. Saucy, *The Case for Progressive Dispensationalism*, 50.

50. Ibid.

51. See Arnold G. Fruchtenbaum, *Israelology* (Tustin, CA: Ariel Ministries, 1996), 702.

52. John Feinberg, "Systems of Discontinuity," 73.

53. Fruchtenbaum states, "What replacement theologians need to prove their case is a statement in Scripture that all believers are of 'the seed of Jacob.' Such teaching would indicate that the church is spiritual Israel or that Gentile Christians are spiritual Jews." Fruchtenbaum, "Israel and the Church," 126–27.

Chapter Two

What Is Dispensationalism Not?

Michael Vlach

Recently while jogging on a treadmill at the local health club, I intently listened to a well-known Bible teacher on my iPhone. During a Q&A session, someone asked him his thoughts on dispensationalism. He responded that one of his biggest problems with dispensationalism was its doctrine of salvation. In particular, he argued that dispensationalism taught trichotomism—the belief that humans are comprised of three parts: body, soul, and spirit. He asserted that since dispensationalism teaches that the soul and spirit are distinct, this leads to the view that Christians could live carnal lives soulishly while living for God's glory spiritually. After hearing this, I replayed his comments to see if I had understood him correctly. And yes, he said what I thought he had said. For him, dispensationalism was intrinsically linked with the belief that the soul and spirit are distinct parts of the human constitution, which could lead to ungodly living.

Unfortunately, this man was seriously mistaken. Trichotomism is not a necessary belief of dispensationalism—not even close. I wondered how or where he came up with such a notion. Sadly, his audience would leave that day thinking that dispensationalism advocates a faulty view of salvation. This is just one of many examples where dispensationalism has been seriously misrepresented.

Throughout its history, dispensationalism has often been linked with peripheral views that are not foundational to its theology, especially in regard to the doctrine of salvation. Such claims reveal an ignorance of the true nature of dispensationalism. So, this chapter will point out some of the common myths or misunderstandings about dispensational theology that need to be eliminated from any factual discussions of dispensationalism.

Dispensationalism and Other Doctrines

Not every theological system has a direct relationship to every area of Christian theology. For example, Reformed theology has specific views on the doctrines of Scripture, God's sovereignty, and salvation. But Reformed theology does not lead to any particular view of eschatology. For example, Reformed theologians can be Amillennialists, Postmillennialists, or Premillennialists. Any attempt to link Reformed theology to a specific millennial view would be mistaken since Reformed theology is not inherently related to a specific millennial perspective.

Dispensationalism does not have a direct relationship to every category of theology. It is inherently linked to some areas of theology, but is unrelated to others. It is primarily concerned with the doctrines of ecclesiology (church) and eschatology (end times). It is also closely linked with hermeneutics and principles of Bible interpretation. But one doctrine that is not inherently related to dispensationalism is soteriology, the doctrine of salvation. As John Feinberg, a leading dispensationalist, writes:

> Dispensationalism becomes very important in regard to ecclesiology and eschatology, but is really not about [other categories of systematic theology]. Some think salvation is at the heart of dispensationalism, because they erroneously think dispensationalism teaches multiple methods of salva-

> tion. Those who properly understand the position realize that its emphasis lies elsewhere.[1]

John MacArthur asserts that eschatology and ecclesiology, not soteriology, are at the heart of dispensationalism:

> So dispensationalism shapes one's *eschatology* and *ecclesiology*. That is the extent of it. Pure dispensationalism has no ramifications for the doctrines of God, man, sin, or sanctification. More significantly, true dispensationalism makes no relevant contribution to *soteriology*, or the doctrine of salvation.[2]

O. T. Allis, a nondispensationalist, echoes the conclusions of Feinberg and MacArthur: "The primary features of this movement [dispensationalism] were two in number. The one related to the Church. . . . The other had to do with prophecy."[3]

That dispensationalism primarily addresses ecclesiology and eschatology (and not soteriology) is also evidenced in the works of other leading dispensationalists who have addressed the essence of dispensationalism. For example, Charles Ryrie's book *Dispensationalism Today* devoted a chapter to "Salvation," but the chapter was mostly a refutation of the charge that dispensationalism taught multiple ways of salvation. Ryrie does not argue that dispensationalism inherently leads to any soteriological viewpoint. In his 1993 work, *The Case for Progressive Dispensationalism*, Robert L. Saucy discussed ecclesiological, eschatological, and hermeneutical issues related to dispensationalism, but he promoted no particular dispensational soteriology.[4]

In a 1992 book edited by Blaising and Bock, *Dispensationalism, Israel and the Church: The Search for Definition*, various dispensational authors wrote on ecclesiological, eschatological, and hermeneutical issues, but none argued for a specific dispensational soteriology.[5] The same is true for Blaising and Bock's 1993 book, *Progressive Dispensationalism*.[6] Except for addressing misconceptions about dispensational views on law and grace, there was no direct discussion of any dispensational soteriology. Paul Enns, a dispensationalist, devoted a chapter to "Dispensational Theology" in his 1989 book *The Moody Handbook of Theology*.[7] He offered one paragraph on the issue of salvation. The thrust of the paragraph, though, was to refute the misperception that dispensationalism taught multiple ways of salvation. No specific dispensational soteriology was mentioned. These works by leading dispensationalists are important because they reveal what is at the heart of dispensationalism. When leading dispensationalists wrote about dispensationalism, they did not link dispensationalism with specific soteriological views. When they did address soteriology, it was mostly to answer charges that dispensationalism is linked with faulty views of salvation.

To clarify, I am not asserting that individual dispensationalists do not hold specific soteriological views. A distinction, though, must be made between what individual dispensationalists hold to on various issues in theology and what dispensationalism as a system is based upon. Not heeding this distinction is a fundamental error of those who link dispensationalism with particular soteriological views. They are, as Feinberg puts it, "reacting to what they think dispensationalists hold rather than to the logic of the system itself."[8]

Now let us look at five common myths about dispensationalism.

Myth 1: Dispensationalism Teaches Multiple Ways of Salvation

Ryrie is correct when he claims that "the most frequently heard objection against dispensationalism is that it supposedly teaches several ways of salvation."[9] John Wick Bowman made this accusation in 1956 when he declared that dispensationalists are "clearly left with two methods of salvation."[10] In 1960, Clarence Bass argued that dispensational distinctions between law and grace and Israel and the church "inevitably result in a multiple form of salvation—that men are not saved the same way in all ages."[11] While these accusations are unfounded, we do need to acknowledge that some statements by dispensationalists have been confusing on this issue.[12] This was especially true in the case of the note concerning John 1:17 in the 1909 *Scofield Reference Bible*:

> As a dispensation grace begins with the death and resurrection of Christ (Romans 3:24–26; 4:24, 25). The point of testing is no longer legal obedience as the condition of salvation, but acceptance or rejection of Christ, with good works as a fruit of salvation.[13]

Some saw in this statement an explicit assertion that Scofield—and all dispensationalists by extension—believed in multiple ways of salvation.[14] Significantly, Scofield's views in the *Scofield Reference Bible* were often equated with dispensationalism since he was viewed as the leading dispensationalist of his era. According to Klooster, the perception that dispensationalism taught multiple ways of salvation was commonly held by nondispensationalists until 1965.[15] Around this time, Ryrie published *Dispensationalism Today* where he responded to the charge that dispensationalism taught multiple ways of salvation.[16] Ryrie explained that earlier dispensationalists, including Scofield, did not teach multiple ways of salvation. They made "unguarded statements that would have been more carefully worded if they were being made in the light of today's debate."[17] Ryrie also called on nondispensationalists to acknowledge the significant change in the *New Scofield Reference Bible* regarding John 1:17 in which the controversial wording was removed and a clearer statement of one way of salvation was affirmed. The newer note read:

> Under the former dispensation, law was shown to be powerless to secure righteousness and life for a sinful race (Galatians 3:21–22). Prior to the cross man's salvation was through faith (Genesis 15:6; Romans 4:3), being grounded on Christ's atoning sacrifice, viewed anticipatively by God; . . . now it is clearly revealed that salvation and righteousness are received by faith in the crucified and resurrected Savior.[18]

Since the publishing of *Dispensationalism Today*, other dispensationalists have joined Ryrie in bringing clarity to this issue. As Saucy writes, "While it cannot be denied that there is some unresolved tension in these earlier statements, dispensationalists have more recently been careful to explain that the progression in the dispensations involves no change in the fundamental principle of salvation by grace."[19]

As a result of Ryrie's work, the writings of other dispensationalists, and the *New Scofield Reference Bible* revision, some nondispensationalists became convinced that dispensationalism does not teach multiple ways of salvation. Fred H. Klooster is one example:

> In light of this significant revision in the *New Scofield Reference Bible* and the arguments of such dispensationalists as Ryrie and [John] Feinberg, the old charge should be dropped. One must proceed from the acknowledgement that dispensationalism recognizes a single way of salvation throughout the Scripture. Salvation is now and has always been by grace alone—*sola gratia*! This agreement is a cause for joy; its acknowledgment should not be made grudgingly.[20]

Klooster's perspective was also shared by Anthony Hoekema who wrote, "We gratefully acknowledge their [dispensationalists'] insistence that in every age salvation is only through grace, on the basis of the merits of Christ."[21] Taking into account the *New Scofield Reference Bible* and Ryrie's *Dispensationalism Today*, Daniel Fuller concluded, "In comparing these contemporary statements of dispensationalism with covenant theology, we conclude that there is no longer any substantive difference between the two on the subject of the law and the gospel."[22]

Klooster, Hoekema, and Fuller are to be commended for evaluating this issue objectively. Sadly, not all critics of dispensationalism followed their lead. In his 1991 book, *Wrongly Dividing the Word of Truth: A Critique of Dispensationalism*, John Gerstner accused all dispensationalists of teaching more than one way of salvation. He wrote,

"We must sadly accuse dispensationalists (of all varieties) of teaching, always implicitly and sometimes explicitly, that there is more than one way of salvation and, in the process of developing that theology, excluding the one and only way even from this dispensation of grace."[23] Gerstner does not explain why dispensationalism must lead to a faulty soteriology, but for him that was the case nonetheless. *Contrary to the claims of Gerstner, however, dispensationalism has not and does not teach multiple ways of salvation.* As John Feinberg points out, there is nothing inherent within dispensationalism that leads dispensationalists to conclude that the Bible teaches multiple ways of salvation: "the question of whether dispensationalism necessitates a multiple methods of salvation view, or a single way of salvation position is irrelevant. Soteriology is not the determinative area for dispensationalism."[24]

Myth 2: Dispensationalism Is Inherently Arminian

A second myth often perpetuated is that dispensationalism is inherently linked with Arminianism.[25] Along with this is the claim that dispensationalism is opposed to Calvinism. For example, according to Keith A. Mathison, "Dispensationalism has adopted a semi-Pelagian, Arminian doctrine not based on Scripture."[26] Gerstner viewed dispensationalism as inherently "anti-Calvinistic" and accused it of denying all five points of Calvinism.[27] He also said, "In its views of the creation of man, the Fall, the Atonement, soteriology, and eschatology, this system is a variation of the Arminian system."[28] J. I. Packer appeared impressed with Gerstner's assertions when he stated, "He [Gerstner] sets out to show that Calvinism and dispensationalism are radically opposed, and he proves his point."[29]

The methodology of Mathison and Gerstner is to point to Arminian-like statements from dispensationalists and then declare that dispensationalism is a companion of Arminianism. They are correct that some dispensationalists have promoted certain positions consistent with some aspects of Arminian theology. This point is not in dispute (although the number of dispensationalists who actually adhere line by line to the entire Arminian system is few, at best). However, the real issue is whether dispensationalism is inherently connected with Arminianism. Our assertion is that it is not. We offer three reasons.

First, as we have already indicated, dispensationalism is primarily about ecclesiology, eschatology, and hermeneutics, not soteriology. In addressing whether dispensationalism is related to the Arminianism/Calvinism issue, John Feinberg explains why it is not:

> Neither Calvinism nor Arminianism is at the essence of dispensationalism. . . . This matter is not at the essence of dispensationalism, because Calvinism and Arminianism are very important in regard to the concepts of God, man, sin, and salvation. Dispensationalism becomes very important in regard to ecclesiology and eschatology, but is really not about those other areas.[30]

Second, there are dispensationalists who are Calvinists—even five-point Calvinists. As David L. Turner explains, "There are certain dispensationalists, myself included, who hold Calvinistic theology, including limited atonement."[31] In addition to Turner, the late S. Lewis Johnson Jr. was another dispensationalist who held to all five points of Calvinism.[32] Jeffrey Khoo points out that James Oliver Buswell (1895–1977) was a "dispensational premillennialist" who was also "a true and consistent Reformed scholar . . . a five-point (TULIP) Calvinist."[33] Buswell, a member of the Bible Presbyterian Church, was "perhaps the most prominent Reformed scholar who took a dispensational premillennial view."[34]

Both Mathison and Gerstner deny a connection between dispensationalism and Calvinism, but they do not logically show why dispensationalism is antithetical to Calvinism. Nor do they show why dispensational theologians like Johnson and Buswell cannot be Calvinists. Instead of selecting a few Arminian-like statements from dispensationalists to leave the impression that all dispensationalists are Arminians, the arguments of Gerstner and Mathison would be more impressive if they could logically show why dispensationalism is inherently anti-Calvinistic and why dispensationalists who claim to be Calvinists are not really Calvinists. There is, however, no logical reason why a dispensationalist cannot be a Calvinist. As Richard Mayhue observes, "One may be a five-point Calvinist and still be a consistent dispensationalist."[35]

Finally, some nondispensational scholars have actually documented a close historical connection between dispensationalism and Calvinism. According to Vern Poythress, "Scofield's teachings and notes are. . . . mildly Calvinistic in that they maintain a high view of God's sovereignty."[36] Church historian George M. Marsden says, "Dispensationalism was essentially Reformed in its nineteenth-century origins and had in later nineteenth-century America spread most among revival-oriented Calvinists."[37] C. Norman Kraus declares that "the basic theological affinities of dispensationalism are Calvinistic."[38] In his discussion of Arminianism and Reformed theology, Wayne Grudem says, "Both views are found among . . . Dispensationalists."[39]

We highlight the findings of these scholars not to prove that dispensationalism is inherently Calvinistic but to show that if one wants to press the issue, it can be argued that dispensationalism has a closer historical connection to Calvinism than to Arminianism. In addition, given that dispensationalism does not focus on soteriology, and that many scholars hold to both dispensationalism and Calvinism, the claim that dispensationalism leads to Arminianism is shown to be false. It is simply a myth.

Myth 3: Dispensationalism Is Inherently Antinomian

A third myth about dispensationalism is that it teaches antinomianism. Antinomianism, as Robert D. Linder defines, is "the doctrine that it is not necessary for Christians to preach and/or obey the moral law of the OT."[40] Antinomianism is often associated with the endorsement of lawless behavior.[41] According to Gerstner, dispensationalism is "committed to the non-negotiable doctrine of Antinomianism."[42]

To him, "all traditional dispensationalists teach that converted Christian persons *can* (not may) live in sin throughout their post-conversion lives with no threat to their eternal destiny."[43]

Gerstner went beyond simply arguing that certain dispensationalists teach antinomianism. In his view, dispensationalism is inherently antinomian.[44] Gerstner believes dispensationalism is inherently antinomian because of its assertion that the Christian is not under the Mosaic law and because of its alleged failure "to understand the Reformation doctrines of justification and sanctification."[45] Dispensationalists, he claims, believe that people can be justified without becoming sanctified. This "dualism," according to Gerstner, leads to the belief that Christians can be "carnal."[46]

Gerstner is correct that some dispensationalists in the past have separated justification from sanctification. We must, however, address other issues as well. Are there leading dispensationalists who see justification and sanctification as being inseparable? Also, does dispensationalism drive a dispensationalist to separate justification from sanctification? Contrary to Gerstner's claim, many dispensationalists do see an inseparable connection between justification and sanctification, and many do not accept the view that a person can become justified without also becoming sanctified. Not only is there nothing within dispensationalism that would cause a dispensationalist to separate justification from sanctification, many dispensationalists view justification and sanctification as being inseparable. John MacArthur, for example, argues explicitly against antinomianism and for the view that justification and sanctification are indivisible.[47] For MacArthur, "There is no such thing as a true convert to Christ who is justified but who is not being sanctified."[48] This position is not recent to dispensationalism. The dispensationalist Donald G. Barnhouse declared, "Justification and sanctification are as inseparable as a torso and a head. You can't have one without the other."[49] Alva J. McClain stated that "Justification cannot be separated from sanctification. . . . Justification and sanctification are two aspects of the one work of God in saving men."[50]

Like Gerstner, Curtis Crenshaw and Grover Gunn also assert that there is "an antinomianism inherent in dispensationalism."[51] According to them, dispensationalists reject God's moral law and hold that Christians are free to act carnally:

> Rejecting the moral law, especially OT moral law, results in a number of consequences. They tend to reject the idea that Christ is ruling now by his law (or any law for that matter) as King of kings, relegating this to a future millennium. This in turn leads them to reject His Lordship in salvation and maintain that one can have faith without works (the carnal Christian idea).[52]

There are two responses to this charge of antinomianism. First, we deny that dispensationalism itself is inherently antinomian or that most dispensationalists are antinomians. The tenets of dispensationalism simply do not address the nature of justification or its relation to sanctification. As Feinberg puts it:

> Some argue that dispensationalism entails antinomianism, since dispensationalists claim that the law is done away, for Christ is the end of the law (Romans 10:4). Though some may hold this view, it is hardly the norm or necessitated by dispensationalism.[53]

MacArthur, too, is correct when he says, "It is a gross misunderstanding to assume that antinomianism is at the heart of dispensationalist doctrine."[54]

Second, although most dispensationalists claim that Christians today are not under the Mosaic law, they do not assert that Christians today are without *any* law. Crenshaw and Gunn's claim that dispensationalists reject "moral law" is a misrepresentation of what most dispensationalists believe. Many dispensationalists believe that Christians today are under a new law—the law of Christ in which the moral laws of God are communicated. According to Wayne G. Strickland, the law of Christ "is the new covenant counterpart to the Mosaic Law.

Just as the Mosaic Law was normative for the Jew, the law of Christ is binding for the Christian."[55] According to Blaising, dispensationalism is not antinomian because "while it teaches that Mosaic covenant law has ended dispensationally, it also teaches that it has been replaced by new covenant law."[56] In his summary of the dispensational view of the law, Erickson writes, "The moral law is always in effect . . . although its exact content may vary."[57]

One can try to argue that dispensationalists are in error concerning the relationship of the Mosaic law and the law of Christ, but it is not accurate to charge dispensationalism with saying that Christians today have no law or that Christians can do whatever they want. It should also be noted that the historical connection between dispensationalism and antinomianism may be overstated. As an expert in the history of dispensationalism, Blaising writes, "I am not convinced by Gerstner that Antinomianism as traditionally understood is representative of dispensationalism."[58]

Myth 4: Dispensationalism Leads to Non-Lordship Salvation

A fourth myth about dispensationalism is that it necessarily leads to a non-lordship view of salvation. Although taking different forms, non-lordship theology is usually characterized by the beliefs that repentance and surrender of one's life to the lordship of Christ are not necessary for salvation to occur. Some non-lordship advocates also hold that a person can be saved and not evidence spiritual fruit.[59] According to Gerstner, "All this dispensational defection from the gospel has come to a head in the Lordship controversy."[60] To him, "The gospel of dispensational Antinomianism declares that a person may have Christ as Savior but refuse to accept Him as Lord of one's life."[61]

Clearly, some dispensationalists hold to a non-lordship view of salvation or have non-lordship tendencies. Lewis Sperry Chafer, for example, made statements compatible with a non-lordship view.[62] The most well-known advocate of non-lordship theology is Zane

Hodges. His books *The Gospel Under Siege* and *Absolutely Free* are explicit promotions of non-lordship theology.[63] Again, the issue here is not whether some dispensationalists have held to a non-lordship view, but whether the non-lordship view is a necessary result of dispensationalism. We assert that it is not for two reasons.

First, since dispensationalism is primarily about ecclesiology and eschatology, it does not have a necessary connection to the lordship issue, which is a soteriological matter. Some dispensationalists even challenge whether the more extreme non-lordship view of some dispensationalists is even historically related to dispensationalism. Saucy, for example, claims, "The radical non-lordship position of some contemporary dispensationalists, denying the need in salvation of a 'faith that works' based on James 2:14–26, has never been a part of traditional or classical dispensationalism."[64]

Second, several leading dispensational theologians have explicitly rejected the non-lordship view. John MacArthur and Robert Saucy, for example, have openly argued against the non-lordship position as espoused by Hodges.[65] Strangely, in his assertion that dispensationalism is inherently connected to the non-lordship view, Gerstner cites John MacArthur against other dispensationalists.[66] But the logic here is odd. Gerstner cites the dispensationalist John MacArthur to show that dispensationalism's alleged non-lordship view is wrong. Instead of proving Gerstner's point, though, his use of MacArthur shows that there is diversity within dispensationalism on this issue and that there is no inherent connection between dispensationalism and non-lordship theology.

Myth 5: Dispensationalism Is Primarily about Believing In Seven Dispensations

In his book *What Is Covenant Theology?*, R. C. Sproul offered a comparison between convenant theology and dispensationalism. He defined dispensationalism as follows: "Dispensational theology originally believed that the key to biblical interpretation is 'rightly dividing' the Bible into seven dispensations, defined in the original *Scofield*

Reference Bible as specific testing periods in redemptive history."[67] Unfortunately, Sproul's definition of dispensationalism is very common and, to be fair to Sproul, has often been used by dispensationalists as well. In my opinion, however, this definition shows a lack of understanding of what dispensationalism is really about. As I look at the issues, I am convinced that dispensationalism is not primarily about believing in dispensations or believing that there are seven dispensations. Why do I claim this?

First, believing in dispensations cannot be the sole distinguishing characteristic of dispensationalism since all Christians believe in dispensations. What Christian does not believe there is a dispensational difference between the pre-fall and post-fall world? Who does not see a dispensational distinction between the era before and after Christ's first coming? What Christian does not acknowledge that the present world is different from the coming new heaven and new earth?

Also, dispensationalism is not about acknowledging the Greek term *oikonomia,* which is linked to the word "dispensation." After all, what biblical scholar does not believe that the Greek word *oikonomia* is a biblical term? Thus, acknowledging the word *oikonomia* does not make one a dispensationalist, nor does defining this term reveal the essence of dispensationalism. John Feinberg points out the error in believing "that the word 'dispensation' and talk of differing administrative orders only appears in dispensational thinking."[68] Feinberg is also correct that "Defining the term 'dispensation' no more defines the essence of dispensationalism than defining the term 'covenant' explains the essence of Covenant Theology."[69]

In a similar way, the number of dispensations one holds to should not be considered essential to dispensationalism. Traditionally, dispensationalism has been linked with belief in "seven" dispensations, but others have argued for four or eight or some other number. Personally, I have never agreed with the omission of the Eternal State as a "dispensation" in some dispensational schemas. In addition, I have never been entirely convinced of the "test," "failure," "judgment" criteria for determining a dispensation that is often a part of classical dispensationalism. This seems somewhat arbitrary and results in dispensations that are doubtful while omitting others that appear obvious (like the Eternal State). Thus, one is not required to hold to *seven* dispensations to be a true dispensationalist. Feinberg is correct again when he states, "The number of dispensations is not at the heart of the system."[70]

There are other myths about dispensationalism that could be addressed as well. One is the assumption that dispensationalism necessarily teaches that the Sermon on the Mount applies only to the future millennial kingdom. Lewis Sperry Chafer held this view,[71] and it is true that earlier dispensationalists relegated the Sermon on the Mount (Matt. 5–7) to the future millennium. But most dispensationalists today do not hold this view. Most see the Sermon on the Mount as a kingdom ethic that is applicable to today.[72]

Another myth is that dispensationalism teaches a difference between the kingdom of God and kingdom of heaven. This view of a distinction between the kingdom of God and kingdom of heaven was held by some earlier dispensationalists but is largely rejected by more recent dispensationalists. Again, a distinction needs to be made between what certain dispensationalists believe and what is inherent to the system. As John Martin has observed, "One of the greatest misunderstandings is an assumption that there is a single 'dispensational interpretation' of every passage."[73]

Other claims about dispensationalism reach the level of the absurd. Popular radio host Hank Hanegraaff claimed in his book *Apocalypse Code* that dispensationalism's view of a literal fulfillment of land promises to Israel and belief that Israel will undergo tribulation in the future leads to racism and the promotion of ethnic cleansing.[74] This accusation is silly. Of all the books that I have read on dispensationalism, the charge of racism has never been made by those who have offered serious critiques or explanations of dispensationalism. Dispensationalists believe in a restoration of Israel and a future tribulation period because they believe the Bible teaches these things. This hardly leads to racism. In the Old Testament God explicitly chose Israel from all the nations (see Deut. 7:6). Was God exhibiting racism in the Old Testament since He chose to bless ethnic Israel in a way that He did not the other peoples of the earth? Stephen Sizer in his book *Zion's Christian Soldiers* also makes the incredible assertion that dispensational beliefs result in a total lack of concern for major national and global issues:

> Sadly, the mistaken idea of a secret rapture has generated a lot of bad theology. It is probably the reason why many Christians don't seem to care about climate change or about preserving diminishing supplies of natural resources. They are similarly not worried about the national debt, nuclear war, or world poverty, because they hope to be raptured to heaven and avoid suffering the consequences of the coming global holocaust.[75]

Of course, there are no facts or documentation to back up such a claim. As a dispensationalist, I do care about nuclear war, national debt, natural resources, and the other things Sizer mentions. The same is true for most of the dispensationalists I know. Again, this appears to be a case where a person thinks he understands the implications of dispensationalism but really does not.

In sum, the five points stated above are myths about dispensationalism. They are not at the heart of what dispensationalism represents. Those who desire to study and truly understand dispensationalism should avoid these myths altogether.

Notes

1. John S. Feinberg, "Systems of Discontinuity," in *Continuity and Discontinuity: Perspectives on the Relationship between the Old and New Testaments*, ed. John S. Feinberg (Wheaton, IL: Crossway, 1988), 70–71.
2. John F. MacArthur Jr., *Faith Works: The Gospel according to the Apostles* (Dallas: Word, 1993), 222. See chapter 7 where MacArthur demonstrates that theology proper, especially the element of God's sovereignty, informs dispensationalism, but dispensationalism does not inform theology proper.
3. Oswald T. Allis, *Prophecy and the Church* (Philadelphia: Presbyterian and Reformed, 1945), 9. Klooster, when addressing dispensationalism's views on law and grace, Israel and the church, and the covenants, states, "All of this bears on significant differences in eschatology." Fred H. Klooster, "The Biblical Method of Salvation: A Case for Continuity," in *Continuity and Discontinuity*, 133–34. According

to Richard, "The distinction between Soteriology and ecclesiology as major segments of systematic theology allows dispensationalism to be separated from the soteriological systems (Calvinism, Arminianism, etc.)." Ramesh P. Richard, "Soteriological Inclusivism and Dispensationalism," *Bibliotheca Sacra* 151/601 (January –March 1994): 97, n. 44.

4. Robert L. Saucy, *The Case for Progressive Dispensationalism: The Interface between Dispensational & Nondispensational Theology* (Grand Rapids: Zondervan, 1993).
5. Craig A. Blaising and Darrell L. Bock, eds., *Dispensationalism, Israel and the Church: The Search for Definition* (Grand Rapids: Zondervan, 1992).
6. Craig A. Blaising and Darrell L. Bock, *Progressive Dispensationalism: An Up-To-Date Handbook of Contemporary Dispensational Thought* (Wheaton, IL: Bridgepoint, 1993).
7. Paul Enns, *The Moody Handbook of Theology* (Chicago: Moody, 1989).
8. John S. Feinberg, "Salvation in the Old Testament," in *Tradition and Testament: Essays in Honor of Charles Lee Feinberg*, eds. John S. Feinberg and Paul D. Feinberg (Chicago: Moody, 1981), 48.
9. Charles C. Ryrie, *Dispensationalism* (Chicago: Moody, 1995), 105.
10. See John Wick Bowman, "The Bible and Modern Religions II, Dispensationalism," *Interpretation* 10 (April 1956): 178.
11. Clarence B. Bass, *Backgrounds to Dispensationalism* (Grand Rapids: Eerdmans, 1960), 34. See also J. Barton Payne, *The Imminent Appearing of Christ* (Grand Rapids: Eerdmans, 1962), 31–32.
12. As Feinberg has observed, "In all honesty, however, it must be admitted that statements made by certain dispensationalists in the past appeared to teach multiple ways of salvation." Feinberg, "Salvation in the Old Testament," 42.
13. *Scofield Reference Bible* (New York: Oxford, 1909), 1115 n. 1(2).
14. See William E. Cox, *Why I Left Scofieldism* (Phillipsburg, NJ: P&R, n.d.), 19.
15. Fred Klooster, "The Biblical Method of Salvation: Continuity," in *Continuity and Discontinuity*, 132.
16. Charles C. Ryrie, *Dispensationalism Today* (Chicago: Moody, 1965), 110–31.
17. Ibid., 106–7.
18. *The New Scofield Reference Bible* (New York: Oxford, 1967), 1124 n. 1(2).
19. Saucy, *The Case For Progressive Dispensationalism*, 14.
20. Klooster, "The Biblical Method of Salvation: Continuity," 133. Klooster even asserted that there is "significant evangelical agreement" between dispensationalists and Reformed theologians on the issue of "a single way of salvation," 133.
21. Anthony A. Hoekema, *The Bible and the Future* (Grand Rapids: Eerdmans, 1979), 194.
22. Daniel Fuller, *Gospel and Law: Contrast or Continuum?* (Grand Rapids: Eerdmans, 1980), 45. Erickson writes, "Some critics of dispensationalism have imputed to its supporters a belief in new ways or channels of salvation. More correctly, however, dispensationalists say that while new light has been shed upon the relationship between God and man, no new way of entering into that relationship has

ever been insinuated." Millard J. Erickson, *A Basic Guide to Eschatology: Making Sense of the Millennium* (Grand Rapids: Baker, 1998), 110.

23. John H. Gerstner, *Wrongly Dividing the Word of Truth: A Critique of Dispensationalism* (Brentwood, TN: Wolgemuth & Hyatt, 1991), 168.

24. John Feinberg, "Salvation in the Old Testament," 48. It is not correct, as Gerstner and some older nondispensationalists have asserted, that the dispensational distinctions between Israel and the church naturally lead to multiple ways of salvation. Distinctions between groups can exist without different methods of salvation being present. No evidence exists that any leading dispensational theologians ever taught that the Israel/church distinctions included the idea of different methods of salvation for the two groups.

25. Arminianism takes its name from Jacobus Arminius (1560–1609) and the movement that followed his teachings. Arminianism is known for the following views: conditional election is based on the foreknowledge of God; God's grace can be resisted; Christ's atonement was universal in scope; man has a free will—through prevenient grace he can cooperate with God; and man can lose his salvation through disobedience. Arminianism was condemned by the Synod of Dort in 1619.

26. Keith A. Mathison, *Dispensationalism: Rightly Dividing the People of God?* (Phillipsburg, NJ: P&R, 1995), 50–51.

27. Gerstner, *Wrongly Dividing the Word of Truth*, 115.

28. Ibid.

29. Ibid., back cover.

30. John Feinberg, "Systems of Discontinuity," 70.

31. David L. Turner, "'Dubious Evangelicalism'? A Response to John Gerstner's Critique of Dispensationalism," *Grace Theological Journal* 12:2 (fall 1991): 268.

32. S. Lewis Johnson Jr., "The Testimony of John to Jesus," *Believers Bible Bulletin* (December 20, 1981), 3.

33. Jeffrey Khoo, "Dispensational Premillennialism in Reformed Theology: The Contribution of J. O. Buswell to the Millennial Debate," *Journal of the Evangelical Theological Society* 44:4 (January 2001): 714.

34. Ibid., 698. Khoo himself is a dispensationalist who is also Reformed: "As a Bible-Presbyterian minister, I am Reformed and hold to the covenant system of theology. In the area of eschatology, I hold to a premillennial view that sees a distinction between Israel as God's chosen nation and the Church as the spiritual body of Christ. As regards the rapture, I take the pretribulational view." Khoo, 716.

35. Richard L. Mayhue, "Who Is Wrong?" A Review of John Gerstner's *Wrongly Dividing the Word of Truth*, *The Master's Seminary Journal* 3 (spring 1992): 89.

36. Vern S. Poythress, *Understanding Dispensationalists*, 2nd ed. (Phillipsburg, NJ: P&R, 1994), 20.

37. George M. Marsden, "Introduction: Reformed and American," in *Reformed Theology in America: A History of Its Modern Development*, 2d ed., ed., George M. Marsden (Grand Rapids: Baker, 1997), 8.

38. C. Norman Kraus, *Dispensationalism in America* (Richmond, VA: John Knox, 1958), 59.
39. Wayne Grudem, *Systematic Theology: An Introduction to Biblical Doctrine* (Grand Rapids: Zondervan, 1994), 338.
40. Robert D. Linder, "Antinomianism," in *Evangelical Dictionary of Theology*, ed. Walter A. Elwell (Grand Rapids: Baker, 1984), 57. The term comes from the Greek *anti* (against) and *nomos* (law).
41. See Robert A. Pyne, "Antinomianism and Dispensationalism," *Bibliotheca Sacra* 153 (April–June 1996): 141.
42. Gerstner, *Wrongly Dividing the Word of Truth*, v.
43. Ibid., 240.
44. As R. C. Sproul writes, "One of the most serious charges Gerstner levels at dispensationalism is the charge that its system of theology is inherently antinomian." Gerstner, *Wrongly Dividing the Word of Truth*, with a foreword by R. C. Sproul, x.
45. Gerstner, *Wrongly Dividing the Word of Truth*, 244.
46. Ibid., 245.
47. MacArthur, *Faith Works*, 93–98.
48. Ibid., 114.
49. Donald G. Barnhouse, *Romans* (Grand Rapids: Eerdmans, 1961), 3:10–12.
50. Alva J. McClain, *Romans: The Gospel of God's Grace* (Winona Lake, IN: BMH, 1973), 141.
51. Curtis Crenshaw and Grover E. Gunn, *Dispensationalism Today, Yesterday, and Tomorrow* (Memphis: Footstool, 1995), 92.
52. Ibid., 83–84.
53. John Feinberg, "Systems of Discontinuity," 71.
54. MacArthur, *Faith Works*, 225. According to MacArthur, "The men who taught me in seminary were all dispensationalists. Yet none of them would have defended no-lordship teaching."
55. Wayne G. Strickland, "The Inauguration of the Law of Christ with the Gospel of Christ: A Dispensational View," in *The Law, the Gospel, and the Modern Christian: Five Views*, ed. Wayne G. Strickland (Grand Rapids: Zondervan, 1993), 277. Feinberg writes, "Dispensationalists claim that the believer is under the Law of Christ as outlined in the NT. As in the case of the Mosaic Code, the Law of Christ embodies the timelessly true moral principles of God which are instantiated in both codes. But as a separate code the Law of Christ excludes the ceremonial and civil aspects of the Mosaic Code. Dispensationalism is neither antinomian nor entails it." "Systems of Discontinuity," 71.
56. Blaising and Bock, *Progressive Dispensationalism*, 199. Strickland also states, "The moral law expressed in the Mosaic law under the old covenant has its parallel in the law of Christ under the new covenant, so that the believer today may know God's moral will." "The Inauguration of the Law of Christ with the Gospel of Christ: A Dispensational View," 277.
57. Erickson, *A Basic Guide to Eschatology*, 110.

58. Craig A. Blaising, "Dispensationalism: The Search for Definition," in *Dispensationalism, Israel and the Church*, 14 n. 3.

59. Belcher relates six main characteristics of non-lordship theology: (1) the call to salvation and the call to discipleship are distinct; (2) the believer has the choice to produce or not produce fruit in his life; (3) lack of spiritual fruit is no sign a person is lost; (4) repentance is not a condition of salvation; (5) the concept of lordship is not a condition of salvation but should follow the experience of salvation by faith; and (6) those who possess true saving faith can live in habitual sin or even apostatize from the faith. Richard P. Belcher, *A Layman's Guide to the Lordship Controversy* (Southbridge, MA: Crowne Publications, 1990), 22–23.

60. Gerstner, *Wrongly Dividing the Word of Truth*, 293.

61. Ibid., 292.

62. Chafer said, "The error of imposing Christ's Lordship upon the unsaved is disastrous. . . ." Lewis Sperry Chafer, *Systematic Theology* (Dallas: Dallas Seminary Press, 1948), 3:385.

63. Zane Hodges, *The Gospel Under Siege: Faith and Works in Tension*, 2d ed. (Dallas: Redencion Viva, 1992); *Absolutely Free!* (Dallas: Redencion Viva, 1989).

64. Saucy, *The Case for Progressive Dispensationalism*, 16 n. 7.

65. Saucy refers to the "error of non-lordship salvation." Saucy, *The Case for Progressive Dispensationalism*, 15–16 n. 8; See MacArthur, *Faith Works.*

66. Gerstner, *Wrongly Dividing the Word of Truth*, 294–95.

67. R. C. Sproul, *What Is Reformed Theology: Understanding the Basics* (Grand Rapids: Baker, 1997), 99.

68. John Feinberg, "Systems of Discontinuity," 69.

69. Ibid.

70. Ibid., 70.

71. Lewis S. Chafer, *Systematic Theology*, 5:98.

72. See John A. Martin, "Christ, the Fulfillment of the Law in the Sermon on the Mount," in *Dispensationalism, Israel and the Church*, 248–63.

73. Ibid., 249 n. 2.

74. Hank Hanegraaff, *Apocalypse Code: Find Out What the Bible Really Says about the End Times and Why It Matters Today* (Nashville: Thomas Nelson, 2007), xx–xxii.

75. Stephen Sizer, *Zion's Christian Soldiers?* (Nottingham, England: Inter-Varsity, 2007), 136–37.

Chapter Three

WHY FUTURISTIC PREMILLENNIALISM?

Richard Mayhue

During my childhood years, I loved the challenge of jigsaw puzzles. Early on, a basic strategy emerged that usually led to successfully completing the puzzle. First, I found the most obvious, most determinative pieces for the puzzle that would guide all my further efforts. This involved identifying the four unique corner pieces. Second, I located the next most obvious pieces, which turned out to be the few with one straight edge—the border pieces. With these two steps complete, the jigsaw puzzle picture took on a basic shape and design to which the multitude of remaining pieces conformed and could not change.

The same approach works well in solving the millennial-view puzzle. Four basic views prevail today: Postmillennialism, Amillennialism, Historic Premillennialism, and Futuristic Premillennialism. I intend to define each of the four perspectives, and then explain which one is biblically preferable and why.

The terms "millennium" and "millennialism" come from the Latin word *mille*, meaning "one thousand." Biblically, they point to the Greek phrase *chilia etē*, "one thousand years," which appears six times in Revelation (20:2, 3, 4, 5, 6, 7). The prefix "post" in Postmillennialism refers to Christ's second coming after the millennium, which on this view refers to the kingdom of the church age. The prefix "a" in Amillennialism indicates that there is no millennium on earth before or after Christ's second coming. Both of the "pre" positions (Historic Premillennialism and Futuristic Premillennialism) believe that there is a millennial period on earth that is preceded by Christ's second coming.

Postmillennialism teaches that the kingdom of God is currently being advanced with increasing triumph in the world through gospel preaching and the ministry of the church. Christ now rules over this "golden age" of undetermined length from heaven and will return to earth at the end—thus a Postmillennial return. The church is considered to be spiritual Israel, having inherited the promises made to Abraham and David, which were abrogated for Israel because of their national disobedience. Therefore, there will be no future for a national Israel with any biblical significance. When Christ returns at the end of the millennium, then the rapture, second advent, general resurrection, and judgment all take place in rapid sequence, and finally comes the eternal state.

Amillennialism teaches that the church is now spiritual Israel, having inherited God's promises to Abraham and David that were forfeited by Israel because of continued disobedience. Christ rules over this spiritual kingdom from heaven, and the redemptive work of Christ continues on earth, but without the optimism of Postmillennialism. There is no expectation of a restored national Israel that will have prophetic significance. The affairs of earth will deteriorate until Christ intervenes at His second coming. All of the end-time events—for example, the rapture, general resurrection, and the judgment—happen in a short span of time as the immediate prelude to eternity future.

Historic Premillennialism teaches that Christ will return to rapture the church, judge living unbelievers, and set up an earthly kingdom (some say it will be one thousand years in length, while others believe one thousand is a symbolic number meaning "a long time"). Christ now rules over the earth from heaven and in the future will rule over a millennium on earth where little distinction is made between the church and restored national Israel. At the end of the millennium, there is the resurrection of unbelievers and the final judgment, which is followed by the eternal state. This category of Premillennialism generally interprets Revelation 6–18 in a "historic" sense, i.e., that Revelation 6–18 should be interpreted as past events in church history rather than future ones—thus the name "Historic Premillennialism."

Advocates of *Futuristic Premillennialism*, also called Dispensational Premillennialism, use a consistent grammatical-historical approach to both the Old and New Testament Scriptures by which the Bible is interpreted normally throughout, regardless of whether the subject matter is eschatological (future-related) or not. Therefore, God's promises to Abraham and David are viewed in a futuristic sense as anticipating a restored nation of Israel. In this pattern, the rapture comes first (see chapter 4, "Why a Pretribulation Rapture?"), followed by Christ's second coming at the end of the seven-year tribulation period, biblically spoken of as Daniel's seventieth week. After judging the earth and its inhabitants, Christ rules over the earth for one thousand years (the millennium) from His Davidic throne in Jerusalem. At the end of the millennium, Satan rebels one final time but is instantly defeated. Then comes the resurrection and judgment of all unbelievers at the Great White Throne, which is followed by the New Jerusalem and the eternal state. (See chart on p. 12.)

The remainder of this chapter will apply the three rules of conquering jigsaw puzzles to solving the prophetic puzzle. There are four unmistakable corner pieces that connect to four distinct border pieces. These eight pieces correspond to my contention that there are eight defining biblical reasons to champion Futuristic Premillennialism as the actual future plan of God. Then all of the less obvious, detailed-but-not-defining pieces can be worked on, although they will not alter the broad, basic pattern that this chapter outlines. It will not be any one or two reasons that make the case for Futuristic Premillennialism compelling, but rather the combined strength of them all. We might never know or understand every minute detail of God's prophetic plan, but we can know the basics. The purpose of this primer is to help you be certain about the fundamentals of biblical prophecy.

A Consistent Hermeneutic

Futuristic Premillennialism is distinct because it is the only option out of the four major views that results from (1) dealing with all Scripture inductively, (2) consistently employing the time-tested grammatical-historical hermeneutical approach, (3) engaging all the Scriptures with the principles and skills of unprejudiced exegesis, and (4) not having to shift to a double-meaning hermeneutic when dealing with ecclesiology and eschatology. This is the first "corner piece" to our puzzle.

In other words, Futuristic Premillennialism takes a "normal" or "plain" approach to all the Scriptures, all of the time, which means that Futuristic Premillennialism:

- Takes the biblical text at face value.
- Interprets the biblical text in context.
- Recognizes symbolic language/speech figures and the reality they express.
- Uses clear texts to interpret the unclear/more difficult.
- Allows for the progress of revelation without dramatically altering the meaning of previous revelation.
- Allows for double fulfillment of prophecies (near/far)—for example, two advents of Christ in Isaiah 61—without resorting to double meanings in a primary sense.

Futuristic Premillennialism is more attractive hermeneutically because it alone allows for the greatest consistency in two biblical realms:

- Approaching any book of the Bible with the same general interpretive approach whether it be (1) the unvarnished history of Joshua, (2) the figurative language of Solomon's

Song, or (3) the prophetic books—both major and minor prophets.

- Approaching any topic of systematic theology with the same general interpretive schema rather than switching when one encounters ecclesiology or eschatology as do the other three major options.

Futuristic Premillennialism is more attractive hermeneutically because it does not involve or require:

- A preunderstanding of alleged biblical covenants (such as redemption, grace, works) made in eternity past for which there is no widely persuasive biblical evidence and which are at best vaguely inferential.

- Allegorical interpretation (a third- and fourth-century AD aberration introduced by Origen and Augustine). Compare Galatians 4:24–31, where Paul employs allegory with apostolic sanction but with clear interpretive meaning used only as an illustration.

- Forced historical interpretations on texts in (1) the major and minor prophets, (2) the Olivet Discourse, and (3) Revelation. For example, Revelation 11:1–2 interpreted as the destruction of Jerusalem in AD 70 rather than a future time in the first half of Daniel's seventieth week.

- A minimization of the typical or analogical use of the Old Testament by the New Testament (e.g., Matt. 2:15/Hos. 11:1 and Matt. 2:14–18/Jer. 31:15).

The final and ultimate feature that makes Futuristic Premillennialism both unique and more attractive than the other options is its conformity to a proven paradigm of how Old Testament prophecies were actually fulfilled. Such prophecies came to pass in accordance with a normal hermeneutic, as employed by Futuristic Premillennialism. For example:

- Old Testament prophecies fulfilled in Old Testament history
  Genesis 17:6—from Abraham would come kings
  Daniel 2—world kingdoms
  Habakkuk—in regard to Babylon and Judah

- Old Testament prophecies fulfilled in Christ's earthly life and ministry
  Tribe of Judah—Genesis 49:10
  Born in Bethlehem—Micah 5:2
  Crucifixion—Psalm 22

Even Covenantalists admit the correctness of the Premillennial outcome, if a consistent, normal hermeneutic is used. For example:

O. T. Allis in *Prophecy and the Church:*[1]
". . . the Old Testament prophecies if literally interpreted cannot be regarded as having been fulfilled or as being capable of fulfillment in this present age."

Floyd E. Hamilton in *The Basis of the Millennial Faith:*[2]
"Now we must frankly admit that a literal interpretation of the Old Testament prophecies gives us just such a picture of an earthly reign of the Messiah as the premillennialist pictures."

Loraine Boettner in *The Meaning of the Millennium:*[3]
"It is generally agreed that if the prophecies are taken literally, they do foretell a restoration of the nation of Israel in the land of Palestine with the Jews having a prominent place in that kingdom and ruling over the other nations."

Based on what they knew of Old Testament prophetic material, the first-century BC Jewish community was not looking for the first advent of Christ as presented in the Gospels. Rather, they believed that Messiah's second coming was near and would end Jewish tribulation at the hands of other nations, and establish the Davidic kingdom (2 Sam. 7:12–17) on earth.

The following features summarize their biblical expectations concerning Messiah.[4]

- A season of extreme tribulation would prevail prior to Messiah's arrival.
- In the midst of this upheaval, Elijah would arrive as the forerunner and announcer of Messiah.
- Messiah would then come to earth.
- The nations would rise up against Messiah.
- A coalition of nations would be defeated and destroyed.
- Jerusalem would be reoccupied and rebuilt.
- The Jewish Diaspora would return to Jerusalem.
- Israel would become the capital of the world.
- A time of peace and prosperity would be inaugurated.

Interestingly, this is very similar to what Futuristic Premillennialism expects will happen at the time of Messiah's second arrival. Approaches based on a Covenantal understanding—including Amillennialism, Historic Premillennialism, and Postmillennialism—propose very different outcomes.

Futuristic Premillennialism versus Covenantalism

Consider the question, "Why would a Futuristic Premillennialist and a Covenantalist—both saved and godly people—who agree on about 80 percent of their theological beliefs take such opposite views when dealing with ecclesiology and eschatology?"

- The first reason is the Covenantalist's preunderstanding of the covenant(s) of grace/redemption, which in reality have no biblical basis.

- The second reason is the use of a double-meaning hermeneutic that is required to achieve the appropriate outcomes demanded by a Covenantal preunderstanding.

- The third factor is replacement theology or supercessionism—Israel is replaced by the church, which inherits Israel's spiritual blessings.

Futuristic Premillennialism, on the other hand, comes to the text with no other preunderstanding than a consistent grammatical-historical hermeneutic that is employed consistently throughout the Scriptures in all realms of theology.

Let me clarify the point by quoting well-known theologian J. I. Packer.

> What is covenant theology? The straightforward, if provocative answer to that question is that it is what is nowadays called a hermeneutic—that is, a way of reading the whole Bible that is itself part of the overall interpretation of the Bible that it undergirds. A successful hermeneutic is a consistent interpretative procedure yielding a consistent understanding of Scripture that in turn confirms the propriety of the procedure itself. . . . Once Christians have got this far, the covenant theology of the Scriptures is something that they can hardly miss.[5]

Dr. Packer has engaged in what logicians call "circular reasoning," meaning that one begins with an assumption that guarantees he will reach a particular conclusion. If one's hermeneutic is one's theology, then one's theology determines one's hermeneutic; this way of thinking is a logical fallacy that inevitably leads to erroneous and unsound conclusions.

A theology is *not* a hermeneutic. Such thinking undermines proper Bible interpretation. Actually, good hermeneutics (principles of interpreting literature) applied by skillful exegesis (artful application of interpretive principles) can lead to a theology, but not the reverse. Unfortunately, Dr. Packer and all who follow his lead have put the proverbial theological cart before the hermeneutical horse.

However, every Amillennialist, Historic Premillennialist, and Postmillennialist follows this process, knowingly or unknowingly, in part or in whole, when it comes to dealing with the identity of the church (ecclesiology) and the future of Israel (eschatology). When they do not reach their predetermined theological end using normal hermeneutics (which has served them well in all other areas of theology), they change their hermeneutic to yield the predetermined conclusions they began with. This produces a prejudiced approach to interpretation in order to validate a predetermined conclusion. This is an unacceptable, inconsistent, and invalid manner in which to interpret the Bible. Thus, it is rejected in every way and usage by Futuristic Premillennialism. Only a consistent hermeneutic can lead to a God-intended interpretation of the sacred text. For Futuristic Premillennialism, a consistent grammatical-historical hermeneutic to interpret all of Scripture is a presupposition, not a predetermined theology.

Futuristic Premillennialism does not require new special rules of interpretation when it comes to prophetic texts. The biblical text is taken at normal face value, in its context, recognizing symbolic language and speech figures, plus the reality that they represent. It allows the interpreter to take the same general approach to the history of Joshua, or the highly figurative images of Solomon's Song, or the prophetic books.

Therefore, unless some clear, uncontested mandate from Scripture changes how one interprets second-coming prophecies (and there is none), then prophetic Scripture should be interpreted consistently throughout the Bible. Only Futuristic Premillennialism does so.

An Impartial Exegesis

The text of Revelation 20:1–10 (see chapter 6, "What about Revelation 20?") might well be considered the pinnacle of millennial studies. For here one encounters a unique historical period that is designated as "one thousand years" (20:2, 3, 4, 5, 6, 7).

Several important questions require answers in order to interpret this number and this text accurately. First, it needs to be asked if this period of time is yet future or has already been fulfilled? Next, is this period actually one thousand years in length or does the term represent another length of time, say, five thousand years? Finally, how has the "one thousand" of Revelation 20:1–10 been interpreted in the past? The answers to these questions make up our second corner piece.

The Time of Fulfillment

Peculiar events occur during this special segment of time. An angel binds Satan with a great chain (20:1–2). Satan is then incarcerated in the abyss, which is shut and sealed (20:3). Thus, Satan no longer deceives the nations until the one thousand years transpire. The tribulation martyrs are resurrected to reign with Christ (20:4, 6). When the one thousand years end, Satan is released for a short time to once again deceive the nations (20:3, 7–8).

We begin with the question, "Has this already been fulfilled?" Most who hold a form of "Covenant" theology respond affirmatively and point to Christ's victory over Satan at the cross as the starting point. Texts such as Matthew 12:22–29 are employed to bolster the position that Satan is *now* bound in fulfillment of Revelation 20.

While it is true that Christ won the victory at Calvary and Satan's doom was eternally settled, it is not true that Satan has been incapacitated in the manner demanded by the text. Satan still entices men to lie (Acts 5:3). He is blinding the minds of unbelievers to the gospel of the glory of Christ in God (2 Cor. 4:4). He currently disguises himself as an angel of light to deceive the church (2 Cor. 11:2–3, 13–15). The devil hinders ministers of God (1 Thess. 2:18) and roams about the earth to devour its population (1 Pet. 5:8). To any unbiased student of Scripture, Revelation 20 could not refer to the present time in light of these abundant testimonies of Satan's present, frenetic pace.

Therefore, we can conclude that Revelation 20 looks to some future time of special containment. Since it is yet ahead, we ask, "How long will this time last?"

The Length of Time

The bottom line in this discussion asks, "Does *chilia etē* in Revelation 20 really mean a literal one thousand years?" Let's begin the discussion by looking at biblical numbers in general and then narrow the focus to Revelation and "one thousand" in particular.

It is commonly understood as a basic rule of hermeneutics that numbers should be accepted at face value, i.e., conveying a mathematical quantity, unless there is substantial evidence to warrant otherwise. This dictum for interpreting biblical numbers is generally accepted as the proper starting point.

This rule holds true throughout the Bible, including Revelation. A survey of numbers in the Apocalypse supports this. For instance, seven churches and seven angels in Revelation 1 refer to seven literal churches and their messengers. Twelve tribes and twelve apostles refer to actual, historical numbers (21:12, 14). Ten days (2:10), five months (9:5), one-third of mankind (9:15), two witnesses (11:3), forty-two months (11:2),1260 days (11:3), twelve stars (12:1), ten horns (13:1), two hundred miles (14:20), three demons (16:13), and five fallen kings (17:9–10) all use numbers in their normal sense. Out of the scores of numbers in Revelation, only two (seven spirits in 1:4 and 666 in 13:18) are conclusively used in a symbolic fashion. While this line of reasoning does not prove that "one thousand" in Revelation 20 should be taken normally, it does put the burden of proof on those who disagree with accepting "one thousand" as one thousand.

Not only are numbers in general to be taken normally in Revelation, but more specifically numbers referring to time. In Revelation 4–20 there are at least twenty-five references to measurements of time. Only two of these demand to be understood in something other than a literal sense, and these do not involve actual numbers. The "great day of their wrath" (6:17) would likely exceed twenty-four hours and "the hour of His judgment" (14:7) seemingly extends beyond sixty minutes. There is nothing, however, in the phrase "one thousand years" that suggests a symbolic interpretation.

This next point is very important. Never in the Bible is "year" used with a numerical adjective when it does not refer to the actual period of time that it mathematically represents. Unless evidence to the contrary can be provided, Revelation 20 is not the one exception in the entire Scripture.

Also, the number "one thousand" is not used elsewhere in the Bible with a symbolic sense. Job 9:3; 33:23; Psalms 50:10; 90:4; Ecclesiastes 6:6; 7:28; and 2 Peter 3:8 have been used in support of the idea that one thousand in our text is used symbolically. However, these attempts fail because in each of these texts one thousand is used in its normal sense to make a vivid point.

One thousand and its varied combinations are used frequently in both Testaments. No one questions the literal quantity of five thousand believers (Acts 4:4), twenty-three thousand men killed (1 Cor. 10:8), or seven thousand killed (Rev. 11:13). Likewise, there is no exegetical reason to question the normalcy of one thousand years in Revelation 20.

The Testimony of History

From the post-apostolic era, the church understood the "millennium" of Revelation 20 as a literal one thousand years. Papias, Barnabas, Justin Martyr, Irenaeus, and Tertullian all gave evidence of this fact in their writings. The church taught nothing else until the fourth century.

When theologians began to go beyond what the Bible taught about the millennium, when they began to make it a period of time that would be more for the enjoyment of man than for the glory of God, some reacted to correct this excess by interpreting this time as something less than an actual historical period. In the fifth century, Augustine popularized the approach that reasoned that the church inherited the blessings promised to Israel and that they are spiritual, not earthly. He taught that Revelation 20 referred to this time.

However, even Augustine understood from Revelation 20 that this period lasted one thousand literal years. So Augustine, called by many the father of Amillennialism, took the one thousand years normally. Even to this day some non-Premillennialists interpret Revelation 20 to be one thousand actual years in length.

In light of the above discussion, we conclude that the one thousand years of Revelation 20 requires a future fulfillment since a fair-minded appraisal of the text and history determines that it has not yet occurred. Further, a survey of numbers in the Bible and Revelation pointedly demands that the one thousand years be understood in a normal sense. This position receives further substantiation through the early church's interpretation of this text, which aligns with the Futuristic Premillennial view.

God's Unconditional Covenants[6]

God, who is faithful to keep (Deut. 7:9; 1 Kings 8:23; 2 Chron. 6:14; Neh. 1:5; 9:32; Dan. 9:4) covenants (Rom. 9:4; Gal. 4:24; Eph. 2:12), explicitly made six distinct covenants with promises to Israel: (1) Noahic (Gen. 6:18; 9:8–17); (2) Abrahamic (Gen. 15:1–21; 17:1–22; 26:2–5, 24; 28:13–17); (3) Mosaic (Ex. 19–20, 24); (4) Priestly (Num. 25:10–13); (5) Davidic (2 Sam. 7:12–16); and (6) new (Jer. 31:31–34). Five are unconditional, irrevocable, everlasting, and by grace; only the Mosaic covenant was conditional, revocable, temporary, and by works. The Bible never mentions any alleged covenant of grace or of redemption nor does Scripture address a supposed Edenic (also known as covenant of works) or Adamic covenant in the over 280 uses of "covenant" in the Old Testament and over thirty appearances in the New. The Abrahamic, Davidic, and new covenants speak to the issue of Futuristic Premillennialism, so let's examine them in detail.

Abrahamic Covenant

God made the autonomous, sacred (Luke 1:72) Abrahamic covenant unilaterally (Gen. 15:7–17) with Abraham, Isaac, and Jacob (Ex. 2:24; Lev. 26:42; Ps. 105:9–10), and it is stated or reaffirmed at least eight times (Gen. 12:1–3; 13:14–17; 15:1–21; 17:1–21; 22:15–18; 26:2–5, 24; 28:13–17; 35:10–12). This covenant was everlasting

(Gen. 17:7–8, 13, 19; 1 Chr. 16:15, 17; Pss. 105:8, 10; 111:5, 9; Is. 24:5); irrevocable (Heb. 6:13–18); superior to the Mosaic covenant (Rom. 4:13; Gal. 3:17); immediately conditional (Gen. 17:14; Lev. 26:43; 2 Kings 13:23; Pss. 74:20; 106:45; Is. 24:5), but ultimately unconditional (Lev. 26:44; Deut. 4:31; Jer. 33:25–26; Ezek. 16:60); whose sign is circumcision (Gen. 17:9–14; Acts 7:8). This covenant promised: 1) Abrahamic descendants ethnically (Gen. 13:15; 15:18; 17:2, 7; 22:17; 26:3; 28:13–14; 35:11–12); 2) Abrahamic descendants redemptively (Rom. 4:11; Gal. 3:7, 26–29); 3) the Savior (Gal. 3:16); 4) a nation (Gen. 12:2; 17:4; 35:11); 5) land (Gen. 12:1; 13:15, 17; 15:18; 17:8; 26:3; 28:13; 35:12; Ex. 6:4; Lev. 26:42; Ps. 105:11); 6) personal blessing and protection (Gen. 12:3; 28:15; 35:12; Pss. 105:14–15; 106:44–46); and 7) blessings to the nations (Gen. 12:3; 17:4–6; 22:18; 26:4; 28:14; 35:11), especially redemption (Ps. 111:9; Rom. 4:16–18; Gal. 3:8).

Davidic Covenant

With absolute unconditionality (2 Sam. 7:15; 1 Chr. 17:13; Ps. 89:33–37), God promised David (2 Sam. 7:12–16; 1 Chr. 17:11–14) that a descendant (2 Sam. 7:12, 16; 1 Chr. 17:11, 14) would be enthroned (2 Sam. 7:13, 16; 1 Chr. 17:12, 14) to rule over Israel and the world (2 Sam. 7:12, 16; 1 Chr. 17:11, 14). This Davidic covenant is autonomous and unilateral (2 Sam. 23:5; 2 Chr. 13:5; Ps. 89:3, 28, 34); irrevocable (2 Sam. 7:15; 1 Chr. 17:13; Ps. 89:34; Jer. 33:20–22, 25–26); and everlasting (2 Sam. 7:13, 16; 23:5; 1 Chr. 17:12, 14; 2 Chr. 13:5; 21:7; Ps. 89:28, 36). However, the covenant was immediately conditional (2 Sam. 7:14; 1 Kings 2:3–4; Pss. 89:30–32, 39; 132:12) since sinful descendants were disqualified. While the covenant is not explicitly named in the New Testament (cf. Acts 2:30), it appears clear that Jesus Christ is the specific Davidic seed (Matt. 1:1; John 7:42) whom God intends to enthrone (Matt. 19:28; 25:31; Luke 1:32; John 18:37) for a future, earthly rule over Israel and the nations (Ps. 110:2; Zech. 14:9; Luke 1:33; Rev. 11:15; 12:5; 19:15–16) during the millennial kingdom (Rev. 20:1–10).

New Covenant

The unconditional, unilateral (Ezek. 20:37; 37:26), everlasting (Is. 55:3; 59:21; 61:8; Jer. 32:40; 50:5; Ezek. 16:60; 37:26; Heb. 9:15; 13:20), and irrevocable (Is. 54:10; Heb. 7:22) new covenant assumes nullification, due to Israel's sin, of the conditional Old/Mosaic covenant (Jer. 31:32; Ezek. 44:7; Zech. 11:10–11). Originally made with Israel (Jer. 31:31) and containing redemptive blessings of both salvation (Is. 49:8; Jer. 31:34) and prosperity (Is. 49:8; Jer. 32:40ff.; 50:5; Ezek. 34:25; Hos. 2:18ff.), this autonomous covenant later allowed the New Testament church to participate salvifically (cf. Rom. 11:11–32) through Christ, the messenger (Mal. 3:1) and mediator (Heb. 8:6; 9:15; 12:24) of a better covenant (Heb. 7:22; 8:6) purchased with the blood and death of this unique High Priest (Zech. 9:11; Matt. 26:28; 1 Cor. 11:25; Heb. 9:15; 10:29; 12:24; 13:20). Old Testament believers anticipated (Heb. 9:15) Christ's life-giving sacrifice (2 Cor. 3:6) involving: (1) grace (Heb. 10:29); (2) peace (Is. 54:10; Ezek. 34:25; 37:26); (3) the Spirit (Is. 59:21); (4) redemption (Is. 49:8; Jer. 31:34; Heb. 10:29); (5) removing sin (Jer. 31:34; Rom. 11:27; Heb. 10:17); (6) a new heart (Jer. 31:33; Heb. 8:10; 10:16); and (7) a new relationship with God (Jer. 31:33; Ezek. 16:62; 37:26–27; Heb. 8:10). This covenant pictures Israel's new betrothal to God (Hos. 2:19–20) initiated by the same divine mercy as the Davidic covenant (Is. 55:3).

Israel's Future

Both the Abrahamic and Davidic covenants were intended to be unconditional in their ultimate effect. Nowhere does Scripture suggest that Israel forsook God's blessings forever and that these blessings have now allegedly been made spiritual and inherited by the church. To say otherwise, in effect, is to misrepresent God's intentions.

The Abrahamic covenant is called an everlasting covenant in which God gave Abraham and his descendants the land of Israel as an everlasting possession (Gen. 17:7–8). God's promise to Abraham is corroborated in 1 Chronicles 16:15–17 and Psalm 105:8–15. By this covenant, a people and a land are promised for Israel.

The Davidic covenant of 2 Samuel 7:8–16 is called an everlasting covenant in 2 Samuel 23:5; 2 Chronicles 21:7; and Psalm 89:3–4, 19–29, 36. By this covenant, a throne is promised for Israel.

The apostle Paul said it best when speaking about Israel, "For I do not want you, brethren, to be uninformed of this mystery . . . for the gifts and the calling of God are irrevocable" (Rom. 11:25, 29). Only Futuristic Premillennialism takes the unconditional nature of God's eternal covenants and their irreversibility seriously.

God's Uncompromising Promises

The fourth and final defining corner piece to the prophetic puzzle focuses on God's undeniable promises to an ancient nation that He would soon severely judge. Israel understood that there would be a time in the future when they as a nation and a people would be restored. Then, the long-awaited Messiah would come and rule from Jerusalem, seated on David's throne, over Israel and the entire world.

The following Old Testament texts need no explanation as they clearly point to a Futuristic Premillennial hope for Israel.

Jeremiah 24:6–7
For I will set My eyes on them for good, and I will bring them again to this land; and I will build them up and not overthrow them, and I will plant them and not pluck them up. I will give them a heart to know Me, for I am the LORD; and they will be My people, and I will be their God, for they will return to Me with their whole heart.

Jeremiah 31:12
They will come and shout for joy on the height of Zion, and they will be radiant over the bounty of the LORD—over the grain, and the new wine, and the oil, and over the young of the flock and the herd; and their life will be like a watered garden, and they will never languish again.

Jeremiah 31:40
The whole valley of the dead bodies and of the ashes, and all the fields as far as the brook Kidron, to the corner of the Horse Gate toward the east, shall be holy to the LORD; it will not be plucked up or overthrown anymore forever.

Ezekiel 34:28–29
They will no longer be a prey to the nations, and the beasts of the earth will not devour them; but they will live securely, and no one will make them afraid. I will establish for them a renowned planting place, and they will not again be victims of famine in the land, and they will not endure the insults of the nations anymore.

Ezekiel 37:25
They will live on the land that I gave to Jacob My servant, in which your fathers lived; and they will live on it, they, and their sons, and their sons' sons, forever; and David My servant will be their prince forever.

Joel 2:26–27
You will have plenty to eat and be satisfied and praise the name of the LORD your God, who has dealt wondrously with you; then My people will never be put to shame. Thus you will know that I am in the midst of Israel, and that I am the LORD your God, and there is no other; and My people will never be put to shame.

Joel 3:18–20
And in that day the mountains will drip with sweet wine, and the hills will flow with milk, and all the brooks of Judah will flow with water; and a spring will go out from the house of the LORD to water the valley of Shittim. Egypt will become a waste, and Edom will become a desolate wilderness, because of the violence done to the sons of Judah, in whose land they have

shed innocent blood. But Judah will be inhabited forever and Jerusalem for all generations.

Amos 9:11–15

"In that day I will raise up the fallen booth of David, and wall up its breaches; I will also raise up its ruins and rebuild it as in the days of old; that they may possess the remnant of Edom and all the nations who are called by My name," declares the LORD who does this. "Behold, days are coming," declares the LORD, "when the plowman will overtake the reaper and the treader of grapes him who sows seed; when the mountains will drip sweet wine and all the hills will be dissolved. Also I will restore the captivity of My people Israel, and they will rebuild the ruined cities and live in them; they will also plant vineyards and drink their wine, and make gardens and eat their fruit. I will also plant them on their land, and they will not again be rooted out from their land which I have given them," says the LORD your God.

Zephaniah 3:14–20

Shout for joy, O daughter of Zion! Shout in triumph, O Israel! Rejoice and exult with all your heart, O daughter of Jerusalem! The LORD has taken away His judgments against you, He has cleared away your enemies. The King of Israel, the LORD, is in your midst; you will fear disaster no more. In that day it will be said to Jerusalem: "Do not be afraid, O Zion; do not let your hands fall limp. The LORD your God is in your midst, a victorious warrior. He will exult over you with joy, He will be quiet in His love, He will rejoice over you with shouts of joy. I will gather those who grieve about the appointed feasts—they came from you, O Zion; the reproach of exile is a burden on them. Behold, I am going to deal at that time with all your oppressors, I will save the lame and gather the outcast, and I will turn their shame into praise and renown in all the earth. At that time I will bring you in, even at the time when I gather you together; indeed, I will give you renown and praise among all the peoples

> of the earth, when I restore your fortunes before your eyes," says the LORD.

Zechariah 14:1, 9, 11

> Behold, a day is coming for the LORD when the spoil taken from you will be divided among you. And the LORD will be king over all the earth; in that day the LORD will be the only one, and His name the only one. People will live in it, and there will no longer be a curse, for Jerusalem will dwell in security.

Let me be so bold as to say that *if* God does not fulfill these promises to Israel as a people and a nation, He has failed to keep His word. This is a strong statement and not meant to offend but to shock people who believe otherwise into seeing how unbiblical their eschatology really is. No Bible-believing, Christ-confessing Amillennialist, Futuristic Premillennialist, Historic Premillennialist, or Postmillennialist would believe that God is a liar. We would all believe that He is the truth, speaks the truth, and does not lie like men (Num. 23:19; 1 Sam. 15:29; Titus 1:2).

Yet Amillennial, Historic Premillennial, and Postmillennial adherents unwittingly allow their theology proper statements about God's attributes of being true and speaking truth to be contradicted by their eschatology of denying Israel's restoration to their ancient land with a Davidic King, the Messiah, in a one-thousand-year kingdom.

God is not a liar and, therefore, His promises to Israel are true and surely yet to be fulfilled (2 Cor. 1:20). Amillennialists, Historic Premillennialists, and Postmillennialists need to readjust their eschatology to conform to the truth and true nature of God.

Israel's Preservation

Now, to the border pieces of the prophetic puzzle. Israel is the most persecuted ethnic group in history. From the Egyptians of Moses' day to the WWII atrocities of Hitler, the Jewish race has often been on the brink of elimination. Since the Assyrian captivity (ca. 722 BC), the nation has never regained any degree of its former sovereign rule such as it had with the united monarchy of David and Solomon.

Today, Jews comprise less than one-half of 1 percent of the world's population. The boundaries of Israel are approximately 165 miles (N–S) by 50 miles (E–W). But, they have not been destroyed by countless attempts of genocide nor has their ethnic identity been lost. They remain a recognized people in an identifiable land that traces both elements back to Abraham in Genesis 12. Some have called this remarkable preservation the "greatest miracle of all."

But preservation involves only one-half of the story. God promised *preservation* so that He could ultimately institute *restoration*. To this hour, a return with the characteristics enumerated in Scripture has not occurred—not in the ancient returns from Babylon nor the modern return in 1948.

The Old Testament uses very specific language to describe the uniqueness of the restoration promised, provided, and empowered by God.

- An irreversible restoration (Jer. 31:40; Amos 9:15).
- An everlasting restoration (Ezek. 37:25).
- A shameless and abundant restoration (Joel 2:26–27).
- An internationally acclaimed restoration (Zeph. 3:20).

The Amillennial, Postmillennial, and Historic Premillennial approach to these passages amounts to downplaying their literal and historical aspects while emphasizing their spiritual or theological significance. However, this is a major contaminate in the ointment of their eschatology. But to Futuristic Premillennialism, the promise of Israel's dramatic restoration according to God's promises in Scripture represents a very clear and crucial part of the prophetic puzzle.

Both Ezekiel and Jeremiah provide some of the most compelling testimony that Futuristic Premillennialism unmistakably results from God's plan and Scripture's teaching. Ezekiel 37:15–28 lays out restoration details like no other text in the Bible, as illustrated in the following chart.

ISRAEL'S RESTORATION ACCORDING TO EZEKIEL 37	
Unified nation vv. 19, 22	Davidic king vv. 24, 25
Global rescue vv. 20, 21	Obedient citizens v. 24
Reclaimed real estate v. 21	Permanent residency v. 25
One king v. 22	Covenant of peace v. 26
Righteous people v. 23	Place of God's dwelling v. 27
True worship v. 23	International recognition v. 28

This passage cannot be explained away as having already been fulfilled. Nothing in Israel's past history since the Assyrian and Babylonian exiles comes remotely close in kind to this scenario that Ezekiel describes in meticulous detail. Nor can it be explained as having to do with the church's inherited blessing, forfeited by unceasingly sinful Israel. The detail prohibits any attempt at spiritualizing away the intent and context found here.

Even more persuasive are two passages in Jeremiah (31:35–37; 33:19–26). One rehearses Abrahamic promises (31:35–37) and the other Davidic features (33:19–26). The first involves preserving Abraham's seed (both personally and nationally) and the second speaks to restoring the Davidic kingship. Both preservation and restoration are as sure as:

- The fixed order of day and night (31:35; 33:20, 25).
- The immeasurable heights of heaven and depths of earth (31:37; 33:22).

Over two hundred years ago, Frederick II (1712–1786), the Great King of Prussia (1740–1786), discussed with his chaplain the truth of the Bible. The king had become skeptical about Christianity, largely through the influence of the French atheist Voltaire. So he said to his chaplain, "If your Bible is really true, it ought to be capable of very easy proof. So often, when I have asked for proof of the inspiration of the Bible, I have been given some large tome that I have neither the time nor desire to read. If your Bible is really from God, you should be able to demonstrate the fact simply. Give me proof for the inspiration of the Bible in a word."

The chaplain replied, "Your majesty, it is possible for me to answer your request literally. I can give you the proof you ask for in one word."

Frederick was amazed at this response. "What is this magic word that carries such a weight of proof?" he asked.

"Israel," said the chaplain.

Frederick was silent.

Israel's miraculous preservation through the millennia is an assured sign that God will also ultimately restore Israel, as clearly taught by the prophets and upheld by Futuristic Premillennialism.

Israel's Exclusivity in Deuteronomy 28

Amillennialism, Historic Premillennialism, and Postmillennialism claim that God's curses in Deuteronomy 28:15–68 were meant for Israel (historically), but the promised blessings in 28:1–14 were for the church (spiritually). However, four observations demonstrate these conclusions to be unbiblical.

- There is no hermeneutical warrant to interpret Deuteronomy 28 both historically and spiritually.
- There is no exegetical evidence whatsoever to connect Deuteronomy 28 to the New Testament church.
- In fact, Israel did experience both historical blessings (cf. Josh. 21:45; 23:14; 1 Kings 8:56) and historical curses (cf. Josh. 23:15–16).
- The New Testament never associates Deuteronomy 28 with the church (i.e., New Testament writers never quote Deut. 28).

On the other hand, there are three major biblical observations that confirm the Futuristic Premillennial position that Israel (as a current Christ-rejecting nation) still experiences the curses of Deuteronomy 28.

- God intended the curses to last "forever" (Deut. 28:46) in the sense of a very long, extended period of time, but not for all eternity.
- The Shekinah Glory departed the temple in Jerusalem (Ezek. 8–11) and will not return until the time of Messiah (Is. 11:11; Zech. 14:11), which is yet future.
- The curses of Deuteronomy 28 will cease only when Israel returns to the land in submission to the earthly rule of Messiah (Jer. 32:36–44; Ezek. 20:39–44; 28:25–26).

Two passages in Scripture deal with the end of curses. First, Zechariah 14:11: ". . . there will no longer be a curse, for Jerusalem will dwell in security." This refers to the curses of Deuteronomy 28. The millennial kingdom of Christ will be the promised time of blessing for Israel. Second, Revelation 22:3, ". . . there will no longer be any curse," referring to the Edenic curse of Genesis 3:8–21 upon the whole earth and the entire human population. Eternity future, the subject of Revelation 21–22, will be without human sin and thus without God's curse.

Israel's Fixed Identity

Grace Community Church was picketed several years past by a group holding placards proclaiming that "The church is Israel now." A well-known Christian author and radio Bible personality teaches that "The church is the true Israel of God." So goes the Amillennial, Postmillennial, and Historic Premillennial view of Israel and the church. They teach that the church has superseded Israel as the one people of God (cf. chapter 5, "What about Israel?"). But, is this claim scripturally true?

For a variety of biblical reasons, it can be confidently taught that the church has not replaced Israel.

- The book of Acts speaks frequently of the church (nineteen times) and Israel (twenty times). Beginning at Pentecost, "church" always refers to those people (Jew and Gentile) who are believers in Christ; "Israel" always refers to the Jewish nation, historically and ethnically. The terms are never used synonymously nor interchangeably.
- Never in the entire New Testament is the church called "spiritual Israel" or the "new Israel." Furthermore, never in the whole New Testament is "Israel" ever called "the church."
- "Church" is mentioned nineteen times in Revelation 1–3. "Church" is not later confused with "Israel" in Revelation 6–19. Interestingly, there is no mention of "church" from Revelation 3:22 until 22:16.

Some have proposed that Romans 9:6 speaks of the church as Israel, ". . . they are not all Israel who are descended from Israel." However, Paul's distinction here is between ethnic Jews whose lineage can be traced to Abraham only in a physical sense and ethnic Jews who have both a physical and spiritual heritage in Abraham. In Galatians 6:16, Paul uses the phrase "Israel of God." Some have concluded that Paul is equating Israel with the church here, when in fact he is referring to the believing Jews in the church congregation.[7]

Robert Louis Stevenson, famous Scottish author of the nineteenth century, wrote these striking words about the less-than-sensible equation of the church with "spiritual Israel."

> I cannot understand how you theologians and preachers can apply to the Church—or the multiplicity of churches—Scripture promises which, in their plain meaning, must apply to God's chosen people Israel, and to Palestine; and which, consequently, must still be future. . . . The prophetic books are full of teachings which, if they are interpreted lit-

> erally, would be inspiring, and a magnificent assurance of a great and glorious future; but which, as they are spiritualized, become farcical—as applied to the Church, they are a comedy.[8]

Christ's Coming and Reigning Sequence

Four significant "second coming" texts (two in the Old Testament and two in the New Testament) teach this sequence of events: Christ comes first and then afterward reigns, as illustrated in the following chart.

CHRIST COMES	CHRIST REIGNS
Daniel 2:34–35	Daniel 2:44–45
Zechariah 14:5	Zechariah 14:9
Matthew 24:27, 30, 37, 39, 42, 44	Matthew 25:31
Revelation 19:11–16	Revelation 20:4

This is what Futuristic Premillennialism teaches. However, Amillennialism and Postmillennialism teach that Christ first reigns in heaven and then comes to judge without reigning on earth before eternity future. This signature sequence of Amillennialism and Postmillennialism contradicts a clear teaching of Scripture. Historic Premillennialism proposes that Christ first reigns in the Davidic covenant sense in heaven, then comes, and subsequently rules again on earth.

Only Futuristic Premillennialism follows the biblical pattern of first coming and then reigning.

A Final Word

These four corner and four border pieces of the prophetic puzzle significantly shape the biblical pattern of future events.

- A Consistent Hermeneutic
- An Impartial Exegesis
- God's Unconditional Covenants
- God's Uncompromising Promises
    - Israel's Preservation
    - Israel's Exclusivity in Deuteronomy 28
    - Israel's Fixed Identity
    - Christ's Coming and Reigning Sequence

When the puzzle is completed, it reveals a detailed portrait of Christ ruling over His global, millennial kingdom from the Davidic throne in Jerusalem, just as God promised and Futuristic Premillennialism anticipates.

Notes

1. O. T. Allis, *Prophecy and the Church* (1945; repr., Nutley, NJ: Presbyterian and Reformed, 1977), 238.
2. Floyd E. Hamilton, *The Basis of the Millennial Faith* (Grand Rapids: Eerdmans, 1942), 38.
3. Loraine Boettner, "Postmillennialism," in *The Meaning of the Millennium: Four Views*, ed. Robert G. Clouse (Downers Grove, IL: IVP, 1977), 95.
4. Emil Schürer, *A History of the Jewish People in the Time of Jesus Christ*, 5 vols., rev. ed. (1890; repr., Edinburgh: T&T Clark, 1998), 2:2:126–87.
5. J. I. Packer, "Introduction: On Covenant Theology," in *The Economy of the Covenants between God and Man*, 2 vols., Herman Witsius (1677; repr., Escondido, CA: den Dulk Christian Foundation, 1990), 1:1–2.
6. Renald E. Showers, *There Really Is a Difference! A Comparison of Covenant and Dispensational Theology* (Bellmawr, NJ: Friends of Israel, 1990) provides a superlative treatment of "covenants"—both biblical and unbiblical.
7. S. Lewis Johnson, "Paul and 'The Israel of God': An Exegetical and Eschatological Case Study," in *Essays in Honor of J. Dwight Pentecost*, eds. Stanley D. Toussaint and Charles H. Dyer (Chicago: Moody, 1986), 181–96.
8. Quoted in S. J. Whitmee, "'Tusitala', R.L.S.—A New Phase," *The Atlantic Monthly* 131 (March 1923): 348.

Chapter Four

WHY A PRETRIBULATION RAPTURE?

Richard Mayhue

Every rapture position has its overzealous defenders who have employed unacceptable reasoning or methodology to prove their point. Pretribulationism is no exception. Some of the less-than-satisfactory flaws that have been observed on all sides of the rapture debate include:

- Putting nonbiblical, historical documents on an equal par with Scripture to gain a greater sense of authority for one's conclusion or even to refute a biblical presentation.
- Reading current events into the Scripture to prove one's point.
- Inserting one's predetermined position, without first proving it, into a Scripture passage to gain apparent biblical support.
- Attacking the character of one who holds a particular view in order to discredit the view.
- Accusing an advocate of an opposing view of holding certain unacceptable interpretations or beliefs, when in fact

they do not, in order to falsely demonstrate their supposed poor scholarship.
- Employing selective data to make one's point, when full disclosure would have actually weakened the conclusion.
- Drawing unwarranted and erroneous implications from the Greek NT text that are used to override the more obvious and determinative conclusions that are derived from the passage's context.

This presentation seeks to avoid these all-too-common missteps. The following questions will be raised and answered in this attempt to present a convincing response to the query at hand, "Why a pretribulational rapture?"

- What does "rapture" mean?
- Will there be an eschatological rapture?
- Will the rapture be partial or full?
- Will the rapture be pre, mid, or post in relationship to Daniel's seventieth week?

The scope of this chapter does not allow for discussing the chief deficiencies of other positions. However, this discussion describes the exegetical superiority of pretribulationism as taught in major eschatological texts such as Matthew 24–25, 1 Corinthians 15, 1 Thessalonians 4, and Revelation 3:6–18. No single reason alone makes pretribulationism compelling, but rather the combined force of all the lines of reasoning to be presented.

What Does "Rapture" Mean?

The English noun and verb "rapture" comes from the Latin word *raptura*, which in Latin Bibles translates the Greek word *harpazō* that is used fourteen times in the New Testament. The basic idea of the word is "to suddenly remove or snatch away." The New Testament uses it in reference to stealing or plundering (Matt. 11:12; 12:29;

13:19; John 10:12, 28, 29) and removing (John 6:15; Acts 8:39; 23:10; Jude 23).

The third use focuses on being caught up to heaven. It is used of Paul's third heaven experience (2 Cor. 12:2, 4) and Christ's ascension to heaven (Rev. 12:5). Obviously, *harpazō* is the perfect word then to describe God suddenly taking up the church from earth to heaven as the first part of Christ's second coming. However, the term itself contains no hint of the rapture's timing in relationship to Daniel's seventieth week.

Will There Be a Future Rapture?

First Thessalonians 4:16–17 unquestionably refers to a rapture that is eschatological in nature. Here, *harpazō* is translated "caught up."

> For the Lord Himself will descend from heaven with a shout, with the voice of the archangel and with the trumpet of God, and the dead in Christ shall rise first. Then we who are alive and remain shall be caught up together with them in the clouds to meet the Lord in the air, and so we shall always be with the Lord.

Without employing *harpazō*, but using similar contextual language, 1 Corinthians 15:51–52 refers to the same eschatological event as 1 Thessalonians 4:16–17.

> Behold, I tell you a mystery; we will not all sleep, but we will all be changed, in a moment, in the twinkling of an eye, at the last trumpet; for the trumpet will sound, and the dead will be raised imperishable, and we will be changed.

Thus, it can be assuredly concluded that Scripture points to the fact of an eschatological rapture, even though neither of these foundational texts contain any explicit time indicators.

Will the Rapture Be Partial or Full?

Some have suggested that the rapture spoken of in 1 Thessalonians 4:16–17 and 1 Corinthians 15:51–52 will only be a partial rapture, not a rapture of all who believe. They reason that participation in the rapture is not based upon one's true salvation but rather is conditional, based upon one's deserving conduct.

This theory rests on New Testament passages that stress obedient watching and waiting, e.g., Matthew 25:1–13, 1 Thessalonians 5:4–8, and Hebrews 9:28. The result would be that only part of the church is raptured and those who are not raptured would endure through a portion of, or through the entire, seventieth week of Daniel. However, these biblical texts that supposedly teach a partial rapture are better understood as differentiating between true believers who are raptured and merely professing ones who remain behind. Texts that refer to the final aspect of Christ's second coming are often mistakenly used to support the partial rapture theory.

The partial rapture theory fails to be convincing because the allegedly supporting passages do not support the conclusion. Several other considerations also undermine this position. First, 1 Corinthians 15:51 says that "all" will be changed, not just some. Second, a partial rapture would logically demand a parallel partial resurrection, which is nowhere taught in Scripture. Third, a partial rapture would minimize and possibly eliminate the need for the judgment seat of Christ because the group of true believers taken at the rapture receives a greater reward than the group of true (but needing further spiritual refining) believers left on earth. Fourth, it creates a purgatory of sorts on earth for those believers left behind. Fifth, a partial rapture is nowhere clearly and explicitly taught in Scripture. Therefore, we conclude that the rapture will be full and complete, not just partial.

Will the Rapture Be Pre, Mid, or Post in Relationship to Daniel's Seventieth Week?

The following seven evidences will point to a pretribulation rapture. In this writer's opinion, they create a far more compelling case than the reasoning given for any other possible time of the rapture.

The Church Is Not Mentioned in Revelation 6–19 as Being on Earth

The common New Testament term for *church* (*ekklēsia*) is used nineteen times in Revelation 1–3, and primarily deals with the historical church of the first century, toward the end of the apostle John's life (about AD 95). However, "church" (*ekklēsia*) appears only once more in the twenty-two-chapter book, and that at the very end (22:16) when John again addresses the first-century church. Interestingly, nowhere during the period of Daniel's seventieth week is the term for "church" used for believers on earth (cf. Rev. 6–19).

It is remarkable and totally unexpected that John would shift from detailed instructions for the church to absolute silence about the church for the fourteen chapters describing Daniel's seventieth week (Rev. 6–19) if, in fact, the church continued into the tribulation. If the church will experience the tribulation of Daniel's seventieth week, then surely the most detailed study of tribulation events would include an account of the church's role. But it doesn't! The only timing of the rapture that would account for this frequent mention of "church" in Revelation 1–3 and total absence of the "church" on earth until Revelation 22:16 is a pretribulation rapture that will relocate the church from earth to heaven prior to Daniel's seventieth week.

Today, the church universal is God's human channel of redemptive truth. Revelation gives certain indications that the Jewish remnant will be God's human instrument during Daniel's seventieth week. The unbiased reader would certainly be impressed by the abrupt shift from the "church" in Revelation 2–3 to the 144,000 Jews from the twelve tribes in Revelation 7 and 14. We would certainly ask, "Why?"

Further, because Revelation 12 is a mini-synopsis of the entire tribulation period and because the woman who gave birth to the male child (Rev. 12:13) is Israel, then logically and topically the tribulation period focuses on the nation of Israel and not the church. Thus, it seems to be highly inconsistent and incorrect to argue that the church was absent from the first sixty-nine weeks of Daniel but is present in the seventieth. The best explanation of the church's absence is that a pretribulation rapture has removed the church from the earth prior to Daniel's seventieth week.

The Rapture Is Rendered Inconsequential If It Is Posttribulational

If God miraculously preserves the church through the tribulation (as is postulated by posttribulationism), why have a rapture? If it is to avoid the wrath of God at Armageddon, then why would God not continue to protect the saints on earth just as He protected Israel (see Exod. 8:22; 9:4, 26; 10:23; 11:7) from His wrath poured out upon Pharaoh and Egypt. Further, if the purpose of the rapture is for living saints to avoid Armageddon (again, as suggested by posttribulationism), why also resurrect the saints who are already immune at the same time?

Also, if the rapture took place in connection with our Lord's posttribulational coming, the subsequent separation of the sheep from the goats (see Matt. 25:31ff.) would be redundant. Separation would have taken place in the very act of the translation (rapture) of the church.

In addition, if all tribulation believers are raptured and glorified just prior to the inauguration of the millennial kingdom, who then will populate and propagate the kingdom? The Scriptures indicate that the living unbelievers will be judged at the end of the tribulation and removed from the earth (see Matt. 13:41–42; 25:41). Yet, they also teach that children will be born to believers during the millennium and that these children will be capable of sin (see Is. 65:20; Rev. 20:7–10). This would not be possible if all believers on earth had been glorified through a posttribulational rapture.

Finally, the posttribulational paradigm of the church being raptured and then immediately brought back to earth leaves no time for the Bema (judgment) seat of Christ to occur (1 Cor. 3:10–15; 2 Cor. 5:10), nor the Marriage Supper (Rev. 19:6–10). Thus, it can be concluded that a posttribulation occurrence of the rapture makes no logical sense, is incongruous with the sheep-goat judgment, and, in fact, eliminates two critical end-time events. A pretribulational rapture, however, avoids all of these insurmountable difficulties.

The Epistles Contain No Preparatory Warnings of an Impending Tribulation for Church Age Believers

God's instructions to the church through the Epistles contain a variety of warnings, but never are believers warned to prepare for entering and enduring the tribulation of Daniel's seventieth week.

They warn vigorously about coming error and false prophets (see Acts 20:29–30; 2 Pet. 2:1; 1 John 4:1–3; Jude 4). They warn against ungodly living (see Eph. 4:25–5:7; 1 Thess. 4:3–8; Heb. 12:1). They even admonish believers to endure in the midst of present tribulation (see 1 Thess. 2:13–14; 2 Thess. 1:4; all of 1 Pet.). However, there is absolute silence on preparing the church for any kind of tribulation like that found in Revelation 6–18.

It would be inconsistent for the Scriptures to be silent on such a traumatic change for the church. If any time of the rapture other than pretribulational were true, one would expect the Epistles to teach the fact of the church in the tribulation, the purpose of the church in the tribulation, and the conduct of the church in the tribulation. However, there is no teaching like this whatsoever. Only a pretribulation rapture satisfactorily explains such obvious silence.

First Thessalonians 4:13–18 Demands a Pretribulational Rapture

For discussion's sake, let us hypothetically suppose that some other rapture timing than pretribulational is true. What then would we expect to find in 1 Thessalonians 4? How does this compare with what we do observe?

First, we would expect the Thessalonians to be joyous over the fact that loved ones are home with the Lord and will not have to endure the horrors of the tribulation. But, we discover the Thessalonians are actually grieving because they fear their loved ones will miss the rapture (vv. 13–15). Only a pretribulation rapture accounts for this grief.

Second, we would expect the Thessalonians to be grieving over their own impending trial rather than grieving over loved ones. Furthermore, we would expect them to be inquisitive about their own future persecution. But, the Thessalonians have no fears nor questions about the coming tribulation.

Third, we would expect Paul, even in the absence of interest or questions by the Thessalonians, to have provided instructions and exhortation for such a supreme test, which would make their present tribulation seem microscopic in comparison. But, there is not one indication of any impending tribulation of this kind.

Therefore, 1 Thessalonians 4 only fits the model of a pretribulation rapture. It is incompatible with any other time for the rapture.

John 14:1–3 Parallels 1 Thessalonians 4:13–18

John 14:1–3 refers to Christ's coming again. It is not a promise to all believers that they shall go to Him at death. It does refer to the rapture of the church. Note the close parallels between the promises of John 14:1–3 and 1 Thessalonians 4:13–18. First, the promise of a presence with Christ: ". . . that where I am, there you may be also" (John 14:3). ". . . we shall always be with the Lord" (1 Thess. 4:17). Second, the promise of comfort: "Do not let your heart be troubled; . . ." (John 14:1). "Therefore comfort one another with these words" (1 Thess. 4:18).

Jesus instructed the disciples that He was going to His Father's house (heaven) to prepare a place for them. He promised them that He would return and receive them so that they could be with Him wherever He was.

The phrase "where I am," while implying continued presence in general, here means presence in heaven in particular. Our Lord told the Pharisees in John 7:34, "Where I am, you cannot come." He was not talking about His present abode on earth but rather His resurrected presence at the right hand of the Father. In John 14:3 "where I am" must mean "in heaven," given the context of 14:1–3.

A posttribulation rapture demands that the saints meet Christ in the air and immediately descend to earth without experiencing what our Lord promised in John 14. Since John 14 refers to the rapture, only a pretribulation rapture satisfies the language of John 14:1–3 and allows raptured saints to dwell for a meaningful time with Christ in His Father's house.

The Nature of Events at Christ's Posttribulational Coming Radically Differs from That of the Rapture

If one compares what happens at the rapture in 1 Thessalonians 4:13–18 and 1 Corinthians 15:50–58 with what happens in the final events of Christ's second coming in Matthew 24–25, at least eight significant contrasts or differences can be observed. These differences demand that the rapture occur at a significantly different time than the final event of Christ's second coming.

- At the rapture, Christ comes in the air and returns to heaven (1 Thess. 4:17), while at the final event of the second coming Christ comes to the earth to dwell and reign (Matt. 25:31–32).
- At the rapture, Christ gathers His own (1 Thess. 4:16–17), while at the final event of the second coming angels gather the elect (Matt. 24:31).
- At the rapture, Christ comes to reward (1 Thess. 4:17), while at the final event of the second coming Christ comes to judge (Matt. 25:31–46).
- At the rapture, resurrection is prominent (1 Thess. 4:15–16), while at the final event of the second coming resurrection is not mentioned.
- At the rapture, believers depart the earth (1 Thess. 4:15–17), while at the final event of the second coming unbelievers are taken away from the earth (Matt. 24:37–41).
- At the rapture, unbelievers remain on earth (implied), while at the final event of the second coming believers remain on earth (Matt. 25:34).

- At the rapture, there is no mention of establishing Christ's kingdom on earth, while at the final event of the second coming Christ has come to set up His kingdom on earth (Matt. 25:31, 34).
- At the rapture, believers will receive glorified bodies (cf. 1 Cor. 15:51–57), while at the final event of the second coming no one will receive glorified bodies.

Additionally, several of Christ's parables in Matthew 13 confirm differences between the rapture and the final event of Christ's second coming.

- In the parable of the wheat and tares, the tares (unbelievers) are taken out from among the wheat (believers) at the climax of the second coming (Matt. 13:30, 40), while believers are removed from among unbelievers at the rapture (1 Thess. 4:15–17).
- In the parable of the dragnet, the bad fish (unbelievers) are taken out from among the good fish (believers) at the culmination of Christ's second coming (Matt. 13:48–50), while believers are removed from among unbelievers at the rapture (1 Thess. 4:15–17).

Finally, there is no mention of the rapture in either of the most detailed second coming texts—Matthew 24 and Revelation 19. This is to be expected in light of the observations above that compellingly point to a pretribulational rapture.

Revelation 3:10 Promises That the Church Will Be Removed Prior to Daniel's Seventieth Week

The church of Philadelphia (Rev. 3:7–13) in our view refers both to the first-century church in that location, as well as to the future church that will experience the rapture. This is an example of near/far prophetic fulfillment, and makes the most sense of the warning of tribulation that will "come upon the whole world" (Rev. 3:10)—which did not occur in the first century. The issue here is whether the phrase "keep you from (*tēreō ek*) the hour of testing" means "a continuing safe state outside of" or "safe emergence from within."

The Greek preposition *ek* ("from") has the basic idea of emergence. But this is not true in every case. Two notable exceptions are found in 2 Corinthians 1:10 and 1 Thessalonians 1:10. In the Corinthian passage, Paul rehearses his rescue from death by God. Now Paul did not emerge from a state of death but rather was rescued from that potential danger.

Even more convincing is 1 Thessalonians 1:10. Here Paul states that Jesus is rescuing believers out of the wrath to come. The idea is not emergence out of, but rather protection from entrance into.

Therefore, *ek* can be understood to mean either "a continuing state outside of" or "emergence from within." Thus no rapture position can be dogmatic on this point; all positions remain possible.

It has been argued that if John had meant "to keep from," he would have used *tēreō apo* (cf. James 1:27, "to keep oneself [unstained] by [the world]). But it is equally true that if John had meant "protection within," he would have used *tēreō* with *en*, *eis*, or *dia*. It is submitted that the greater burden of proof lies with other positions since their solution of immunity within in no way explains the use of *ek*.

First, *ek* is much closer to *apo* in meaning than it is to *en*, *eis*, or *dia*. The two frequently overlap, and in modern Greek *apo* is absorbing *ek*. When combined with *tēreō*, *ek* much more closely approximates *apo* than it does *en*, *eis*, or *dia*. Hence, "to keep from" is the more likely meaning.

Second, the phrase *tēreō en* is used three times in the New Testament (see Acts 12:5; 1 Pet. 1:4; Jude 21). In each instance, it implies previous existence within with a view to continuation within. Now, if *tēreō en* means "continued existence within," *tēreō ek* quite logically and obviously means to maintain an existence *outside*.

John 17:15 ("I do not ask You to take them out of the world, but to keep [*tēreō*] them from [*ek*] the evil one") is the only other passage in the New Testament where *tēreō ek* occurs. This word combination does not occur in the Septuagint. We can assume that whatever the phrase means here, it will also have the same meaning in Revelation 3:10.

But if *tēreō ek* were to mean "previous existence within" in John 17:15, then it would contradict 1 John 5:19 where the statement is made that believers are of God and unbelievers are in the power of the evil one. That is, *tēreō ek* would imply that the disciplies had "continuing existence" within the evil one. But, of course, 1 John 5:19 says just the opposite. Rather, John 17:15 records the Lord's petition to keep them *outside* of the evil one.

Since John 17:15 means "to keep outside" of the evil one, then the parallel thought in Revelation 3:10 is to keep the church outside of the hour of testing. Therefore, only a pretribulation rapture would fulfill the promise.

If Revelation 3:10 means "immunity" or "protection within" as other positions insist, then several contradictions result. First, if protection in Revelation 3:10 is limited to protection from God's wrath only and not Satan's, then Revelation 3:10 denies our Lord's request in John 17:15.

Second, if it is argued that Revelation 3:10 means total immunity from trials, how can this be reconciled with Revelation 6:9–11 and 7:14 where martyrs abound? The wholesale martyrdom of saints during the tribulation demands that the promise to the Philadelphia church be interpreted as "keeping out of" the hour of testing, not "keeping within." The saints martyred during the tribulation are those who come to Christ following the rapture, after the church is taken away.

Answers to Difficult Questions

Over the last three decades, I have collected and interacted with some of the most significant objections to pretribulationism. In what follows, the challenges are raised and then answered.

Since the phrase "to meet the Lord" in 1 Thessalonians 4:17 (apantaō *and* apantēsis) *can refer to a friendly city going out to meet the visiting king and escorting him back to the city, does not this phrase point decidedly to a posttribulational rapture?*

First, this Greek verb/noun can refer to either meeting within a city (Mark 14:13; Luke 17:12) or going out of the city to meet and return back (Matt. 25:6; Acts 28:15). So the use of this particular word is not at all decisive. Second, remember that Christ is coming to a hostile people who will eventually fight against him at Armageddon. So, the pretribulation rapture best pictures the king rescuing, by a rapture, His faithful followers who are trapped in a hostile world and who will later accompany Him when He returns to conquer His enemies and set up His kingdom (cf. Rev. 19:11–16).

Why does Paul write in 1 Thessalonians 5:6 for believers to be alert for "the day of the Lord" if they would not be in it according to pretribulationism?

Paul exhorts believers in 1 Thessalonians 5:6 to be alert and to live godly lives in the context of the day of the Lord, just as Peter does in 2 Peter 3:14–15 where the day of the Lord experience is clearly at the end of the millennium since the old heavens and earth will be destroyed and replaced with the new. In both cases, they are exhortations to present godly living for true believers in the light of God's future judgment on unbelievers. Thus, these texts are not relevant to determining the timing of the rapture.

Doesn't Matthew 24:37–42, where people are taken out of the world, teach a posttribulational rapture?

In fact, Matthew 24:37–42 refers to the judgment of unbelievers at Christ's second coming. First, the historical allusion to Noah (vv. 37–39) shows that Noah and his family were left alive while the whole world was taken away in death and judgment. This is exactly the sequence to be expected at Christ's second coming as taught in the parable of the wheat and tares (Matt. 13:24–43), the parable of the dragnet (Matt. 13:47–50), and the sheep-goat nation judgment (Matt. 25:31–46). In all of these cases, at the final event in Christ's second coming, unbelievers are taken away in judgment and righteous believers remain. Hence, this passage does not address the rapture.

Doesn't a pretribulational rapture result in two second comings of Christ while Scripture teaches only one second coming?

Not at all. No matter what rapture position one holds, Christ's second coming is one event that occurs in two parts—Christ coming in the air to rapture the church (1 Thess. 4:13–18) and Christ coming to earth to conquer, judge, and set up His kingdom (Matt. 24–25).

When Jeremiah writes (30:7), "And it is the time of Jacob's distress, but he will be saved from it," is this not the same kind of language used in Revelation 3:10 (keep from) and would not Revelation 3:10 then point to a posttribulational rapture?

The Septuagint (LXX) translates the Hebrew text of Jeremiah with the phrase *sōzō apo*. In the case of Israel, they will be saved through the judgment and emerge out of it as the people of God over whom Christ will reign as promised to David (2 Sam. 7:8–17) and prophesied by Ezekiel (37:11–28). Because *sōzō apo* means "protected in the midst of," this has no bearing on the meaning of a different verb and preposition used in Revelation 3:10 (*tēreō ek*). (See the earlier discussion on Revelation 3:10.) Finally, there is no necessary equation of Israel's outcome and God's plan for the church.

If pretribulationism is true, why is there no mention of the "church" in heaven in Revelation 4–19?

It is true that the word for "church" (*ekklēsia*) is not used of the church in heaven in Revelation 4–19. However, that does not mean the church is not present. There are at least two distinct appearances of the church in heaven. First, the twenty-four elders in Revelation 4–5 symbolize the church. Second, the phrase "you saints and apostles and prophets" in Revelation 18:20 clearly refers to the church in heaven. The rapture scenario that best accounts for the church being in heaven in these texts is a pretribulational rapture.

Why is Revelation addressed to the church, if the church will not experience the tribulation of Revelation 6–19 due to a pretribulational rapture?

God frequently warned Israel in the OT of impending judgment, even though the generation who received the prophecy would not experience it. As mentioned in the second question above, both Paul (1 Thess. 5:6) and Peter (2 Pet. 3:14–15) used a future judgment that the people to whom they wrote would not experience to exhort God's people to present godly living. The same pattern was followed by John in Revelation. The church was alerted to God's future judgment of sin on earth as a basis for the church to teach pure doctrine and live holy lives (Revelation 2–3).

If the day of the Lord occurs at the end of Daniel's seventieth week, doesn't the chronological sequence of 1 Thessalonians 4 and 1 Thessalonians 5 teach a posttribulational rapture?

First, regardless of whether the day of the Lord begins at the beginning or the end of Daniel's seventieth week, this point does not necessarily determine the time of the rapture. Second, the grammar of 1 Thessalonians 5:1 argues against a close chronological sequence with 1 Thessalonians 4 by the use of *peri de* ("now as to," occuring eighteen times in the New Testament). In all but four cases an obvious change in time or topic is implied (see, for example, Matt. 22:31; 24:36; Mark 12:26; 13:32). This prepositional phrase is used by Paul eight times. Every other Pauline use indicates a change in topic. Therefore, it is expected that Paul's use of *peri de* in 1 Thessalonians 5:1 also indicates a change in topic and time from 1 Thessalonians 4. This is consistent with his earlier use of *peri de* in this epistle (cf. 4:9).

In 1 Thessalonians 4:13–18, Paul has described the circumstances of deceased loved ones at the time of the rapture. But in

5:1 and the following verses, Paul shifts to the day of the Lord and the subsequent judgment upon unbelievers. This is a totally different topic than the rapture and an event that will occur at a different time than the rapture.[1] If 1 Thessalonians 4:13–5:11 is to be taken as one unit of thought as some have suggested, then Paul's use of *peri de* means nothing. However, because *peri de* appears here, it is best interpreted as a major shift in thought within the broad topic of eschatology; only a pretribulation rapture would account for this.

Is there any relationship between the rapture trumpet of 1 Thessalonians 4:17/1 Corinthians 15:52 and the trumpet of Joel 2:1, or the trumpet of Matthew 24:31, or the trumpet of Revelation 11:15? If so, doesn't this contradict a pretribulation rapture?

A careful study of the almost one hundred uses of "trumpet/trumpets" in the Old Testament will quickly instruct the student of Scripture not to hastily equate the trumpets in any two texts without a great deal of corroborating contextual evidence. For example, there is the trumpet used for warning (Jer. 6:1); the trumpet used for worship/praise (2 Chron. 20:28; Pss. 81:3; 150:3; Is. 27:13); the trumpet used for victory (1 Sam. 13:3); the trumpet used for recall (2 Sam. 2:28; 18:16); the trumpet used for rejoicing (2 Sam. 6:15); for announcements (2 Sam. 20:1; 1 Kings 1:34; 2 Kings 9:13); and dispersement (2 Sam. 20:22), to name a few.

After looking at the texts in question, it appears that each trumpet is used for a distinct purpose that is unique and different from the other three. The trumpet of Joel 2:1 is a trumpet of alarm that the day of the Lord is near (cf. Jer. 6:1). The trumpet of 1 Thessalonians 4:16/1 Corinthians 15:52 is a trumpet that announces the approaching king (cf. Ps. 47:5) so that people may go out to greet Him. The trumpet of Matthew 24:31 is a trumpet call to assembly (cf. Ex. 19:16; Neh. 4:20; Joel 2:15). The trumpet of Revelation 11:15 is the seventh in a series of seven and announces victory (cf. 1 Sam. 13:3). There is no compelling reason to equate the rapture trumpet with any of the other three trumpets. Therefore, these texts cannot be used to determine the time of the rapture.

Doesn't the promise of deliverance for church saints in 2 Thessalonians 1:6–10, at the time when Jesus returns with His angels to judge the world, point to a rapture after the tribulation?

Paul is not writing a detailed, chronological, or even precise prophetic treatise here, but rather is wanting to give the Thessalonians hope that, in the end, God's righteousness would prevail. Like Old Testament prophets (cf. Is. 61:1–2; 2 Pet. 1:10–11), Paul has compressed the details so that the range of time is not apparent, nor are all of the details. The apostle is plainly assuring the Thessalonians that there will certainly be a coming day of retribution for their persecutors. As a result, this text has no bearing on determining the time of the rapture.

Doesn't Revelation 14:14 teach a midtribulational rapture?

While the language certainly refers to Christ, the context is of judgment, similar to Revelation 19:11–16. The context of the rapture, however, is one of blessing for the saints. (See the eight major differences/contrasts between the rapture and the last event of Christ's second coming discussed above.) Consequently, Revelation 14:14 does not refer to a midtribulational rapture.

Isn't a midtribulational view actually a pretribulational view, since the "great tribulation" (Matt. 24:21; Rev. 7:14) does not begin until the middle of Daniel's seventieth week?

To say that real tribulation does not begin until the midpoint of Daniel's seventieth week is to make an arbitrary delineation, and also to contradict the testimony of at least the first four seals of Revelation 6:1–8 that picture the tribulation triggered by Christ from heaven. These seals are described as "birth pangs" and "tribulation" in Matthew 24:8–9. While the ultimate intensity of tribulation is in the final half of Daniel's seventieth week, the entire period is marked by tribulation. Thus, the only true pretribulation position is the one that places the rapture prior to Daniel's seventieth week.

If the church partakes of the first resurrection, and if the first resurrection is described in Revelation 20:4–5, does this not point to a posttribulational resurrection/rapture?

The use of the phrase "first resurrection" in Revelation 20:5–6 refers specifically to the posttribulational resurrection of those who believed in Christ during Daniel's seventieth week, as made clear by the language of Revelation 20:4. Nothing in this phrase limits the "first resurrection" only to this group of people or to this time. The "first resurrection," which is contrasted with the "second death" (Rev. 20:6, 14; 21:8)—that is, the resurrection of all unbelievers—is made up of several additional categories of people who were resurrected at various times. These include: (1) Christ the firstfruits (1 Cor. 15:23); (2) church saints at the rapture (1 Cor. 15:23, 50–58); and (3) OT saints at the end of Daniel's seventieth week (Ezek. 37:12–14; Dan. 12:2). This text, then, does not point to a posttribulational resurrection/rapture.

Notes

1. The rapture occurs just prior to the beginning of Daniel's seventieth week, while the day of the Lord begins at the end of Daniel's seventieth week. See Richard L. Mayhue, "The Bible's Watchword: Day of the Lord," *The Master's Seminary Journal* 22:1 (spring 2011): 65–88.

Chapter Five

What about Israel?

Michael Vlach

A pastor from another generation was preaching on the kingship of Christ when he eloquently and powerfully cut loose with this beautiful summarization.

> The Bible says my King is a seven-way king. He's the King of the Jews. That's a racial king. He's the King of Israel. That's a national king. He's the King of righteousness. That's a spiritual king. He's the King of the ages. That's an eternal king. He's the King of heaven. That's a celestial king. He's the King of glory. That's a magnificent king. He's the King of kings and He's the Lord of lords. That's a divine king. That's my divine King.[1]

The purpose of this chapter is to establish that Israel is the people and nation over which the King of kings and Lord of lords will one day rule.

Few topics in Christian theology are as controversial and important as Israel. In fact, Israel is the primary issue that separates Futuristic

Premillennialism from non-dispensational systems like Amillennialism, Historic Premillennialism, and Postmillennialism. The key question is, "Does the nation Israel still possess significance in the plan of God or has the nation's significance been superseded and transcended by Jesus in such a way that there is no future role for the nation in the plan of God?" Futuristic Premillennialism affirms the former while the other views claim the latter.

The biblical evidence shows that Futuristic Premillennialism is correct in holding that the nation Israel remains important to God's purposes. In fact, one cannot have a proper understanding of God's plans for the ages unless he has an informed view of how God is using Israel to accomplish His purposes. This includes grasping the relationship between the nation Israel and Jesus the ultimate Israelite who, as Israel's head, restores the nation to a future place of service and leadership among the nations. This is where Futuristic Premillennialism makes a significant contribution to understanding theology and where other theological systems have largely failed. Those who do not hold to Futuristic Premillennialism have wrongly concluded that Jesus' identification with Israel has meant the end of national Israel's role and significance,[2] while Futuristic Premillennialists assert that Jesus' identity as "Israel" is part of a corporate solidarity in which the one (Jesus) and the many (the nation Israel) are related to each other without the One swallowing up the significance of the many.

The main point in this chapter is that the Bible, including both Testaments, often and explicitly teaches the salvation and restoration of the nation Israel. We also will establish that God created Israel to be a *means* for worldwide blessing. As Robert Martin-Achard declared, "The choice of Israel . . . belongs to the realm of means not ends."[3] This includes being the vehicle through which Jesus would come. And it also involves Israel having a strategic role to the nations as Christ exercises His righteous rule over these nations. Thus, Israel is a means for blessings to the world, but Israel is not an end in itself. It is not God's purpose to make everyone who believes "Israel."

A Word about Nations in the Bible

Many non-dispensationalists struggle with the idea that the nation Israel could have any future role to play in God's purposes. For them, the unity that all believers have in Christ must mean there can be no restoration of Israel. But before we examine what the Bible has to say about Israel, it is important to have a correct understanding of nations. For if one errs in understanding how God views nations, he will err in regard to Israel as a nation in God's plan. Our proposition is this—there is nothing wrong with or unspiritual about the concept of nations. In fact, God has a purpose for nations. And if He has a purpose for nations, there should be no problem understanding that He has a future plan for the nation Israel. The salvific unity that all believers experience in Christ (see Eph. 2:11–22) in no way rules out God's future dealings with nations, including Israel, because spiritual unity in Christ does not rule out diversity in other areas. Unity and diversity can exist in perfect harmony. We see this with other categories. Believing men and women are equal in their standing with Christ (see Gal. 3:28) but there are still distinctions in how they function in the church (see 1 Tim. 2:9–15). Likewise, within a local church all Christians share equally in salvation blessings but elders and leaders within the church have roles not shared by others in the congregation (see Heb. 13:17). The Trinity itself evidences both unity (one God) and diversity (three persons). One of the strengths of Futuristic Premillennialism is its understanding that God intends to glorify Himself through both unity and diversity. Both can exist in harmony and when they do they also reflect the unity and diversity within the Godhead.

Although they are a post-fall development, nations are not inherently bad or something that must be transcended or diminish in significance with the coming of Christ. Yes, there is much emphasis in the Bible on individual salvation, but this is not mutually exclusive with God's plans for nations. In fact, nations were created by God. Paul declared that "He [God] made from one man every nation of mankind to live on all the face of the earth" (Acts 17:26a). Isaiah

19:24–25 indicates that a day is coming when the traditional enemies of Israel, Egypt, and Assyria will join Israel as the people of God:

> In that day Israel will be the third party with Egypt and Assyria, a blessing in the midst of the earth, whom the LORD of hosts has blessed, saying, "Blessed is Egypt My people, and Assyria the work of My hands, and Israel My inheritance."

Notice that in the last days Egypt will become "My people" and Assyria will become "the work of My hands." These nations will become the people of God alongside Israel who is still God's "inheritance." The believing nations do not become "Israel," but they exist as God's people alongside Israel to the glory of God. So not only does God have a future for Israel, He has a plan for other nations too, even the traditional enemies of Israel like Egypt and Assyria. In Zechariah 2:11, God declared, "Many nations will join themselves to the LORD in that day and will become My people." Zechariah 14 indicates that on the day when "the LORD will be king over all the earth" (v. 9), "nations" (including Egypt) will "go up from year to year to worship the King" (v. 16).

But are God's plans for nations transcended by the coming of Jesus and the New Testament era? There is no evidence that they are. Repeatedly, God's plans for the nation Israel are affirmed (see Matt. 19:28; Luke 1:32–33; Acts 1:6; Rom. 11:26–27). Revelation 21:24–26 even affirms the presence of nations in the Eternal State:

> The nations will walk by its [the New Jerusalem's] light, and the kings of the earth will bring their glory into it. In the daytime (for there will be no night there) its gates will never be closed; and they will bring the glory and the honor of the nations into it.

These "nations" (plural) will walk by the light of the New Jerusalem and the "kings of the earth" will bring their cultural contributions from their homelands to the great city. These nations are united in that they are all saved the same way—through faith alone in Christ alone. But this spiritual unity does not erase all ethnic and geographical distinctions. The scriptural evidence for nations in God's future plans is so significant that even the Amillennialist theologian Anthony Hoekema recognized the existence of nations. In regard to Revelation 21:24, 26, Hoekema asked, "Is it too much to say that, according to these verses, the unique contributions of *each nation* to the life of the present earth will enrich the life of the new earth?"[4] These contributions include "the best products of culture and art which this earth has produced."[5]

This understanding that multiple nations have a role in God's future purposes leads to an important theological implication: *If one recognizes that there are nations in the future with specific roles and identities, why would there not be a special role and identity for the nation Israel?* In response to Hoekema's declaration concerning the presence of nations and culture on the new earth, Barry Horner rightly points out that "the mention of distinctive national contributions . . . would surely have to include the cultural benefactions of Israel!"[6] Horner's point is well taken. If there are nations on the new earth, why would Israel not be one of these nations contributing to the new order? Moreover, the presence of plural nations in the eternal state indicates that it is not God's purpose to make everyone Israel as non-dispensationalists often claim. There is no indication that the nations in Revelation 21 and 22 are all identified as "Israel." Israel's role is to bring blessings to the nations, not to make everybody Israel. In sum, as we approach the topic of Israel, we should set aside any unbiblical notions or assumptions that nations are unspiritual or something that must be transcended. Both Testaments affirm a future for nations.

The Nation Israel as a Means for Worldwide Blessings

A proper understanding of Israel and God's purposes for Israel must be rooted in a correct interpretation of Genesis 12:1–3. For it is here that we find the purpose for Abraham and Israel:

> Now the LORD said to Abram, "Go forth from your country, and from your relatives and from your father's house, to the land which I will show you; and I will make you a great nation, and I will bless you, and make your name great; and so you shall be a blessing; and I will bless those who bless you, and the one who curses you I will curse. And in you all the families of the earth will be blessed."

This passage introduces the Abrahamic covenant. Here God promises Abraham personal blessings including a great name. God also tells Abraham, "I will make you a great nation." As the book of Genesis unfolds, it becomes evident that this "great nation" is Israel, the descendants of Abraham through Isaac and Jacob. Significantly, the *purpose* of Abraham and the great nation that would come from him is found in verse 3b: "And in you all the families of the earth will be blessed." Dumbrell points out that the Hebrew grammar here indicates the intended purpose of Abraham and the great nation:

> [T]he clause is most probably to be taken as a result clause indicating what will be the consummation of the promises that the preceding verses have announced. That is to say, the personal promises given to Abram have final world blessing as their aim.[7]

Thus, Genesis 12:2–3 indicates that the purpose of Abraham and the great nation to come from him (Israel) is a worldwide blessing. As Christopher Wright points out: "Beyond doubt, then, there was a universal purpose in God's election of Abraham, and therefore also a universal dimension to the very existence of Israel. Israel as a people was called into existence because of God's mission to bless the nations and restore his creation."[8]

The implications of this passage for the people of God concept are significant. First, from the very beginning, the Abrahamic covenant was intended for both Israel and the Gentiles. It is not just for Israel alone, although the covenant would be mediated through Israel. Later, when we see the Abrahamic covenant related to believing Gentiles (see Gal. 3:7–9, 29), this should not surprise us or make us conclude that Gentiles are now part of Israel. Nor should we conclude that the promises of the Abrahamic covenant have now been transferred from Israel to the church. God's purpose with the Abrahamic covenant is not to make the Gentiles part of Israel, as non-dispensationalists often believe. Instead, the purpose of Abraham and Israel is to bring blessings to the Gentiles as Gentiles. Second, God does not intend for Israel to be an end in itself. Israel is not an end but a means—a means for worldwide blessings. This promise that Abraham's seed would be the vehicle for blessings to Gentiles is explicitly stated again in three other sections of Genesis:

> In your seed all the nations of the earth shall be blessed, because you have obeyed My voice. (Gen. 22:18)

> I will multiply your descendants as the stars of heaven, and will give your descendants all these lands; and by your descendants all the nations of the earth shall be blessed. (26:4)

> Your descendants will also be like the dust of the earth, and you will spread out to the west and to the east and to the north and to the south; and in you and in your descendants shall all the families of the earth be blessed. (28:14)

Israel's purpose as a vehicle for blessings to the nations is also seen in Exodus 19:6 where God states, "and you shall be to Me a kingdom of priests and a holy nation." Israel was to be a sparkling testimony of God to the other nations. Deuteronomy 26:19 declares, "He will set you [Israel] high above all nations which He has made, for praise, fame, and honor." Psalm 67 relates, "God be gracious to us [Israel] and bless us. . . . That Your way may be known on the earth, Your salvation among all nations. . . . That all the ends of the earth may fear Him" (Ps. 67:1, 2, 7). These passages should lead us to conclude, as Tuvya Zaretsky has noted, that "The purpose of God for Israel as revealed in the Bible was that they would be a vehicle to shine forth the light of His revelation to the nations and the delivery system for God's Savior, the Messiah."[9]

The Restoration of Israel in the Old Testament

Deuteronomy 30:1–6 is a strategic passage regarding God's plans for Israel:

> When all these things happen to you—the blessings and curses I have set before you—and you come to your senses [while you are] in all the nations where the LORD your God has driven you, and you and your children return to the LORD your God and obey Him with all your heart and all your soul by doing everything I am giving you today, then He will restore your fortunes, have compassion on you, and gather you again from all the peoples where the LORD your God has scattered you. Even if your exiles are at the ends of the earth, He will gather you and bring you back from there. The LORD your God will bring you into the land your fathers possessed, and you will take possession of it. He will cause you to prosper and multiply you more than [He did] your fathers. The LORD your God will circumcise your heart and the hearts of your descendants, and you will love Him with all your heart and all your soul so that you will live. (HCSB)

This section details a "big picture" prophecy concerning Israel's future. God had dramatically delivered Israel from Egypt. He had also given Israel the Mosaic law. In Deuteronomy 28–29 God described the blessings that would come upon Israel if the nation obeyed Him. He also discussed the curses that would result because of disobedience. God then described what the distant future would hold for Israel. After experiencing blessings and curses, God would banish Israel to all the nations because of disobedience. But a time would come when Israel would return to God and He would restore Israel. This includes a *spiritual salvation* ("your God will circumcise your heart") and a *physical restoration* ("into the land your fathers possessed"). In sum, God promised Israel that after a period of banishment the nation would be saved and restored to its Promised Land. This passage should steer us clear from any theology that claims that God has replaced or superseded the nation Israel because of Israel's disobedience. Both Israel's rebellion and restoration are predicted and both will come to pass. Other passages reaffirm the expectation of Deuteronomy 30:1–6. Ezekiel 36:22–30 predicts that after a period of dispersion Israel will experience salvation and a restoration to her land:

> "Therefore, say to the house of Israel: This is what the LORD GOD says: It is not for your sake that I will act, house of Israel, but for My holy name, which you profaned among the nations where you went. I will honor the holiness of My great name, which has been profaned among the nations—the name you have profaned among them. The nations will know that I am Yahweh"—the declaration of the Lord GOD —"when I demonstrate My holiness through you in their sight. For I will take you from the nations and gather you from all the countries, and will bring you into your own land. I will also sprinkle clean water on you, and you will be clean. I will cleanse you from all your impurities and all your idols. I will give you a new heart and put a new spirit within you; I will remove your heart of stone and give you a heart of flesh. I will place My Spirit within you and cause you to follow My statutes and carefully observe My ordinances. Then you will live in the land that I gave your fathers; you will be My people, and I will be your God. I will save you from all your uncleanness. I will summon the grain and make it plentiful, and will not bring famine on you. I will also make the fruit of the trees and the produce of the field plentiful, so that you will no longer experience reproach among the nations on account of famine." (HCSB)

Jeremiah 30:1–3 also tells of a restoration of Israel to the land:

> [This is] the word that came to Jeremiah from the LORD. This is what the LORD, the God of Israel, says: "Write down on a scroll all the words that I have spoken to you, for the days are certainly coming"—[this is] the LORD's declaration—"when I will restore the fortunes of My people Israel and Judah"—the LORD's declaration. "I will restore them to the land I gave to their ancestors and they will possess it." (HCSB)

Joel 3:20 indicates that as a result of the day of the Lord (3:18) "Judah will be inhabited forever, and Jerusalem from generation to generation" (HCSB). In Zephaniah 3:20 God promises again to "restore" the "fortunes" of Israel (HCSB). When examining these and other restoration texts in the Bible, certain truths emerge: (1) the restoration of Israel involves both spiritual salvation and physical blessings including possession of the land of promise; (2) the promise of restoration is not based on Israel's greatness but on God's choice and God's character; and (3) the promise for restoration takes place after the period of Israel's disobedience. As the passages above and many others indicate, the restoration of Israel is a major theme in the Old Testament. It is an explicit doctrine.

Jesus the Servant and the Nation Israel

Another important passage for a proper understanding of Israel is Isaiah 49:3–6. This section discusses the relationship between the Servant of Israel (Jesus) and the nation Israel:

> He said to Me, "You are My Servant, Israel, in Whom I will show My glory." But I said, "I have toiled in vain, I have spent My strength for nothing and vanity; yet surely the justice due to Me is with the LORD, and My reward with My God." And now says the LORD, who formed Me from the womb to be His Servant, to bring Jacob back to Him, so that Israel might be gathered to

> Him (for I am honored in the sight of the LORD, and My God is My strength), He says, "It is too small a thing that You should be My Servant to raise up the tribes of Jacob and to restore the preserved ones of Israel; I will also make You a light of the nations so that My salvation may reach to the end of the earth."

According to verse 3, the Lord is speaking to "My Servant Israel." The Amillennialist Robert Strimple is right when he states that Christ "is the suffering Servant of the LORD."[10] Verse 5 then states one of the purposes of this "Servant." The Servant's role is "to bring Jacob back to Him, so that Israel might be gathered to Him." Verse 6 also states that the role of the Servant is "to raise up the tribes of Jacob and to restore the preserved ones of Israel." God will also "make" the Servant be "a light of the nations." *What is significant here is that the Servant is clearly linked with Israel (v. 3), yet He is also distinct in some way since He is the one who will "restore" Israel.* The nation Israel cannot restore itself, for it is sinful. But the Servant—who is Jesus Christ, the true Israel—can restore the nation Israel and bring blessings for the nations. Thus, this passage teaches that Jesus, the true Israel, will restore the nation Israel and bring light to the nations. He will also restore Israel to her land (Isaiah 49:8).

Thus, the presence of Jesus does not mean that the people of Israel lose their significance. It is not Jesus' goal for everything to be absorbed into Himself. On the contrary, the people of Israel are saved and restored to their land and made what they were supposed to be *because of* Jesus Christ. In regard to Israel, Robert Saucy rightly points to the concept of "corporate personality" in which the head ministers to the body so that the body may accomplish its mission.[11] This means that Israel, who was given a mission to the nations, will be able to accomplish its mission because of the Servant—Jesus Christ. Thus, Isaiah 49:3–6 explicitly contradicts the argument of non-dispensationalists that Christ as true Israel means the end of national Israel's significance. Not only does Christ as true Israel not mean the end of the nation Israel in the plan of God, but the presence of Christ means the restoration of the nation Israel.

The Restoration of Israel in the New Testament

The New Testament tells of the coming of Jesus, the Servant, and the One who represents everything Israel was intended to be. The connection between Jesus and Israel is clearly seen in Matthew 2:15 where Jesus' calling and coming out of Egypt is connected with the nation Israel's historical exit from Egypt (cf. Hos. 11:1): "Out of Egypt I called My son." Jesus' connection with Israel is that of a corporate solidarity or personality in which there is a relationship between the head (Jesus) and the many (the people of Israel). Jesus is singularly the representative of Israel, but He is also the One who represents and restores the people of Israel.

The Gospels and Acts

When the angel Gabriel appeared to Mary, he indicated that the child born to her would one day reign over Israel: "He will be great and will be called the Son of the Most High; and the Lord God will give Him the throne of His father David" (Luke 1:32). Jesus' words in Matthew 19:28 and Luke 22:29–30 show that Jesus expected a restoration of national Israel:

> And Jesus said to them, "Truly I say to you, that you who have followed Me, in the regeneration when the Son of Man will sit on His glorious throne, you also shall sit upon twelve thrones, judging the twelve tribes of Israel." (Matt. 19:28)

> "and just as My Father has granted Me a kingdom, I grant you that you may eat and drink at My table in My kingdom, and you will sit on thrones judging the twelve tribes of Israel." (Luke 22:29–30)

In these passages Jesus is speaking about what will take place in the future. In the day when the earth experiences "regeneration" and the "kingdom" is established, the apostles will sit on twelve thrones "judging the twelve tribes of Israel." This is explicit and powerful testimony for the restoration of Israel. Israel's restoration is linked with the second coming, the renewal of the planet, and the coming kingdom of God.

Matthew 23:37–39 and Luke 13:34–35 also are evidence that Jesus expected a future restoration of Israel. Matthew 23:37–39 records Jesus' words to the inhabitants of Jerusalem:

> "Jerusalem, Jerusalem, who kills the prophets and stones those who are sent to her! How often I wanted to gather your children together, the way a hen gathers her chicks under her wings, and you were unwilling. Behold, your house is being left to you desolate! For I say to you, from now on you will not see Me until you say, 'BLESSED IS HE WHO COMES IN THE NAME OF THE LORD!'"

The text in Luke 13:34–35 is similar:

> "O Jerusalem, Jerusalem, the city that kills the prophets and stones those sent to her! How often I wanted to gather your children together, just as a hen gathers her brood under her wings, and you would not have it! Behold, your house is left to you desolate; and I say to you, you will not see Me until the time comes when you say, 'BLESSED IS HE WHO COMES IN THE NAME OF THE LORD!'"

In these two parallel texts, Jesus announced that desolation would come to Jerusalem and its temple because the inhabitants of the city rejected Him. Jesus also announced that He would be hidden from the people of Jerusalem until the day they say, "Blessed is He who comes in the name of the LORD!" The prediction that the Jews will one day cry out that Jesus is "blessed" is clear, but what is the context of their cry? Is this the exclamation of disobedient Jews facing eschatological judgment, or is it the cry of a repentant Israel at the time of its restoration? The latter view is correct. Craig L. Blomberg notes that Jesus' words in Matthew 23:39 indicate "genuine belief" on the part of Israel.[12] This declaration of blessedness upon Jesus will come from a repentant nation at the time of its restoration. Thus Robert Gundry is correct that Matthew 23:37–39 refers to "Israel's restoration in the kingdom of the Son of man."[13] In reference to Luke 13:35, Robert C. Tannehill also rightly declares, "This lament over Jerusalem includes a continuing hope that a restored Jerusalem will find this salvation."[14]

Another passage that supports the idea of a restoration of national Israel is Acts 1:6–7 where the apostles asked Jesus an important question:

> So when they had come together, they asked Him, "Lord, at this time are You restoring the kingdom to Israel?" He said to them, "It is not for you to know times or periods that the Father has set by His own authority." (HCSB)

After Jesus' resurrection, on His day of ascension into heaven, the apostles fully expected a restoration of the nation Israel. Jesus' response includes no rebuke or correction for this belief, thus affirming their understanding. This belief was not misguided for two reasons. First, Acts 1:3 states that Jesus met with the disciples for a period of "forty days" after His resurrection "speaking about the kingdom of God." It seems unlikely that the disciples could be totally misguided in their perceptions of the kingdom after having received forty days of instruction about the kingdom from the risen Lord. If Jesus had taught some spiritual kingdom or redefinition of the kingdom that did not involve national Israel, how could their question be so off target? Second, the lack of correction from Jesus in Acts 1:7 is validation that the disciples were correct in their beliefs about Israel's restoration for the simple reason that Jesus offers no rebuke or correction for their idea. If the disciples were wrong about a future restoration of the kingdom to Israel, Jesus would probably have corrected their misconception as He did on other occasions. But Jesus gives no correction at all. He does state that the disciples were not to know the *timing* of the restoration of the kingdom to Israel. Thus, J. Bradley Chance is correct that "Jesus' response challenges the hope for an immediate restoration of Israel. It does not challenge the hope of such a restoration itself."[15]

Romans 9–11

Romans 9–11 offers more explicit evidence of a future for the nation Israel. With 9:3b–4, Paul refers to "my kinsmen according to the flesh, who are Israelites, to whom belongs the adoption as sons, and the glory and the covenants and the giving of the Law and the temple service and the promises." As Paul writes his letter to the Romans, the era of the church was underway and Israel's rejection of Christ was well established. But Paul says there are certain things that still "belong" to his fellow Israelites. Using the present tense Paul includes "adoption as sons," "glory," "the covenants," "the giving of the Law," "the temple service," and "the promises." These still belong to Israel. Paul's words are not a statement that unbelieving Jews are saved or are currently in a right relationship with God, but they do indicate that God's commitment to the nation is not over. So despite their current state of unbelief, God is not done with Israel. He has not revoked His covenants and promises to His people. Those things still belong to Israel.

Romans 11:1 states, "I say then, God has not rejected His people, has He? May it never be!" In case there was any doubt Paul emphatically declares that Israel was still "His people." Paul then makes a strategic statement in Romans 11:11–12:

> I say then, they did not stumble so as to fall, did they? May it never be! But by their transgression salvation has come to the Gentiles, to make them jealous. Now if their transgression is riches for the world and their failure is riches for the Gentiles, how much more will their fulfillment be! (HCSB)

Israel's stumbling is temporary, not permanent. Also, Israel's temporary stumbling has a purpose—to make Israel jealous by bringing salvation to the Gentiles. When Israel's "fulfillment" (salvation and restoration) takes place, even greater blessings will be bestowed upon the world. This shows that God's plans for both Israel and the Gentiles is not completely fulfilled in our current age. Great blessings have currently come to Gentiles as a result of Israel's temporary fall, but when Israel is saved the blessings to the Gentiles will be magnified even more. In other words, if you think the blessings to the Gentiles is great now, just wait until Israel's "fulfillment" comes! Then Paul explicitly predicts this salvation and restoration of Israel in Romans 11:25–27:

> For I do not want you, brethren, to be uninformed of this mystery—so that you will not be wise in your own estimation—that a partial hardening has happened to Israel until the fullness of the Gentiles has come in; and so all Israel will be saved; just as it is written, "THE DELIVERER WILL COME FROM ZION, HE WILL REMOVE UNGODLINESS FROM JACOB." "THIS IS MY COVENANT WITH THEM, WHEN I TAKE AWAY THEIR SINS."

Israel's salvation is not only explicitly declared—"All Israel will be saved"—it is linked with the promises of the Old Testament, showing that God's promises will be literally fulfilled. Paul also mentions that Israel's salvation is linked with God's sovereign, electing purposes: "from the standpoint of God's choice they are beloved for the sake of the fathers" (11:28). God has a future for His covenant people, Israel, because God is faithful to the promises He made to the Jewish patriarchs and His electing purposes stand true.

In sum, Romans 9–11 is powerful testimony for the future of the nation Israel and a strong refutation of any "replacement theology" in which the church is viewed as replacing or superseding Israel. The scholar C. E. B. Cranfield declared that these chapters are a strong rebuttal to any idea that the church has replaced Israel in God's plans:

> It is only where the Church persists in refusing to learn this message, where it secretly—perhaps quite unconsciously—

> believes that its own existence is based on human achievement, and so fails to understand God's mercy to itself, that it is unable to believe in God's mercy for still unbelieving Israel, and so entertains the ugly and unscriptural notion that God has cast off His people Israel and simply replaced it by the Christian Church. These three chapters [Rom. 9–11] emphatically forbid us to speak of the Church as having once and for all taken the place of the Jewish people.[16]

Revelation

When we come to the last book of the Bible, Revelation (ca. AD 95), it is clear that Israel is still important to God's purposes. Revelation 7:4–8 specifically foretells the sealing of the twelve tribes of Israel during the time of tribulation upon the world:

> And I heard the number of those who were sealed, one hundred and forty-four thousand sealed from every tribe of the sons of Israel: from the tribe of Judah, twelve thousand were sealed, from the tribe of Reuben twelve thousand, from the tribe of Gad twelve thousand, from the tribe of Asher twelve thousand, from the tribe of Naphtali twelve thousand, from the tribe of Manasseh twelve thousand, from the tribe of Simeon twelve thousand, from the tribe of Levi twelve thousand, from the tribe of Issachar twelve thousand, from the tribe of Zebulun twelve thousand, from the tribe of Joseph twelve thousand, from the tribe of Benjamin, twelve thousand were sealed.

The specific mentioning of each of the twelve tribes of Israel, which have a role of witness in the difficult days of the coming tribulation period, emphasizes the continuing importance of the tribes of Israel in the plan of God. This is not a reference to Gentiles or the "church militant" as some assert.[17] Immediately after this Revelation 7:9 states, "After this I looked, and there was a vast multitude from every nation, tribe, people, and language, which no one could number, standing before the throne and before the Lamb" (HCSB). Thus, John distinguishes Jews

(Rev. 7:4–8) and Gentiles (Rev. 7:9). The group in 7:4–8 consists of ethnic Jews while the group in 7:9 is a multitude from "every nation." Plus, the group in 7:4–8 is a specific and relatively small number—a group of 144,000, while the group in 7:9 is "a great multitude which no one could count." These are not the same groups of people.

Revelation 21:10–14 also emphasizes the continuing relevance of the tribes of Israel in God's plan:

> And he carried me away in the Spirit to a great and high mountain, and showed me the holy city, Jerusalem, coming down out of heaven from God, having the glory of God. Her brilliance was like a very costly stone, as a stone of crystal-clear jasper. It had a great and high wall, with twelve gates, and at the gates twelve angels; and names were written on them, which are the names of the twelve tribes of the sons of Israel. There were three gates on the east and three gates on the north and three gates on the south and three gates on the west. And the wall of the city had twelve foundation stones, and on them were the twelve names of the twelve apostles of the Lamb.

This passage is significant because of its reference to the "twelve tribes of the sons of Israel" (v. 12) in the eternal state. Robert L. Thomas points out that the names of Israel serve "explicit notice of the distinct role of national Israel in this eternal city in fulfillment of their distinctive role in history throughout the centuries of their existence (cf. 7:1–8)."[18] The twelve tribes of Israel are distinguished from the "twelve apostles of the Lamb" of verse 14. This shows that Israel's distinct identity is still maintained even in the eternal state. This passage also rules out any idea that the twelve tribes of Israel were only a temporary type that has been superseded by the twelve apostles. The twelve tribes of Israel, who are the foundation of national Israel, are viewed as distinct from the twelve apostles.

Conclusion

As this survey has shown, the salvation and restoration of the nation Israel is an explicit biblical doctrine. It is found from Genesis through Revelation. Israel's future is linked with the ultimate Israelite, Jesus Christ, who restores the nation and brings blessings to the nations of the earth. May our response to the unbiblical idea that the nation Israel no longer has a place in God's plans be that of the apostle Paul who declared, "God has not rejected His people, has He? May it never be!" (Rom. 11:1).

Notes

1. S. M. Lockridge, "Seven-Way King," online at http://thatsmyking.wordpress.com/words/.
2. For example, Kim Riddlebarger argues against a literal fulfillment of Old Testament physical promises to the nation Israel based on his understanding of Christ as the "true Israel": "The ramifications for this on one's millennial view should now be obvious. The New Testament writers claimed that Jesus was the true Israel of God and the fulfillment of Old Testament prophecies. So what remains of the dispensationalists' case that these prophecies will yet be fulfilled in a future millennium? They vanish in Jesus Christ, who has fulfilled them." Kim Riddlebarger, *A Case for Amillennialism: Understanding the End Times* (Grand Rapids: Baker, 2003), 70.
3. Robert Martin-Achard, *A Light to the Nations* (Edinburgh: Oliver and Boyd, 1962), 40–41.
4. Anthony A. Hoekema, *The Bible and the Future* (Grand Rapids: Eerdmans, 1979), 286. Emphases added.
5. Ibid.
6. Barry E. Horner, *Future Israel: Why Christian Anti-Judaism Must Be Challenged* (Nashville: B&H Academic, 2007), 217.
7. William J. Dumbrell, *Covenant and Creation: A Theology of the Old Testament Covenants* (Nashville: Thomas Nelson, 1984), 65.
8. Christopher J. H. Wright, *The Mission of God: Unlocking the Bible's Grand Narrative* (Downers Grove, IL: IVP), 251.
9. Tuvya Zaretsky, "Israel the People," in *Israel: The Land and the People: An Evangelical Affirmation of God's Promises*, ed. H. Wayne House (Grand Rapids: Kregel, 1998), 49.
10. Robert B. Strimple, "Amillennialism," *Three Views on the Millennium and Beyond*, ed. Darrell L. Bock (Grand Rapids: Zondervan, 1999), 87.

11. Robert L. Saucy, "Israel and the Church: A Case for Discontinuity," in *Continuity and Discontinuity: Perspectives on the Relationship between the Old and New Testaments*, ed. John S. Feinberg (Wheaton, IL: Crossway, 1988), 242.
12. Craig L. Blomberg, "Matthew," in *Commentary on the New Testament Use of the Old Testament*, eds. G. K. Beale and D. A. Carson (Grand Rapids: Baker, 2007), 85.
13. Robert H. Gundry, *Matthew: A Commentary on His Literary and Theological Arts* (Grand Rapids: Eerdmans, 1982), 394.
14. Robert C. Tannehill, *Luke*, ANTC (Nashville: Abingdon, 1996), 226–27.
15. J. Bradley Chance, *Jerusalem, the Temple, and the New Age in Luke–Acts* (Macon, GA: Mercer University Press, 1988), 133.
16. C. E. B. Cranfield, *A Critical and Exegetical Commentary on the Epistle to the Romans*, ICC (Edinburgh: T. & T. Clark, 1975–79), 2:448.
17. See G. K. Beale and Sean M. McDonough, "Revelation," in *Commentary on the New Testament Use of the Old Testament*, eds. G. K. Beale and D. A. Carson (Grand Rapids: Baker, 2007), 1107.
18. Robert L. Thomas, *Revelation 8–22: An Exegetical Commentary* (Chicago: Moody, 1995), 463.

Chapter Six

WHAT ABOUT REVELATION 20?

Matthew Waymeyer

Several years ago some friends of mine rented an adventure movie to watch with their two daughters. During an intense scene early in the film, the girls became afraid and were no longer sure they wanted to finish the DVD. So their parents did something creative—they fast-forwarded to the very end and showed their daughters that the main characters were alive and well in the final scene. Then they reset the movie and resumed where they had left off. Now the girls were able to make it through the scary parts because they knew for sure how everything would turn out in the end.

That's precisely what God does in the book of Revelation. In order to strengthen and encourage the persecuted church, He reveals a series of visions in which He fast-forwards to the end of time and shows His people that when all is said and done, the Lord Jesus Christ is victorious over everything that is evil. And knowing this—knowing the end from the beginning—is part of what enables the church to stand firm and persevere through times of suffering. In the end, Jesus wins!

In one of these visions—found in Revelation 20:1–6—the Lord

shows the apostle John what is commonly known as the millennial reign of Christ.[1] In this monumental passage, John describes a thousand-year period of time when Satan will be bound in the abyss (vv. 1–3) and the Lord Jesus Christ will reign upon the earth (vv. 4–6). This vision has become a focal point in the debate between the various millennial positions, being labeled by one leading Amillennialist as the most important biblical passage on the subject of the millennium.[2]

A key distinction in the discussion concerns the timing of the thousand-year reign of Christ. According to Futuristic Premillennialism, the visions in Revelation 19–22 will occur in the same order that they are written, and therefore the millennial kingdom of Revelation 20 is yet future. After the seven-year period of tribulation (Rev. 6–19), Jesus will return in glory (19:11–16), bringing judgment to the false prophet, the beast, and the unbelieving armies of the earth (19:17–21). Satan will be imprisoned in the abyss for a thousand years (20:1–3), and Jesus will establish His kingdom on earth where He will reign with the saints in perfect righteousness (20:4–6). At the end of the thousand years, Satan will be released and defeated once and for all (20:7–10); the wicked will be resurrected, judged, and thrown into the lake of fire (20:11–15); then the eternal state of the new heaven and earth will begin (21–22). This is the Futuristic Premillennial view of Revelation 20.

In contrast, Amillennialism and Postmillennialism contend that the thousand-year reign of Christ takes place during the present age, extending from the time of His first coming to the time of the second coming. More specifically, they believe that even though the return of Christ is described at the end of chapter 19, Revelation 20:1 brings the reader back to the beginning of the current age so that the millennial kingdom is a present reality. In terms of timing, then, the key difference is that Amillennialism and Postmillennialism affirm that the thousand years of Revelation 20 is *present*, whereas Futuristic Premillennialism maintains it is *future*.[3]

This chapter will examine several key features in Revelation 20 to demonstrate that this passage clearly teaches that the thousand-year reign of Christ will take place after His second coming, as held by

Futuristic Premillennialism. Central to this assertion are (1) the timing of Satan's binding, (2) the nature of the first resurrection, (3) the duration of the thousand years, and (4) the chronology of John's visions.

The Timing of Satan's Binding

In Revelation 20:1–3, John's vision focuses on the status of Satan during the millennial reign of Christ. The apostle writes:

> Then I saw an angel coming down from heaven, holding the key of the abyss and a great chain in his hand. And he laid hold of the dragon, the serpent of old, who is the devil and Satan, and bound him for a thousand years; and he threw him into the abyss, and shut *it* and sealed *it* over him, so that he would not deceive the nations any longer, until the thousand years were completed; after these things he must be released for a short time.

A primary question involves the timing of Satan's binding. Put simply, is it now or in the future? In other words, is Satan currently bound in the abyss during the present age, or will his thousand-year imprisonment take place after the second coming of Christ? Amillennialism and Postmillennialism see the binding of Satan as a present reality—the millennium is *now*—whereas Futuristic Premillennialism sees it as future.

Satan's imprisonment cannot be considered a present reality because the events of Revelation 20:1–3 are incompatible with the New Testament's portrayal of his influence during the present age. According to John's vision, Satan will be cut off entirely from all earthly activity during the thousand years. The imagery of him being cast into the abyss and having it shut and sealed over him provides a vivid picture of a total removal of his influence on earth. In fact, if a vision were intended to teach that Satan would be rendered completely inactive during the thousand years, it is difficult to imagine how this could be portrayed more clearly.

The specific location of Satan's imprisonment makes this especially clear. The word *abyss* refers to a prison for evil spirits; when evil spirits are confined in the abyss, the Bible indicates that they are prevented from roaming free on earth. This is evident in Luke 8 where Jesus encountered a demon-possessed man. When Jesus began conversing with the demons indwelling this man, they pleaded with Him not to command them to depart into the abyss but rather permit them to enter a nearby herd of swine (vv. 31–32). The reason for the demons' request was not because they were so determined to kill the swine, but rather because imprisonment in the abyss would have cut them off from having any influence in this world—at least as long as they were *in* the abyss—whereas a departure into the swine would allow them to continue to roam free and wreak havoc upon the earth.

The same can be seen in the book of Revelation. In Revelation 9:1–3, a multitude of demons must first be released from the abyss before causing harm on the earth. Prior to that release, however, the demons have no earthly influence whatsoever. Similarly, in Revelation 20, Satan must first be "released from his prison" (v. 7) before he can "come out to deceive the nations" (v. 8). But as long as he is confined in the abyss, the devil is not able to depart from his prison and therefore his activity on earth is completely nonexistent.

In contrast, the New Testament makes it quite clear that Satan—who is described as "the god of this world" (2 Cor. 4:4) and "the ruler of this world" (John 12:31; 14:30; 16:11; cf. 1 John 4:4)—is extremely active on earth during the present age. He not only "prowls around like a roaring lion, seeking someone to devour" (1 Pet. 5:8), but is also involved in a host of other activities: he tells lies (John 8:44); he tempts believers to sin (1 Cor. 7:5; Eph. 4:27); he disguises himself as an angel of light (2 Cor. 11:13–15); he seeks to deceive the children of God (2 Cor. 11:3); he snatches the gospel from unbelieving hearts (Matt. 13:19; Mark 4:15; Luke 8:12; cf. 1 Thess. 3:5); he takes advantage of believers (2 Cor. 2:11); he influences people to lie (Acts 5:3); he holds unbelievers under his power (Acts 26:18; Eph. 2:2; 1 John 5:19); he buffets the servants of God (2 Cor. 12:7); he thwarts the progress of ministry (1 Thess. 2:18); he seeks to destroy the faith of believers (Luke 22:31); he wages war against the church (Eph. 6:11–17); and he traps and deceives people, holding them captive to do his will (2 Tim. 2:26). It is impossible to reconcile this portrayal of Satan's activities with the view that he is currently sealed in the abyss.

Amillennialists and Postmillennialists have responded to this incongruity by insisting that the binding of Satan only prevents him from deceiving the nations, which leaves him free to engage in these other activities. After all, that is the only stated purpose of Satan's binding in Revelation 20:3—"that he would not deceive the nations any longer." In this way, Amillennialists and Postmillennialists say that Satan's activity in the present age is *limited*, but not eliminated.

One problem with this argument is that it focuses on the stated purpose in verse 3 while ignoring the actual location of Satan's imprisonment. If the warden of a prison puts a prisoner in solitary confinement for the stated purpose of preventing him from killing other prisoners, this does not mean that he is free to steal from them and do other such activities. After all, the location of solitary confinement completely removes him from the rest of the prison and cuts him off entirely from the other prisoners. In the same way, the degree of Satan's restriction in Revelation 20 is determined not by the stated purpose alone, but also by the location of his imprisonment—the abyss—which removes the devil from earth and cuts him off from any influence there.[4]

Additionally, the New Testament teaches that Satan *is* involved in deceiving the nations during the present age. According to 2 Corinthians 4:4, Satan "has blinded the minds of the unbelieving so that they might not see the light of the gospel of the glory of Christ." In other words, Satan is presently deceiving the unbelievers that make up the nations of this world by blinding them and keeping them from embracing the gospel. Furthermore, the book of Revelation teaches that Satan and his demons will continue to deceive the nations right up to the time when Jesus returns to establish His kingdom and Satan is cast into the abyss (Rev. 12:9; 13:14; 18:23; 19:20). If Satan is prevented from deceiving the nations during the millennial reign of Christ and yet he is currently deceiving the nations in the present age, the thousand years of Revelation 20 cannot be taking place right now. The binding of Satan must be future.[5]

The Nature of the First Resurrection

In Revelation 20:4–6, the apostle John refers to individuals who "came to life and reigned with Christ for a thousand years" (v. 4), describing this coming to life as "the first resurrection" (v. 5).[6] According to Futuristic Premillennialism, this is the first of two physical resurrections in Revelation 20, resurrections that are separated by a thousand years. The first is a resurrection of the righteous—the faithful believers who are martyred during the tribulation (v. 4)—and the second is a resurrection of the wicked who will stand before the throne of final judgment after the millennial kingdom (vv. 11–15). As John writes: "They came to life and reigned with Christ for a thousand years. The rest of the dead did not come to life until the thousand years were completed" (vv. 4–5).

Amillennialists and Postmillennialists reject this idea of two physical resurrections separated by a thousand years, insisting instead that "the first resurrection" at the beginning of the thousand years is not physical but rather spiritual. They explain the spiritual nature of this resurrection in various ways, but the most common view is that the first resurrection refers to the regeneration of believers at the point of conversion. In this way, the first resurrection takes place during the present age when those who are spiritually dead are made alive in Christ (John 5:25; Eph. 2:4–6; Col. 2:12–13; 1 John 3:14) and live to reign with Him in the present millennial kingdom.

But there are several difficulties with this view. First, the word translated "resurrection" (*anastasis*) is used forty-one other times in the New Testament and never is it used to refer to regeneration. This objection is not conclusive—because it is theoretically possible that John is using this word in a unique way—but it does place the burden of proof on those who say it is used this way in Revelation 20.

A second problem concerns the coming to life of "the rest of the dead" at the beginning of verse 5. When John says that these individuals "came to life" (*ezēsan*), interpreters agree that this word refers to a physical resurrection. Because John uses the same form of the same Greek word (*ezēsan*) to refer to the coming to life of the individuals in verse 4, it stands to reason that this "first resurrection" must be a physical resurrection as well. Otherwise, "we are faced with the problem of the same word being used in the same context with two entirely different meanings, with no indication whatsoever as to the change of meaning."[7] Futuristic Premillennialism doesn't have this problem, because it sees the verb *ezēsan* as referring to a physical resurrection in both verses—a resurrection of the righteous in verse 4 and a resurrection of the wicked in verse 5.

Third, this passage indicates that the entire group of individuals who are raised in the first resurrection are resurrected together at the beginning of the millennium and reign together with Christ for the entirety of the thousand years (Rev. 20:4–6). This is clear from the grammar of the passage.[8] However, according to the view that the first resurrection equals regeneration, believers are regenerated *throughout* the thousand years (which is seen as the present age) so that the entrance of the saints into this reign is distributed throughout the millennium. This simply does not fit with John's vision as he describes it.

Lastly, according to the view that the first resurrection refers to regeneration, the individuals described in verse 4 are not regenerated by the Holy Spirit until after they are martyred. In this way, the regeneration view introduces "the absurdity of having souls being regenerated *after* they've been beheaded for their faithfulness to Christ!"[9]

In contrast, there are several reasons why the "first resurrection" must refer to a physical resurrection: (1) this is consistent with the use of the word "resurrection" (*anastasis*), which refers to physical resurrection forty-one out of forty-two times in the New Testament; (2) the word translated "they came to life" (*ezēsan*) refers to the same kind of resurrection in verse 5 as it does in verse 4—a physical resurrection; (3) it makes perfect sense of the terminology "*first* resurrection," which obviously implies a second resurrection, the resurrection of the wicked a thousand years later; and (4) it fits the context in which John sees those who were killed in the physical realm coming back to life in the physical realm.

The most common objection to Futuristic Premillennialism's view of two physical resurrections in Revelation 20 is that elsewhere the Bible teaches a single, general resurrection in which the righteous and the wicked will be raised at the same time (Dan. 12:2; John 5:28–29; Acts 24:15). As one Postmillennialist asks: "Why should we believe that the New Testament everywhere teaches a general, singular resurrection on the last day, only to discover later . . . that there are actually two specific, distantly separated resurrections for different classes of people?"[10]

In response to this objection, Daniel 12:2, John 5:28–29, and Acts 24:15 do not actually preclude the possibility of two distinct resurrections separated by a period of time. In fact, all three passages speak of a resurrection of the righteous and a resurrection of the wicked—and always in that same order (the same as in Rev. 20)—and they neither state nor require that the two resurrections happen at the same time.[11]

It is helpful to remember that later revelation in Scripture will sometimes clarify that there is actually a gap of time that separates two events predicted in earlier revelation—two events that initially appeared as if they would occur at the same time. For example, there is no clear evidence in the Old Testament alone that there would be two separate comings of the Messiah separated by a significant period of time. But once you come to the later revelation of the New Testament, you realize that what the Old Testament writers seemed to depict as a single event must now be recognized as involving two events. In the same way, when it comes to the future resurrection, what the earlier writers of Scripture seemed to depict as a single resurrection (a general resurrection of the righteous and the wicked) must now be recognized as involving two resurrections (a resurrection of the righteous and then a resurrection of the wicked a thousand years later).

To illustrate, imagine driving down a freeway in the desert. Off in the distance, you see two mountains on the horizon and the freeway going right down the middle of them. The two mountains appear to be right next to each other, one on the left and one on the right, but as you draw near, you see that the one on the right is actually closer than the one on the left. In fact, as you drive *past* the one on the right, you find that there is a thousand-yard gap between the two mountains—a gap you couldn't see when looking from a distance.

That is exactly what you find in the progress of revelation with the future resurrection of the righteous and the wicked. Earlier in Scripture you see a resurrection of life and a resurrection of judgment, and from a distance it initially appears that the two will occur at the same time (Dan. 12:2; John 5:28–29; Acts 24:15). But now that you're closer—looking at the clear teaching of Revelation 20—you realize that just as there was a thousand yards separating the two mountains, so is there a thousand years separating the two resurrections. This is the only way to harmonize all of what Scripture teaches on the subject of the future resurrection.

The Duration of the Thousand Years

The reign of Christ in Revelation 20 is often called His *millennial* reign because it is described as being a thousand years in length. Amillennialists and Postmillennialists generally say that, in keeping with the symbolic nature of Revelation as a whole, the thousand years should be understood symbolically, representing either a "complete" period of time or an indefinitely long period of time. This raises the question of whether the thousand years in Revelation 20 should be understood literally or figuratively. The significance of this question is obvious: if the thousand years is literal, it cannot refer to the present age, which is already nearly two thousand years long, and therefore it must refer to a period of time that is yet future.

The main argument for the symbolic view is that the book of Revelation is full of symbolism in general and symbolic numbers in particular. Therefore, it is said, the number "one thousand" must be symbolic as well. This argument, however, is overly simplistic. The reality is that the vast majority of the 254 numbers in the book of

Revelation are intended to be understood literally. Furthermore, any time a number is used with a time indicator in Revelation—such as days, months, or years—there is no clear indication that it is symbolic. In addition, nowhere in Scripture—not even in 2 Peter 3:8—is a thousand years used as a symbolic designation.[12]

It is not enough to merely *say* that Revelation is filled with symbolism and therefore that the thousand years must be symbolic; one must provide compelling evidence that it should be understood this way. The only conceivable approach to understanding literature of any kind is to assume the literal sense unless the nature of the language forces the reader to consider a symbolic interpretation.[13] Not only is this the only conceivable approach, but it also reflects the fact that symbolic language is a departure from the literal, and not vice versa.

To determine whether something in Scripture should be interpreted symbolically, it is helpful to ask three questions. First, *does it possess a degree of absurdity when taken literally?* With symbolic language, there is something inherent in the language itself that compels the interpreter to look beyond the literal meaning. This something is a degree of absurdity that causes the interpreter to scratch his head and say, "But how can this be?" Second, *does it possess a degree of clarity when taken symbolically?* Symbolic language is essentially clear and understandable, vividly portraying what it symbolizes. For this reason, interpreting figurative language symbolically brings clarity to the meaning of a text that appeared to be absurd when taken literally. And third, *does it fall into an established category of symbolic language?* Because figures of speech are legitimate departures from the normal use of language, they are limited in number and can be defined in accordance with known examples.[14] For this reason, the interpreter must determine whether the language in question falls into an established category of figurative language, such as simile, metaphor, hyperbole, personification, or anthropomorphism.

For example, when Isaiah 55:12 refers to the trees of the field clapping their hands, the language of the text meets all three criteria for symbolic language—it possesses a degree of absurdity when taken literally (trees don't have hands); it possesses a degree of clarity when taken symbolically (it clearly communicates a time of such joy that even the trees will be clapping); and it falls into an established category of symbolic language (personification—in which a human action is attributed to an inanimate object).

In contrast, the thousand years of Revelation 20 meets none of the proposed criteria. First, there is nothing absurd or nonsensical about the literal interpretation of the thousand years that compels the interpreter to seek something other than the literal meaning. In fact, if God had wanted to communicate that the reign of Christ would last for a literal thousand years, how else could He have done it? What else could He have said?

Second, there is no degree of clarity when the thousand years is taken symbolically. For example, one Postmillennialist describes the symbolic significance of the thousand years like this: "The sacred number seven in combination with the equally sacred number three forms the number of holy perfection [ten], and when this ten is cubed into a thousand [John] has said all he could say to convey to our minds the idea of absolute completeness."[15] But what exactly would lead the interpreter to see these kinds of math equations behind the number one thousand? Furthermore, the common explanation that the thousand years represents "completeness" or "a complete period of time" raises the question, What exactly is completeness? What is a *complete* period of time, and how does it differ from an *incomplete* period of time? What exactly is being communicated by the words "a thousand years"? Most of the symbolic explanations of the thousand years introduce more confusion than clarity.

Third, the symbolic use of the thousand years does not fall into any clear category of symbolic language. The closest possibility appears to be the suggestion that the symbolic interpretation of the thousand years is like the statement: "I've told you a million times!"[16] This figure of speech is known as *hyperbole*, an obvious exaggeration to emphasize a point. But John's use of one thousand years cannot possibly be understood as hyperbole if it's being used to refer to a period of time that is already nearly two thousand years in length!

The number one thousand is not an exaggeration of the number two thousand.

There is simply no compelling reason in the immediate context to interpret the thousand years as anything other than literal. In fact, when the apostle John intends to express an indefinite quantity of something in Revelation 20, he does so not by naming a specific number like one thousand years, but rather by using indefinite expressions like "for a short time" (v. 3) or "the number of them is like the sand of the seashore" (v. 8). John's sixfold use of the specific number one thousand—in contrast to these indefinite phrases for time and numbers—only strengthens the conclusion that the thousand years should be understood literally.

The Chronology of John's Visions

The crux of the debate over the timing of the millennium is ultimately found in the chronological relationship between Revelation 19 and Revelation 20. Most interpreters agree that the visions in Revelation 19:11–21 portray the second coming of Christ. For this reason, if the vision in Revelation 20:1–6 is intended to portray what happens next—*after* the second coming—then obviously the thousand years are yet future and the book of Revelation teaches Premillennialism.

In contrast to the chronological reading of Revelation 19 and 20, Amillennialism and Postmillennialism contend that Revelation 20:1 recapitulates and takes the reader back to the beginning of the present age. In this way, it is said that the thousand years is not future but present, extending from the first coming of Christ to the time of His second coming. This is often referred to as the recapitulation view. The question is whether there are compelling reasons to believe that Revelation 20:1 takes the reader back to the start of the present age.

The most common argument for recapitulation comes from Revelation 12. According to the recapitulation view, the parallels between the casting down of Satan in Revelation 12:7–12 and the casting down of Satan in Revelation 20:1–6 confirm that both passages portray the same events in the present age. For example, both take place in a heavenly scene; both involve an angelic battle with Satan; both refer to him as the dragon and the ancient serpent; both portray him being cast down; and both refer to his "short" period of time. These and other parallels are cited by Amillennialists and Postmillennialists as evidence that Revelation 20:1 takes the reader back to the beginning of the New Testament era.[17]

The problem is that this argument focuses on superficial points of similarity between Revelation 12 and Revelation 20, while ignoring differences between the two passages that make it impossible for them to be describing the same events or time period. Suppose a news magazine were to publish two separate articles about the president of the United States. The first article described how he flew on Air Force One from Washington, DC, to London where he spent the day giving a number of public speeches. A subsequent article described how he flew on Air Force One from London to Hawaii where he spent two weeks vacationing with his family out of the public eye. The discerning reader would not assume that the two articles were describing the same flight simply because they both referred to how (a) the president of the United States (b) flew across the ocean (c) on Air Force One. After all, the point of departure is different, the destination is different, and the substance of the trip is different. The two accounts couldn't possibly be describing the same flight across the ocean.

So it is with the parallels between Revelation 12 and Revelation 20: Even though both passages refer to the casting down of Satan, critical differences preclude the possibility that they refer to the same casting down. For example, in Revelation 12, Satan is cast down from heaven to *earth*, but in Revelation 20 he is cast down from earth into the *abyss*. Unless one is prepared to equate the abyss and the earth, this cannot be the same casting down of Satan. He is on earth in Revelation 12 and in the abyss in Revelation 20, but he cannot be in both places at once.

Another major difference is that the expulsion of Satan from heaven in Revelation 12 has the opposite effect of the casting of Satan into the abyss in Revelation 20. When Satan is cast down to earth in chapter 12, it results in increased deception of the nations (Rev. 12:9).[18]

But when Satan is cast into the abyss in Revelation 20, it prevents him from deceiving the nations any longer (Rev. 20:3). Satan can be deceiving the nations of the world, or he can be sealed in the abyss and unable to deceive those nations, but he cannot be both deceiving and unable to deceive at the same time. The two descriptions are incompatible.

A final difference involves the short amount of time given to Satan in both passages. At the end of Revelation 12:12, John describes Satan being cast down to the earth, "having great wrath, knowing that he has only a short time." In Revelation 20:3, John writes that after Satan is locked in the abyss for a thousand years, "he must be released for a short time." This parallel—"a short time" in 12:12 and "a short time" in 20:3—is cited by those who argue for the recapitulation view. The problem is that these two periods of time do not line up chronologically. In Revelation 12, Satan is cast down to earth for a short time, but in Revelation 20 he is cast into the abyss for a *long* time (the thousand years), and then afterward he is released for a short time. If the recapitulation view is correct, the short time in Revelation 12 coincides with the long time in Revelation 20 (the thousand years), which is then *followed* by a short time. The supposed parallel between the "short time" in Revelation 12 and the "short time" in Revelation 20 offers no support for the recapitulation view and actually presents a problem for it.

In contrast to the recapitulation view, the most natural way to read this section of Revelation is to see a sequential relationship in which the events of chapter 20 follow those of chapter 19. There is nothing in Revelation 20:1 that indicates a chronological break between the two chapters—John simply introduces the next vision with the words "and I saw," just like he does throughout the book of Revelation. In the absence of any clear indication that Revelation 20:1 takes the reader back to the beginning of the present age, it is better to affirm a chronological relationship.

In addition, the sequential view of Revelation 19 and 20 is supported by a number of features in the immediate context. First, John's reference to how Satan's imprisonment will prevent him from deceiving the nations "any longer" (Rev. 20:3) connects this vision to the previous context in a way that suggests a sequential relationship. Because the words "any longer" indicate that Satan was engaged in this deception just prior to being locked in the abyss—and because Revelation 12–19 repeatedly highlights the satanic deception of the nations that will take place throughout the second half of the tribulation (Rev. 12:9; 13:14; 16:14; 18:23; 19:19–20)—this reference to Satan "no longer" deceiving the nations during the thousand years points to a chronological reading of Revelation 19 and 20. This would be similar to a narrative that contained several chapters describing how a dog barked at a cat, followed by a chapter that then described how a man locked the dog in the garage "so that it would bark at the cat *no longer*." The most natural way to read such a narrative would be to see this latter chapter as describing an event that took place subsequent to the events described in the previous chapters.

Second, the description of the lake of fire in Revelation 20:10 also suggests a sequential relationship. At the time of the second coming, prior to the thousand years, the beast and the false prophet will be "thrown alive into the lake of fire which burns with brimstone" (Rev. 19:20). Then, at the conclusion of the thousand years, Satan will be "thrown into the lake of fire and brimstone, *where the beast and the false prophet are also*" (Rev. 20:10; emphasis added). In light of this description, the most natural way to read Revelation 19–20 is to see a chronological sequence in which (1) the beast and false prophet are cast into the lake of fire (Rev. 19:20); (2) Satan is bound and sealed in the abyss for a thousand years (Rev. 20:1–6); (3) Satan is released after the thousand years and defeated by fire from heaven (Rev. 20:7–9); and then (4) Satan is thrown into the lake of fire where the beast and false prophet already are (Rev. 20:10).

Third, the content of Revelation 20:1–6 is simply incompatible with the view that this passage is a description of the current age. The binding of Satan is future rather than present, the "first resurrection" is physical rather than spiritual, and the thousand years is literal rather than symbolic. For these reasons, the content of John's vision in Revelation 20:1–6 will not allow for the recapitulation view, and the events of Revelation 20 must follow after those of Revelation 19.

Conclusion

The disagreement over the millennium will likely continue for some time, but not because of a lack of clarity in Revelation 20:1–6. Any attempt to argue for Amillennialism or Postmillennialism must either downplay the contribution of this passage or reject its straightforward interpretation. When Christ returns to earth in glory, Satan will be cast into the abyss where he will be confined for a thousand years. During this time the Lord Jesus will establish His millennial kingdom and reign from Jerusalem in perfect peace and righteousness. Then, at the conclusion of the thousand years, Satan will be released from the abyss, decisively defeated, and thrown into the lake of fire. The wicked will be judged, the earth will be destroyed, and a new heaven and earth will be established and continue throughout eternity. And in this way, when all is said and done, the Lord Jesus Christ will be victorious over all that is evil.

Notes

1. Jack S. Deere, "Premillennialism in Revelation 20:4–6," *Bibliotheca Sacra* 135 (January–March 1978): 58–73 sets forth an excellent exegetical summary of this text.
2. Kim Riddlebarger, *A Case for Amillennialism: Understanding the End Times* (Grand Rapids: Baker, 2003), 195.
3. At the same time, an important distinction should be made: Amillennialism teaches that the present age *is* the millennial kingdom whereas Postmillennialism teaches that it is *becoming* the millennial kingdom. More specifically, Postmillennialism teaches that the gospel will go forth with increasing success in the present age until most of the world is converted to Christ and the kingdom is fully established. Because Postmillennialists believe that the exact starting point of the millennial kingdom is difficult (if not impossible) to discern, Postmillennialism does not necessarily affirm that the thousand years of Revelation 20 extends throughout the entirety of the present age as Amillennialism does, but it does affirm that the thousand years takes place during the present age. For this reason, some of the arguments in this chapter apply more directly to Amillennialism than to Postmillennialism.
4. This illustration was taken from Charles E. Powell, "Progression Versus Recapitulation in Revelation 20:1–6," *Bibliotheca Sacra* 163 (January–March 2006): 98.
5. Amillennialists typically equate the binding of Satan in Revelation 20 with the binding of the strong man in Matthew 12:29 and assert that both bindings took place at the beginning of the present age when Christ conquered the devil at Calvary (Col. 2:15; Heb. 2:14–15; 1 John 3:8). Although the same verb "bind" (*deō*) is used in both passages, this is where the similarities end. In Matthew 12:29, the

binding of Satan broke the power he had to possess specific individuals and thereby enabled Jesus to deliver those individuals from Satan's control. In contrast, the binding of Satan in Revelation 20 involves incarcerating him in the abyss and preventing him from deceiving the nations. The Amillennial view that the binding of Satan in Revelation 20 refers to the victory of Christ on the cross faces the additional problem of how to explain the release of Satan in Revelation 20:7; for whatever is accomplished in the imprisonment of verse 2 is undone in the release of verse 7.

6. The first part of Revelation 20:5 ("The rest of the dead did not come to life until the thousand years were completed") is parenthetical. Therefore, when John refers to the "first resurrection" in the next part of verse 5, he is pointing back to the coming to life described at the end of verse 4. This is agreed upon by all interpreters.

7. George Eldon Ladd, *A Commentary on the Revelation of John* (Grand Rapids: Eerdmans, 1972), 266.

8. In writing that the saints came to life and reigned with Christ "for a thousand years" (Rev. 20:4), the apostle John uses what Greek grammarians refer to as an accusative of time (see Daniel Wallace, *Greek Grammar beyond the Basics: An Exegetical Syntax of the New Testament* [Grand Rapids: Zondervan, 1996], 201–3). This indicates that the saints will reign with Christ for the entirety of the thousand years (just as Satan will be bound and incarcerated for the entirety of the thousand years). If John had intended to communicate that the saints would reign *during* the thousand years (as Amillennialists and Postmillennialists believe) rather than *throughout the extent* of the thousand years, he would have used a *genitive* of time (see Wallace, 122–24).

9. Alva J. McClain, *The Greatness of the Kingdom: An Inductive Study of the Kingdom of God* (1959; repr., Winona Lake, IN: BMH, 1992), 488; emphasis in original.

10. Kenneth L. Gentry Jr., "A Postmillennial Response to Craig A. Blaising," in *Three Views on the Millennium and Beyond*, ed. Darrell L. Bock (Grand Rapids: Zondervan, 1999), 243.

11. When John states that "an *hour* is coming" when these two resurrections will occur (John 5:28–29), this does not require that both resurrections take place at the same time. After all, John frequently uses the word "hour" to refer to an extended period of time (John 16:2), sometimes as long as the entire present age (John 4:21, 23; 1 John 2:18). In fact, he uses the word "hour" in this very way just three verses earlier in John 5:25.

12. Steve P. Sullivan, "Premillennialism and an Exegesis of Revelation 20:37–40," http://www.pre-trib.org/data/pdf/Sullivan-PremillennialismAndA.pdf.

13. Bernard Ramm, *Protestant Biblical Interpretation: A Textbook of Hermeneutics*, 3rd ed. (Grand Rapids: Baker, 1970), 123.

14. Walter C. Kaiser Jr., *Toward an Exegetical Theology: Biblical Exegesis for Preaching and Teaching* (Grand Rapids: Baker, 1981), 122.

15. B. B. Warfield, "The Millennium and the Apocalypse," in *Biblical Doctrines* (New York: Oxford University Press, 1929), 654.

16. David Chilton, *The Days of Vengeance: An Exposition of the Book of Revelation* (Fort Worth: Dominion Press, 1987), 507.

17. A second objection to the Premillennial view concerns the unbelieving nations in the millennial kingdom: If Revelation 19 and 20 present a sequence of events, and all the nations are destroyed at the end of chapter 19, where do all the unbelievers come from in 20:8 when Satan deceives the nations after his release? Premillennialists have responded to this objection in one of two ways. First, some Premillennialists claim that not all the unbelievers will be destroyed at the second coming of Christ, and therefore the nations will arise from non-glorified survivors of the battle in Revelation 19:17–19. This view appears difficult to sustain, however, in light of the universal language of Revelation 19:18 ("all men, both free men and slaves, and small and great"), as well as other passages that indicate the complete destruction of the wicked at the second coming (Is. 24:22; Zeph. 3:8; 1 Thess. 5:3; 2 Thess. 2:12; Matt. 25:31–46; cf. Matt. 7:21; John 3:3–5). A more likely explanation is that the nations will arise from the offspring of non-glorified saints who originally enter the millennium. According to this view, the church will be raptured and glorified just prior to the seven-year tribulation period (1 Thess. 4:13–18), and those believers who are martyred during the tribulation will be resurrected and glorified at the beginning of the thousand years (Rev. 20:4). But those believers who were converted during the tribulation and yet survive the persecution will enter the millennial kingdom in non-glorified bodies, presumably being resurrected some time later. During the millennium, these individuals will produce offspring who will eventually give rise to the unbelieving nations that rebel against Christ after the thousand years. Although some Amillennialists and Postmillennialists object to the co-existence of glorified and non-glorified people, this is precisely what happened when the risen and glorified Christ ate and interacted with the non-glorified disciples during the forty days between His resurrection and ascension.

18. This deception is then described in Revelation 13–19 (see 13:14; 16:14; 18:23; 19:20).

Chapter Seven

Does Calvinism Lead to Futuristic Premillennialism?[1]

John MacArthur

The legacy of Reformed theology (commonly called "Calvinism") goes back, not just to Reformers like John Calvin or church fathers like Augustine, but to the Bible itself. The glorious doctrines of grace are not primarily products of church history, but the testimony of Scripture—with its repeated emphasis on man's total inability and God's electing and preserving love. Passage after passage, from John 6 to Romans 9 to Ephesians 1, reiterate these great truths with clarity and power.[2] As the notable orphanage-founder and prayer-warrior George Müller explained over a century ago:

> I went to the Word, reading the New Testament from the beginning, with a particular reference to these truths. To my great astonishment I found that the passages which speak decidedly for election and persevering grace, were about four times as many as those which speak apparently against these truths; and even those few, shortly after, when I had examined and understood them, served to confirm me in the above doctrines.[3]

Though Müller had initially rejected Calvinistic doctrines, he soon became overwhelmingly convinced of their veracity through his study of the Scriptures. Along with George Müller, the greatest names in evangelical church history have shared in that Reformed heritage—men like John Knox, John Owen, George Whitefield, Jonathan Edwards, William Carey, Charles Hodge, Charles Spurgeon, and D. Martyn Lloyd-Jones.

But in spite of this prestigious heritage, there are still a few areas in which Reformed theology is in need of further reform. One of the most glaring deficiencies in the history of the Reformed movement is in the realm of eschatology—where, generally speaking, a literal interpretation of the millennial promises made to Israel has been rejected. Instead, an allegorical (or spiritual) hermeneutic has been applied to many prophetic passages, resulting in a predominant commitment to Amillennialism and, to a lesser degree, Postmillennialism.

Even today, if one were to survey leaders of the so-called young, restless, Reformed movement on the issue of eschatology, the consensus would be that there is no consensus. Many conservative evangelical pastors regard the end times as somewhat unimportant, or even dangerous—a hindrance to unity and an issue on which doctrinal clarity is impossible to achieve. But if there is any camp that should be neither confused about nor ambivalent toward eschatology, it is those who are committed to a Reformed understanding of God's sovereignty in election.

After all, Reformed evangelicals are unwavering in their devotion to the glory of God, and very careful regarding categories of doctrine. They are fastidious in hermeneutics and they treat biblical truth with the utmost seriousness. They approach every other area of theology with confidence and determination. So, why would they treat eschatology with consternation or indifference—as if God's revelation regarding the future was either hopelessly ambiguous or didn't matter very much?

The reality is that the end *does* matter. It matters to God—so much so that nearly one-fourth of His Word relates to end-time prophecies. Are these significant passages of prophecy so muddled that the high ground for theologians is simply to recognize the jumble and walk away, abandoning any thought of the perspicuity of Scripture with regard to eschatology? Is working hard to understand prophetic passages a futile endeavor, since they require a spiritualized or allegorized interpretation in order to be understood? Is the truth hidden behind the normal meaning of the words, such that the text actually means something other than what it says?

Eschatology and the Reformed Hermeneutic

The Reformed position has always approached Scripture using a literal hermeneutic—one that takes the Bible at face value and applies the normal rules of language in order to understand the text. John Calvin himself was a staunch defender of the literal method of Bible interpretation. As he explained, "Let us know that the true meaning of Scripture is the genuine and simple one, and let us embrace and hold it tightly. Let us . . . boldly set aside as deadly corruptions, those fictitious expositions which lead us away from the literal sense."[4] His commitment to literal hermeneutics meant he sought the original author's intended meaning. In his commentary on Romans, he asserted, "Since it is almost [the interpreter's] only task to unfold the mind of the writer whom he has undertaken to expound, he misses the mark, or at least strays outside his limits, by the extent to which he leads his readers away from the meaning of the author [of Scripture]."[5]

In interpreting the text, Calvin underscored the seriousness of biblical exposition. He wrote, "It is presumptuous and almost blasphemous to turn the meaning of Scripture around without due care, as though it were some game that we were playing."[6] Moreover, he aggressively opposed an allegorical interpretation of the text.

> This error [of allegory] has been the source of many evils. Not only did it open the way for the adulteration of the natural meaning of Scripture but also set up boldness in allegorizing as the chief exegetical virtue. Thus many of the

> ancients without any restraint played all sorts of games with the sacred Word of God, as if they were tossing a ball to and fro. It also gave heretics a chance to throw the Church into turmoil, for when it is accepted practice for anybody to interpret any passage in any way he desired, any mad idea, however absurd or monstrous, could be introduced under the pretext of allegory. Even good men were carried away by their mistaken fondness for allegories into formulating a great number of perverse opinions.[7]

Thus, he concluded that students of God's Word must "entirely reject the allegories of Origen, and of others like him, which Satan, with the deepest subtlety, has endeavored to introduce into the Church, for the purpose of rendering the doctrine of Scripture ambiguous and destitute of all certainty and firmness."[8]

Futuristic Premillennialists wholeheartedly affirm statements such as these. A literal hermeneutic is the exegetical foundation on which Premillennialism rests. But, significantly, Calvin proved to be *inconsistent* in the application of his own commitment to literal hermeneutics, especially when he came to end-times prophecy. In millennial passages, the Reformer all-too-quickly jettisoned his own literal hermeneutic and used an allegorical approach instead. As he himself explained:

> When the prophets describe the kingdom of Christ, they commonly draw similitudes from the ordinary life of men. . . . But those expressions are allegorical and are accommodated by the prophet to our ignorance, that we may know, by means of those things which are perceived by our senses, those blessings which have so great and surpassing excellence that our minds cannot comprehend them.[9]

For example, in his commentary on Amos 9, Calvin completely abandoned a literal approach to the text, arguing instead that the passage is full of "metaphorical expressions" and "figurative expressions." In his view, the prophet Amos spoke of physical blessings in order to describe to Israel the "spiritual blessings" and "spiritual abundance" of the church. He stated:

> If anyone objects and says, that the Prophet does not speak here allegorically; the answer is ready at hand, even this, — that it is a manner of speaking everywhere found in Scripture, that a happy state is painted as it were before our eyes, by setting before us the conveniences of the present life and earthly blessings: this may especially be observed in the Prophets, for they accommodated their style, as we have already stated, to the capacities of a rude and weak people.[10]

But if Calvin had interpreted Amos 9 and other apocalyptic passages in the same way he interpreted the rest of the Bible, using the literal hermeneutic he championed, he would have inevitably reached Futuristic Premillennial conclusions.[11] After all, a literal hermeneutic, consistently applied, leads to Futuristic Premillennialism—a point that Amillennial scholars have openly admitted over the years. In chapter 3, Richard Mayhue cited the words of Floyd E. Hamilton[12] and O. T. Allis[13] in this regard. To their voices, we might add,

> **Herman Bavinck:** "All the prophets, with equal vigor and force, announce not only the conversion of Israel and the nations but also the return to Palestine, the rebuilding of Jerusalem, the restoration of the temple, the priesthood, and sacrificial worship, and so on. Prophecy pictures for us but one single image of the future. And this image is either to be taken literally as it presents itself [and as Premillennialists take it] . . . or this image calls for a very different interpretation than that attempted by chiliasm [Premillennialism]."[14]

> **William Masselink:** "If all prophecy must be interpreted in a literal way, the Chiliastic [Futuristic Premillennial] views are correct; but if it can be proved that these prophecies have a spiritual meaning, then Chiliasm must be rejected."[15]

> **Anthony Hoekema:** "Amillennialists, on the other hand, believe that though many Old Testament prophecies are indeed to be interpreted literally, many others are to be interpreted in a nonliteral way."[16]

> **Graeme Goldsworthy:** "It could be argued that, though the details may be hard to pin down because of the prophetic preference for poetic imagery and metaphor, the big picture is abundantly clear. On this basis, the literalist asserts that God reveals through the prophets that his kingdom comes with the return of the Jews to Palestine, the rebuilding of Jerusalem, and the restoration of the temple. . . . The literalist must become a futurist, since a literalistic fulfillment of all Old Testament prophecy has not yet taken place."[17]

Loraine Boettner, a Postmillennialist, echoes similar sentiments: "It is generally agreed that if the prophecies are taken literally, they do foretell a restoration of the nation of Israel in the land of Palestine with the Jews having a prominent place in that kingdom and ruling over the other nations."[18]

As these examples demonstrate, Futuristic Premillennialism is the result of the consistent application of literal hermeneutics. Though Calvin strongly advocated the literal approach, he was inconsistent in the application of that hermeneutic. Generations of Reformed theologians have followed his example, adopting an allegorical approach to many prophetic passages.

But, with all due respect to the distinguished Reformer, there is no good reason to change our hermeneutic when we encounter biblical prophecy. We ought to interpret prophecy the same way we interpret history—taking it as a literal record of real (though future) events. As J. C. Ryle rightly remarked,

> All these [prophetic] texts are to my mind plain prophecies of Christ's second coming and kingdom. All are yet without their accomplishment, and all shall yet be literally and

> exactly fulfilled. I say "literally and exactly fulfilled," and I say so advisedly. From the first day that I began to read the Bible with my heart, I have never been able to see these texts, and hundreds like them, in any other light. It always seemed to me that as we take literally the texts foretelling that the walls of Babylon shall be cast down, so we ought to take literally the texts foretelling that the walls of Zion shall be built up—that as according to prophecy the Jews were literally scattered, so according to prophecy the Jews will be literally gathered—and that as the least and minutest predictions were made good on the subject of our Lord's coming to suffer, so the minutest predictions shall be made good which describe our Lord's coming to reign.[19]

As Ryle points out, it is inconsistent to arbitrarily change our method of interpretation when we come to end-times prophecy. Calvin's own reasons for doing so were based on his assumption that those prophecies had not yet been fulfilled in history, and therefore could not be taken literally.[20] By rejecting the possibility of a future fulfillment, Calvin embraced the very hermeneutical error he denounced: the allegorical method.

But the allegorical hermeneutic, even when used in moderation (as Calvin claimed to use it),[21] is full of dangers—because it opens the door to an endless number of possible, spiritualized interpretations. Rather, the text ought to be taken at face value, not in a woodenly literalistic way, but according to the normal use of language. To repeat an excellent line from Calvin, "Let us know that the true meaning of Scripture is the genuine and simple one." If he had applied that principle to every biblical passage, the history of Reformed eschatology would have been radically different.

Those who follow in the Reformed tradition, who hold to a literal approach to Bible interpretation, ought to be the foremost advocates of Futuristic Premillennialism. From the standpoint of hermeneutics, it is inconsistent for them not to be.

Eschatology and the Doctrine of Election

There is a second reason why those who cherish Reformed theology ought to embrace Futuristic Premillennialism, and it centers on the doctrine of election.

Calvinists are known for their unrivaled defense of and delight in the doctrine of election. They cherish God's sovereign grace regarding the church and treasure its inviolable place in God's purpose from predestination to glorification. They aggressively defend the truth of God's faithfulness in fulfilling His promises perfectly and without exception. They understand that the church's election is divine, unilateral, unconditional, and irrevocable. Yet, ironically, they deny the same for the elect nation of Israel—such that the divine promises associated with Israel's election are either forfeited by Israel or spiritualized and transferred to the church. But such a position is not biblically tenable. After all, Scripture uses nearly identical language to describe both the election of Israel and the church; and both elections are based on absolute promises from the same God. Thus, we cannot deny one without calling into question the other.

Yet, Amillennialists and Postmillennialists contend that, in spite of having once been elected, the nation of Israel on account of her disobedience was rejected by God and replaced by a new Israel, the church. Thus we read,

> **William Hendriksen:** "And what about the nation, namely, the old unconverted Israel, the rejecters of the Messiah? . . . In the place of the old covenant people there would arise—was it not already beginning to happen?—'a nation producing its fruit,' a church international, gathered from both Jews and Gentiles."[22]

> **David Hill:** "The Jewish nation, as a corporate entity, had now forfeited its elect status."[23]

> **Jack Dean Kingsbury:** "Consequently, owing to Israel's rejection of the proclamation of the Gospel of the Kingdom by Jesus Messiah, the Son of God, and by his ambassadors, God withdraws his Rule from Israel and Israel ceases to be his chosen people."[24]

> **R. V. G. Tasker:** "Because of this rejection of Jesus the Messiah, which came as the climax of a long series of rejections of the prophets God had sent to it (Matt. 21:35, 36), the old Israel as such would forfeit the right to receive the blessings appertaining to the kingdom of God. These blessings would in consequence be made available to a less exclusive people of God which would contain men of all races and nations (Matt. 21:43); and the murderers of God's Son would themselves be destroyed (Matt. 21:41)."[25]

> **Charles Price:** "The teaching of Jesus in these parables [Matt. 21:1–22:14] is about the rejection of the Jewish people from the focus of God's purpose in the world, and their replacement with a new order, those from the highways and byways who will identify with Christ and be brought into union with him. But the fig tree Israel is cursed."[26]

Statements like these affirm replacement theology—the notion that the nation of Israel was replaced or superseded by the church, such that the church is now Israel. Paul Enns explains,

> Replacement theology is a distinctive of covenant theology. The terminology reflects its teaching that the church has replaced Israel in God's program. They believe that since Israel rejected Jesus as their Messiah, God has replaced Israel with the church. Israel no longer has a future in God's program. The promises that God has made to Israel have been fulfilled in the church.[27]

In other words, through her disobedience, the nation lost her elect status as God's chosen people, along with all of the corresponding blessings promised her in the Old Testament. While individual Jews might still be saved through the church, God is done with Israel as a nation.

But how can these things be? Can election be forfeited? Can the promises of God be annulled, even through the disobedience of men? Was not Israel's apostasy part of God's eternal plan?

This, again, is where Reformed theology—consistently applied—leads to Futuristic Premillennial conclusions. Of all people to be Futuristic Premillennialists, it should be those who affirm sovereign election and the doctrines of grace. Both Amillennialism and Postmillennialism are better suited to an Arminian approach, in which election can be lost based on human choices and behavior. To teach that the Israelites could forfeit God's choosing of them through their own willful actions is consistent with Arminianism. But it is not consistent with Reformed theology. For those who understand that God is sovereign, that He is the only One who can determine who will be saved, and that He alone can save them, neither Amillennialism nor Postmillennialism makes any sense. Both of those views essentially teach that the nation of Israel, on her own, forfeited the promises of God.

When we look at the great reality of election in the Bible, there are only four specific entities that are mentioned as being elect: Christ (Is. 42; 1 Pet. 2:6), the holy angels (1 Tim. 5:21), Israel (Is. 45:4; 65:9, 22), and the church (2 Thess. 1:1 with 2:13). The election of Christ and the angels is eternal, as is God's election of the church. So why would we conclude that Israel's election is temporary, or could be forfeited? Such runs contrary to the very essence of God's faithful character and His sovereign, electing work.

Again, we might appeal to the writings of John Calvin. In his commentary on 1 Corinthians, Calvin explains that "Whatever God begins He carries through to completion. . . . God is unwavering in His purpose. Since that is so, He does not, therefore, make fun of us in calling us, but He will maintain His work for ever."[28] Calvin's remarks on Romans 11:28–29 are even more to the point:

> God was not unmindful of the covenant which He had made with their fathers, and by which He testified that according to His eternal purpose He loved that nation [of Israel]: and this he [Paul] confirms by this remarkable declaration,—that the grace of the divine calling cannot be made void. . . . [T]he counsel of God, by which He had once condescended to choose them for Himself as a peculiar nation, stands firm and immutable. If, therefore, it is completely impossible for the Lord to depart from the covenant which He made with Abraham in the words, "I will be a God unto . . . thy seed" (Gen. 17.7), then He has not wholly turned His kindness away from the Jewish nation.[29]

Thus, even Calvin acknowledged that God's election of Israel could not be undone, in spite of their unbelief.[30]

Herein, then, lies the dilemma. If there is no future for Israel as a nation (as replacement theology asserts), then God's election of the nation has been forfeited. But, as Calvin articulated, such is impossible since the "gifts and the calling of God are irrevocable" (Rom. 11:29). The immutable nature of divine election guarantees that God will not abandon His chosen people. In the words of one mainline Protestant theologian:

> There can be no question [i.e., possibility] of God's having finally rejected the people of his choice—he would then have to reject his own election ([Romans] 11.29)—and of his then having sought out instead another people, the church. Israel's promises remain Israel's promises. They have not been transferred to the church. Nor does the church push Israel out of its place in the divine history.[31]

Not only is there a remnant of Jewish believers in the present (as Calvin acknowledged), but the irrevocable nature of election mandates that the promises God made to Israel in the past will yet be realized in the future. As we've already seen, those promises are to be interpreted literally. Thus the faithful character of God demands that He will yet do exactly what He promised the Old Testament saints He would do.

Is the Church the Same as Israel?

When applied consistently, both the Reformed hermeneutic and the doctrine of election lead us to Futuristic Premillennial conclusions. But this raises an important question, one on which there has been much confusion in Reformed circles. Does the Bible teach that the church is now Israel, such that the blessings promised to Old Testament saints have been transferred to the New Testament church? Or is Israel distinct from the church, such that we should expect the promises made to Israel in the past to be fulfilled for Israel in the future?

The Bible calls God, "the God of Israel," over two hundred times. There are more than two thousand references to Israel in Scripture. Seventy-seven of those occur in the New Testament, and every one of them refers to ethnic Israel, not the church. In fact, the term "Israel" was never used to refer to the church until Justin Martyr did so in his *Dialogue with Trypho* (around AD 160).[32]

Only two passages in the New Testament are widely debated with regard to the meaning of the term "Israel"—Romans 9:6 and Galatians 6:16.[33] (Significantly, in the other seventy-five occurrences, interpreters agree that the term refers to national Israel.) In Romans 9:6, Paul notes that "They are not all Israel who are descended from Israel." Though some interpret this as a reference to the church as a whole, the context makes it clear that the apostle is speaking only about Jewish believers (a distinct group of ethnic Israelites within the larger unbelieving nation). The preceding verses make it certain that Paul has physical descendants of Abraham in view as he pens verse 6. For example, the apostle directly states that he is talking about his "kinsmen according to the flesh" in verse 3. And nothing in the context suggests that he shifts to speak of Gentile Christians. Rather, "the point of the entire section is that while the promises of God to Israel may appear to have failed when one looks at the totality of Israel, which is predominantly unbelieving, there is a remnant [of believing Jews] within Israel."[34]

In Galatians 6:16, both the grammar and context indicate that the "Israel of God" refers to elect Jews and not to the entire church.[35] In that verse, Paul tells his readers, "May peace be on all those who follow this standard, and mercy also be on the Israel of God!" (HCSB). Two groups of people, then, are immediately evident from the grammar of the verse—the "all those who follow" being distinct from the "Israel of God."[36] To the first group, all Christians who abide by the instruction given throughout the epistle, Paul extends the peace of God. But he reserves a special blessing specifically for Jewish believers—knowing that divine mercy will be shown to those who are elect of God. The "Israel of God" then refers to ethnic Jews who are circumcised in their hearts and not just physically (cf. Rom. 2:28–29). They are the true Israelites, the same group Paul distinguishes in Romans 9:6. As in every other instance where he uses the term, Paul intends "Israel" in this verse to refer to national Jews. Contextually, it provides an important closing note at the end of Galatians, a letter in which Paul has been pointedly refuting the Judaizers. Though the Mosaic system is no longer binding on believers (which is Paul's point throughout the letter), the apostle closes by noting that God has nevertheless not done away with His chosen people (cf. Rom. 11:1, 26).[37]

Of course, if God had rejected the nation of Israel, we would expect the Jewish people to have become extinct. Like the Hittites, Amorites, Moabites, and all the rest, the Jews would have disappeared in history and the nation of Israel would never have been reestablished. Yet, this is not what has happened. The Jews have survived, miraculously so, and Israel is now, once again, a nation. While some Amillennialists deny that this has any eschatological significance whatsoever, it has caused others to pause and take notice. As Amillennial writer Kim Riddlebarger admits,

> We cannot repeat the mistakes of the prior generations of amillennarians (such as Bavinck and Berkhof) who both said one of the sure signs that dispensationalism was false was

> that the dispensationalists kept predicting that Israel will become a nation. As we all know, Israel became a sovereign nation in 1948 despite Berkhof's and Bavinck's views to the contrary.[38]

R. C. Sproul has acknowledged similar interest in the reestablishment of the nation:

> I remember sitting on my porch in Boston in 1967, and watching on television the Jewish soldiers coming into Jerusalem, dropping their weapons and rushing to the Wailing Wall, and weeping and weeping. Immediately I telephoned one of my dear friends, a professor of Old Testament theology, who does not believe that modern-day Israel has any significance whatsoever. I asked him, "What do you think now? From 70 AD until 1967, almost 1900 years, Jerusalem has been under the domination and control of Gentiles, and now the Jews have recaptured the city of Jerusalem. Jesus said that Jerusalem will be trodden under foot by the Gentiles, until the fullness of the Gentiles be fulfilled. What's the significance of that?" He replied, "I am going to have to rethink this situation." It was indeed startling.[39]

But what remains startling and confusing to Amillennialists and Postmillennialists fits perfectly within a Premillennial understanding of the future. The survival of the Jews is exactly what we would expect if we apply a consistently literal hermeneutic to biblical prophecy and if we understand God's sovereign election of Israel to be unconditional and distinct from the church.

In recent years, the Spirit of God has been moving in the American church to revive a passion among His people for the doctrines of grace. Now that the glorious high ground of sovereign election in salvation is being rediscovered, it is also time to reestablish the equally high ground of sovereign grace for a future generation of ethnic Israelites in salvation and in the establishment of the messianic earthly kingdom, with the complete fulfillment of all of God's promises to Israel.

This chapter then is a call to those of a Reformed mindset to reconsider their eschatology in light of their commitment to literal hermeneutics and the doctrine of sovereign election. Futuristic Premillennialism is the only conclusion that can be drawn from a literal, historical-grammatical hermeneutic when it is applied consistently. Moreover, of all people, Calvinists should affirm that God's sovereign election cannot be forfeited, for His purposes can never be thwarted. Thus, the promises made to elect Israel must be fulfilled by Israel; just as the promises made to the elect church will be fulfilled for us.

A Personal Note on Futuristic Premillennialism

It is appropriate, I think, to conclude this chapter on a personal note. The more I understand God's sovereign, electing grace, the clearer the study of eschatology becomes. Moreover, the longer I study the Scriptures, the more convinced I become of the Futuristic Premillennial position.

Over the last forty years, I have had the wonderful privilege of studying and preaching through every verse, every phrase, and every word in the New Testament. For all of it, I have applied a literal grammatical-historical hermeneutic—taking the Word of God at face value. As a result, a Futuristic Premillennial understanding of eschatology has had to stand the test of every New Testament verse. But instead of being persuaded against Futuristic Premillennialism, my conviction as to its truthfulness has only been strengthened.

In the Old Testament, I have had opportunities to teach from Genesis through the Psalms and to preach many portions of the Prophets. Working on a study Bible also forced me to filter my eschatology through every single text of God's Word. Again, when I applied the literal hermeneutic to every passage, the results were the same.

Thus, I am a Futuristic Premillennialist for the same reason that I embrace the doctrines of grace. God's Word clearly teaches the sovereign election of the church. But equally clear is His sovereign election of the nation of Israel. Armed with a literal hermeneutic, and fully convinced that God's election cannot be forfeited because His purposes cannot fail, I embrace a Futuristic Premillennial eschatology with the same confidence that I embrace a Reformed soteriology. After all, we are bound to believe what the Scriptures reveal. In this case, a straightforward reading of God's Word leaves me with no other option.

Notes

1. This chapter is adapted from parts of a lecture delivered at the 2007 Shepherds' Conference at Grace Community Church, Sun Valley, California.
2. For an excellent survey of these passages, see Steven J. Lawson, *Foundations of Grace: A Long Line of Godly Men* (Lake Mary, FL: Reformation Trust, 2006).
3. George Müller, *A Narrative of Some of the Lord's Dealings with George Müller, Written by Himself, Jehovah Magnified.* Addresses by George Müller, Complete and Unabridged, 2 vols. (Muskegon, MI: Dust and Ashes, 2003), 1:46.
4. John Calvin, "Commentaries on the Epistles of Paul to the Galatians and Ephesians" in *Calvin's Commentaries*, 22 vols (1853; repr., Grand Rapids: Baker, 1989), 21:136.
5. John Calvin, "Dedicatory Letter to Simon Grynaeus," in Calvin's *Commentary on the Epistle to the Romans* (October 18, 1539), 1. Translation from R. Ward Holder, "The Pauline Epistles," in *Calvin and the Bible*, ed. Donald K. McKim (New York: Cambridge University, 2006), 227.
6. John Calvin, *The Epistles of Paul the Apostle to the Romans and to the Thessalonians*, CNTC, trans. Ross Mackenzie (Grand Rapids: Eerdmans, 1960), 4.
7. John Calvin, "Commentary on 2 Corinthians 3:6;" *Corpus Reformatorum*, 50.40–41. Translation from David Puckett, *John Calvin's Exegesis of the Old Testament* (Louisville, KY: Westminster John Knox Press, 1995), 107.
8. John Calvin, *Genesis*, Crossway Classic Commentaries (1847; repr., Wheaton, IL: Crossway, 2001), 33. Calvin is commenting on the phrase "In Eden" in Gen. 2:8.
9. John Calvin, "Commentary on Isaiah 30:25;" *Corpus Reformatorum*, 36.525. Translation from David Puckett, *John Calvin's Exegesis*, 110.
10. John Calvin, *Commentaries on the Twelve Minor Prophets*, trans. John Owen (1846; repr., Grand Rapids: Baker, 1979), 14:410–13. Calvin is commenting on Amos 9:13–15.
11. Even with regard to the prophets, Calvin explained that instead of using an allegorical method, interpreters "ought reverently and soberly to interpret the prophetic writings and not to fly in the clouds but ever to fix our foot on solid ground" (John Calvin, "Commentary on Zechariah 6:1–3;" *Corpus Reformatorum* 44.202. Translation from David Puckett, *John Calvin's Exegesis*, 108).

12. Floyd E. Hamilton, *The Basis of the Millennial Faith* (Grand Rapids: Eerdmans, 1942), 38.
13. O. T. Allis, *Prophecy and the Church* (1945; repr., Nutley, NJ: Presbyterian and Reformed, 1977), 238.
14. Herman Bavinck, *The Last Things*, ed. John Bolt, trans. John Vriend (Grand Rapids: Baker, 1999).
15. William Masselink, *Why Thousand Years?* (Grand Rapids: Eerdmans, 1930), 31.
16. Anthony Hoekema, "Amillennialism," in *The Meaning of the Millennium: Four Views*, ed. Robert G. Clouse (Downers Grove, IL: IVP, 1977), 172. Hoekema also acknowledged that a chronological approach to the book of Revelation results in Premillennialism: "Let us assume, for example, that the book of Revelation is to be interpreted in an exclusively futuristic sense, referring only to events that are to happen around or at the time of Christ's Second Coming. Let us further assume that what is presented in Revelation 20 must necessarily follow, in chronological order, what was described in chapter 19. We are then virtually compelled to believe that the thousand-year reign depicted in 20:4 must come after the return of Christ described in 19:11." Hoekema, "Amillennialism," 156.
17. Graeme Goldsworthy, *Gospel-Centered Hermeneutics* (Downers Grove, IL: IVP, 2006), 170–71.
18. Loraine Boettner, "Postmillennialism," in *The Meaning of the Millennium: Four Views*, ed. Robert G. Clouse (Downers Grove, IL: IVP, 1977), 95. Another Postmillennialist, Charles Hodge, says similarly, "The literal interpretation of the Old Testament prophecies relating to the restoration of Israel and the future kingdom of Christ, cannot by possibility be carried out." Charles Hodge, *Systematic Theology* (1871–1873; repr., Grand Rapids: Eerdmans, 1972), 3:809.
19. J. C. Ryle, *Wheat or Chaff?* (New York: Robert Carter & Bros., 1853), 85. The same is true with regard to passages like Revelation 20:1–6. Commenting on that passage, John Gill explained: "The space of a thousand years is . . . to be taken, not indefinitely, but definitely, for just this number of years exactly, as appears from their having the article prefixed to them; and are called afterwards, no less than four times, *ta cilia eth*, 'the thousand years,' or these thousand years (Revelation 20:3), and from the things which are attributed to the beginning and ending of these years, which fix the epoch, and period of them; . . . [They] are to be understood literally and definitely, as before, of just such an exact number and term of years" (John Gill, *Gill's Commentary* [1852; repr., Grand Rapids, Baker, 1980], 6:1064–65).
20. David Puckett, *John Calvin's Exegesis*, 113.
21. Ibid. The author explains that "Calvin indicates that the difference between his approach and that of the allegorists is one of degree—he is moderate; they are excessive." Herman Bavinck justified his spiritualized hermeneutic similarly. "The error of the older exegesis [from the allegorists] was not spiritualization as such but the fact that it sought to assign a spiritual meaning to all the illustrative details [of prophecy], in the process, as in the case of Jesus' parables, often losing sight of the main thought." Bavinck, *The Last Things*, 95.

22. William Hendriksen, *Exposition of the Gospel according to Matthew,* NTC (Grand Rapids: Baker, 1973), 786.

23. David Hill, *The Gospel of Matthew* (London: Oliphants, 1972), 301.

24. Jack Dean Kingsbury, *Matthew: Structure, Christology, Kingdom* (Philadelphia: Fortress, 1975), 156.

25. R. V. G. Tasker, *The Gospel according to St. Matthew,* TNTC (Grand Rapids: Eerdmans, 1961), 204.

26. Charles Price, *Matthew* (Ross-shire, Scotland: Christian Focus, 1998), 247.

27. Paul Enns, *Moody Handbook of Theology* (Chicago: Moody, 2008), 537.

28. John Calvin, *The First Epistle of Paul the Apostle to the Corinthians,* CNTC, trans. John W. Fraser (Grand Rapids: Eerdmans, 1960), 23. Calvin is commenting on 1 Corinthians 1:8.

29. Calvin, *The Epistles of Paul the Apostle to the Romans and to the Thessalonians,* 257. Calvin is commenting on Romans 11:29.

30. Along these same lines, Gerhardus Vos remarks, "[T]here still remains reserved for the future a certain fulfillment of the national elective promise. Israel in its racial capacity will again in the future be visited by the saving grace of God [Rom. 11.2, 12, 25]." *Biblical Theology: Old and New Testaments* (Grand Rapids: Eerdmans, 1948), 79.

31. Jürgen Moltmann, *The Way of Jesus Christ* (Minneapolis, MN: Fortress Press, 1993), 35.

32. Justin, *Dialogue with Trypho,* 11.5.

33. At the same time, it should be noted that some interpreters do understand Paul's use of "Israel" in Romans 11:26 as a reference to the church rather than to ethnic Israel. However, because the ten other uses of "Israel" in Romans 9–11 refer to ethnic Israel (9:6 [2x], 27 [3x], 31; 10:19, 21; 11:2, 7, 25), this view is uncommon even among Amillennialists. For further discussion of Paul's use of "Israel" in Romans 11:26, see Harold W. Hoehner, "Israel in Romans 9–11," in *Israel, the Land and the People: An Evangelical Affirmation of God's Promises,* ed. H. Wayne House (Grand Rapids: Kregel, 1998), 145–67; S. Lewis Johnson Jr., "Evidence from Romans 9–11," in *A Case for Premillennialism: A New Consensus,* eds. Donald K. Campbell and Jeffrey L. Townsend (Chicago: Moody, 1992), 199–223; Michael G. Vanlaningham, "Romans 11:25–27 and the Future of Israel in Paul's Thought," *The Master's Seminary Journal* 3 (1992): 141–74; Matt Waymeyer, "The Dual Status of Israel in Romans 11:28," *The Master's Seminary Journal* 16 (2005): 57–71.

34. Robert L. Saucy, "Israel and the Church: A Case for Discontinuity," in *Continuity and Discontinuity,* ed. John Feinberg (Wheaton, IL: Crossway, 1988), 245.

35. Even those who interpret Galatians 6:16 as referring to the church admit that "it is certainly true that nowhere else in the New Testament do we find the term 'Israel' being applied to the church" (Christopher W. Cowan, "Context Is Everything: The 'Israel of God' in Galatians 6:16," *Southern Baptist Journal of Theology* 14:3 [2010]: 80).

36. Though Amillennialists argue for an explicative use of *kai* in this verse, such is very unlikely. As Robert Saucy explains, "This explicative sense is not common, especially in the writings of Paul. Therefore unless there are strong contextual grounds the usual copulative (i.e., 'and') should be retained." Saucy, "Israel and the Church," 246.
37. For a more detailed discussion of why the "Israel of God" in Galatians 6:16 can only refer to Jews, see Hans Dieter Betz, *Galatians* (Philadelphia: Fortress Press, 1979), 323; F. F. Bruce, *Galatians*, NIGTC (Grand Rapids: Eerdmans, 1982); Ernest DeWitt Burton, *Galatians*, ICC (Edinburgh: T&T Clark, 1921); S. Lewis Johnson Jr., "Paul and 'Israel of God'," in *Essays in Honor of J. Dwight Pentecost*, ed. Stanley D. Toussaint and Charles H. Dyer (Chicago: Moody, 1986); Peter Richardson, *Israel in the Apostolic Church* (Cambridge: Cambridge University Press, 1969).
38. Kim Riddlebarger, "Answers to Questions: Part 2," *The Riddleblog*, http://kimriddlebarger.squarespace.com/answers-to-questions-2/.
39. R. C. Sproul, *The Gospel of God: Romans* (Ross-shire, Scotland: Christian Focus, 1999), 191–92.

Chapter Eight

DOES THE NEW TESTAMENT REJECT FUTURISTIC PREMILLENNIALISM?[1]

John MacArthur

Several decades ago, the term "newspaper exegesis" was coined and then used as a straw-man argument against Futuristic Premillennialism.[2] This caricature pictures those of a Futuristic Premillennial persuasion studying with the Bible in one hand and the latest edition of the newspaper in the other.

Reading current events into the Bible and then drawing them out as accurate scriptural interpretations represents a serious charge of hermeneutical and exegetical malpractice. In this chapter, that charge will be found to be without merit for the vast majority of Futuristic Premillennial adherents. To the contrary, it will be demonstrated that interpretive negligence actually characterizes the other eschatological views, in that they, without biblical warrant, read the New Testament into the Old Testament, resulting in an eschatology that fits a predetermined theology. In so doing, they reinterpret the Old Testament in such a way that no one before the time of Christ would have recognized their conclusions.

The prophecies of the Old Testament, taken at face value, inevitably lead to Futuristic Premillennialism. As noted in the previous chapter, this is a point on which Amillennial and Postmillennial scholars agree. Even a brief survey of Old Testament prophecy leaves no question as to what was being described. As Premillennialist John Walvoord explains:

> If interpreted literally, the Old Testament gives a clear picture of the prophetic expectation of Israel. They confidently anticipated the coming of a Savior and Deliverer, a Messiah who would be Prophet, Priest, and King. They expected that He would deliver them from their enemies and usher in a kingdom of righteousness, peace, and prosperity upon a redeemed earth. It is hardly subject to dispute that the Old Testament presents such a picture, not in isolated texts, but in the constantly repeated declaration of most of the prophets. All the major prophets and practically all the minor prophets have Messianic sections picturing the restoration and glory of Israel in this future kingdom. This is so clear to competent students of the Old Testament that it is conceded by practically all parties that the Old Testament presents premillennial doctrine if interpreted literally. The premillennial interpretation offers the only possible literal fulfillment for the hundreds of verses of prophetic testimony.[3]

In light of this historical reality, Amillennialists and Postmillennialists usually respond in one of two ways. On the one hand, some claim that the promises given in the Old Testament, if interpreted as literal, were conditional. Thus, when the nation rejected her Messiah, she simultaneously forfeited any promise of a future kingdom. But, as discussed in the previous chapter, this claim runs contrary to the irrevocable nature of divine election (Rom. 11:29). Israel's rejection of the Messiah was part of God's plan from eternity past, leading to the cross. It did not alter His plan for them as His chosen people. Moreover, Israel's glorious future is predicated on the unconditional promises of the Abrahamic, Davidic, and New covenants (e.g., Ps. 89:29–37; Jer. 30:4–11). God could not revoke those promises without going back on His own word, which is absolutely impossible (Heb. 6:13–18).

On the other hand, many Amillennialists and Postmillennialists respond by rejecting the notion that millennial promises should be interpreted in a literal way. Instead, it is claimed, many Old Testament prophecies ought to be spiritualized, such that any physical descriptions of a future kingdom are understood as metaphors of spiritual blessing. Amillennial scholars justify this approach by appealing to the New Testament, contending that if the interpreter starts there, he will come to understand the Old Testament in an Amillennial way. The purpose of this chapter is to investigate that claim.

In order to do so, it is important to first understand the eschatological mindset of ancient Israel. There is no question that the Jews of the Old Testament interpreted the words of the prophets in a literal way. As a result, they expected a future messianic kingdom on earth. Anticipation for that golden age only escalated throughout the intertestamental period. As one scholar explains,

> During the so-called Intertestamental period, there was developing thought in much Jewish literature of a coming resurrection and the establishment of a "millennial kingdom.". . . For example, a millennial kingdom is spoken of in such works as 1 Enoch 6–36, 91–104, and 2 Enoch 33:1, where it is to be 1,000 years, Pss. Sol. 11:1–8 and Jub. 23:27, where it is again 1,000 years, 4 Ezra 7:28–9, where it is 400 years, and Test. Isaac 6–8, where it is referred to as a millennial banquet.[4]

In the time of Christ, then, the universal expectation of the Jewish people centered on an earthly kingdom in which Messiah would reign over all the nations from Jerusalem.[5] This would have been Mary's perspective when she heard Gabriel's announcement in Luke 1:31–33.[6] It was also the view of the disciples during their time with Jesus—which is why, though driven by selfish motives, they sought for greatness in the kingdom (cf. Matt. 20:21; Mark 10:37; Luke 22:24).

When considering the New Testament's treatment of the millennial issue, it must be done against the backdrop of first-century Jewish eschatology. If the New Testament writers rejected the Futuristic Premillennialism that was so prevalent in their day, we would expect them to denounce it clearly and explicitly (just as they did in response to other issues, like the legalism of the Judaizers). A strong, overt condemnation would be necessary in order to overturn the widespread eschatology of Jewish believers based on the common understanding of Old Testament Scripture that had been passed down to them.[7]

The fact that no such denunciation exists is highly significant, especially when paired with New Testament passages where the literal interpretation of Old Testament prophecy is upheld. Moreover, the most explicit reference to the millennium in all of Scripture resides in the New Testament, in Revelation 20:1–6. If the goal of the New Testament writers was to overturn the prevailing eschatology of their day, as the Amillennial position asserts, they did a very poor job of it—so poor, in fact, that the generations of church fathers who immediately followed after them understood the New Testament in a distinctly Premillennial way.[8] As one writer observes,

> One of the most eloquent testimonies to premillennial truth is found in the absolute silence of the New Testament, and for that matter the early centuries of the church, on any controversy over premillennial teaching. It is admitted that it was universally held by the Jews. It is often admitted that the early church was predominantly premillennial. Yet there is no record of any kind dealing with controversy. It is incredible that if the Jews and the early church were in such a serious error in their interpretation of the Old Testament and in their expectation of a righteous kingdom on earth following the second advent, that there should be no corrective, and that all the evidence should confirm rather than deny such an interpretation.[9]

In the discussion that follows, the teachings of Christ, Peter, Paul, and John will be considered. For each, it will be asked whether or not they rejected Futuristic Premillennialism. It will be seen that, rather than excluding a literal interpretation of the Old Testament promises, the New Testament actually *promotes* and *upholds* the Futuristic Premillennialism of the Jewish prophets.

Did Jesus Reject Futuristic Premillennialism?

Though Jesus often spoke of the kingdom of God in a general sense (as the realm in which God rules or the sphere of salvation), He never denied the reality of the future millennial kingdom.[10] In fact, His promise in Matthew 19:28 was explicitly Premillennial. He told His disciples, "Truly I say to you, that you who have followed Me, in the regeneration when the Son of Man will sit on His glorious throne, you also shall sit upon twelve thrones, judging the twelve tribes of Israel." That promise was reiterated on the night before His death in Luke 22:28–30: "You are those who have stood by Me in My trials; and just as My Father has granted Me a kingdom, I grant you that you may eat and drink at My table in My kingdom, and you will sit on thrones judging the twelve tribes of Israel." The disciples, who shared the millennial expectations of their fellow Jews, would have understood those promises literally.

After the resurrection, the Lord continued to instruct the disciples about the kingdom. Luke, in his brief description of the forty-day period between the resurrection and ascension, explains that this topic was the predominant theme of Christ's teaching. In Acts 1:3 Luke writes, "To these [the apostles] He also presented Himself alive after His suffering, by many convincing proofs, appearing to them over a period of forty days and speaking of the things concerning the kingdom of God." His primary message concerned the kingdom. Though the disciples had been characterized, in the past, by hard heads and hard hearts, such was no longer the case, because Christ "opened their minds to understand the Scriptures" (Luke 24:45).

At the very end of this forty-day period Scripture includes a most instructive passage regarding the millennial kingdom. After having been taught about the kingdom by Christ Himself, and having been granted a supernatural understanding of God's Word, the disciples still understood the messianic kingdom in a literal, Futuristic Premillennial sense. In Acts 1:6 they inquired, "Lord, is it at this time You are restoring the kingdom to Israel?" In their minds, after intensive instruction on the subject by the resurrected Christ Himself, the millennial promises of the Old Testament were still to be understood as literally true. Their only question was *when* these things would come to pass.

It is important to note the manner in which Jesus responded to their question. "He said to them, 'It is not for you to know times or epochs which the Father has fixed by His own authority'" (v. 7). Significantly, Christ did not denounce or correct their millennial expectations. He did not refute their understanding of the *nature* of the kingdom. Instead, He merely explained that they were not privy to knowing the *timing* of that future kingdom.

During the forty days Jesus spent with His disciples, discussing things pertaining to the kingdom, He certainly could have taught them that it was only a spiritual kingdom. Having opened their eyes to understand the Scripture, the Lord could have explained to them that the Old Testament prophets ought to be interpreted in a non-literal way. Yet, He did neither. At the end of this period, the disciples were still convinced that the kingdom would literally be restored to the nation Israel. If Christ had wanted to correct that notion, this would have been the time to do it. Instead, He did nothing of the sort. He refused to answer their question about the timing of the kingdom, but He never refuted their understanding of the nature of it.

Christ's response indicates that the apostles' expectation of a literal, earthly kingdom mirrored His own teaching and the plan of God clearly revealed in the Old Testament. But the timing of the kingdom was still future. In the meantime, the Lord had a specific mission for the disciples to accomplish, which was to be His "witnesses both in Jerusalem, and in all Judea and Samaria, and even to the remotest part of the earth" (Acts 1:8).

Did Peter Reject Futuristic Premillennialism?

From the testimony of Christ, we move to the post-Pentecost testimonies of the apostles. Acts 1:6 indicates that the disciples retained their Premillennial expectations after the resurrection. But what about after the day of Pentecost? Did the establishment of the church in Acts 2 change their understanding of Old Testament prophecy?

Peter's sermon in Acts 3 indicates just the opposite—namely, that the apostles still expected a literal fulfillment of millennial prophecy even after the church was born. After healing a lame man (Acts 3:6–7), Peter began preaching in the temple. Luke records the sermon in Acts 3:12–26. In the middle of his message, Peter told his Jewish hearers: "The things which God announced beforehand by the mouth of all the prophets, that His Christ would suffer, He has thus fulfilled. Therefore repent and return, so that your sins may be wiped away, in order that times of refreshing may come from the presence of the Lord; and that He may send Jesus, the Christ appointed for you, whom heaven must receive until the period of restoration of all things about which God spoke by the mouth of His holy prophets from ancient time" (vv. 18–21).

In those few verses, Peter made two important points. First, he emphasized that the Old Testament prophecies about Jesus' first coming were literally fulfilled (v. 18); thus, the Jews ought also to expect prophecies about Christ's second coming to be fulfilled in a literal way (vv. 20–21). Second, Peter used millennial language—indicating that he was speaking of the earthly kingdom expected by his Jewish audience. Phrases such as "times of refreshing" and "the period of restoration of all things" are millennial phrases, borrowing imagery from the Old Testament, with which Peter's listeners would have been readily familiar.

For example, Ezekiel said the millennial kingdom would be a time of "showers of blessing" (34:26). Joel described it as a time of satisfaction (2:26). Isaiah saw it as an age when "waters will break forth in the wilderness . . . and the scorched land will become a pool, and the thirsty ground springs of water" (35:6–7) and God "will pour water on him that is thirsty" (44:3 KJV). Isaiah 11:6–10 describes the peaceful rest of the kingdom in these familiar words:

> And the wolf will dwell with the lamb, and the leopard will lie down with the young goat, and the calf and the young lion and the fatling together; and a little boy will lead them. Also the cow and the bear will graze, their young will lie down together, and the lion will eat straw like the ox. The nursing child will play by the hole of the cobra, and the weaned child will put his hand on the viper's den. They will not hurt or destroy in all My holy mountain, for the earth will be full of the knowledge of the LORD as the waters cover the sea. Then in that day the nations will resort to the root of Jesse, who will stand as a signal for the peoples; and His resting place will be glorious.

"The period of restoration of all things" is another name for the future earthly reign of Christ, the millennial kingdom. It is reminiscent of our Lord's description of the kingdom as the "regeneration" (Matt. 19:28). It is then that the apostles' question in Acts 1:6 will be answered (cf. Mark 9:12). The kingdom will be marked by peace, joy, holiness, the revelation of God's glory, comfort, justice, knowledge of the Lord, health, prosperity, and freedom from oppression. The universe will be dramatically altered in its physical form (Joel 2:30, 31; 3:14–16; Rev. 16:1–21) as the curse on man and his world will be reversed.

Peter ended his sermon in Acts 3 by reaffirming the fact that the Jews were still God's chosen nation. He said, "It is you who are the sons of the prophets and of the covenant which God made with your fathers, saying to Abraham, 'AND IN YOUR SEED ALL THE FAMILIES OF THE EARTH SHALL BE BLESSED'" (v. 25). Rather than denying a future to national Israel, Peter upheld and affirmed a literal understanding of those Old Testament promises—noting that they would be fulfilled just as literally as the prophecies regarding Christ's first coming. As they heard him preach, his Jewish audience would have known exactly what he meant.

Did Paul Reject Futuristic Premillennialism?

As the Apostle to the Gentiles, Paul perhaps had the greatest incentive to deny a future kingdom for national Israel as he proclaimed the gospel to non-Jewish audiences throughout the Roman Empire. Yet, what did he tell his predominantly Gentile readers in Romans 3:1–4?

> Then what advantage has the Jew? Or what is the benefit of circumcision? Great in every respect. First of all, that they were entrusted with the oracles of God. What then? If some did not believe, their unbelief will not nullify the faithfulness of God, will it? May it never be! Rather, let God be found true, though every man be found a liar, as it is written, "THAT YOU MAY BE JUSTIFIED IN YOUR WORDS, AND PREVAIL WHEN YOU ARE JUDGED."

The fact that some Jews were unfaithful (cf. Rom. 9:6)—such that an entire generation would reject their Messiah—did not nullify the faithfulness of God, nor cancel out His promises to the nation. As Paul asked rhetorically in Romans 11:1, "I say then, God has not rejected His people, has He? May it never be!" The apostle continued by making that point explicit in verses 25–29. There he wrote:

> For I do not want you, brethren, to be uninformed of this mystery—so that you will not be wise in your own estimation—that a partial hardening has happened to Israel until the fullness of the Gentiles has come in; and so all Israel will be saved; just as it is written, "THE DELIVERER WILL COME FROM ZION, HE WILL REMOVE UNGODLINESS FROM JACOB. THIS IS MY COVENANT WITH THEM, WHEN I TAKE AWAY THEIR SINS." From the standpoint of the gospel they are enemies for your sake, but from the standpoint of God's choice they are beloved for the sake of the fathers; for the gifts and the calling of God are irrevocable.

In the context, "all Israel" must be taken to mean just that—a future generation of ethnic Jews who will comprise the entire nation of Israel at the beginning of the millennial kingdom. The common Amillennial view that "all Israel" refers only to a remnant redeemed during the church age does injustice to the text. Paul's declaration about all Israel is set in clear contrast to what he has already said about the believing Jewish remnant whom the Lord has always preserved for Himself. The fact, for instance, that only *some* of the branches (unbelieving Jews) were broken off (v. 17) plainly indicates that a remnant of believing Jews—those not broken off—will continually exist while the fullness of the Gentiles is being completed. These are Jews being redeemed who are not part of the spiritual hardening that has come upon Israel because of her rejection of her Messiah (v. 25).

Before all Israel is saved, its unbelieving, ungodly members will be separated out by God's inerrant hand of judgment (Ezek. 20:33–38; Dan. 12:10; Zech. 13:8–9). Those who hear the preaching of the 144,000 (Rev. 7:1–8; 14:1–5), of other converts (Rev. 7:9), of the two witnesses (Rev. 11:3–13), and of the angel (Rev. 14:6), and thus safely pass under God's rod of judgment will then comprise all Israel, which—in fulfillment of God's sovereign and irrevocable promise—will be completely a nation of believers who are ready for the kingdom of the Messiah Jesus. Then the promises of the new covenant will be finally and fully realized:

> "Behold, days are coming," declares the LORD, "when I will make a new covenant with the house of Israel and with the house of Judah, not like the covenant which I made with their fathers in the day I took them by the hand to bring them out of the land of Egypt, My covenant which they broke, although I was a husband to them," declares the LORD. "But this is the covenant which I will make with the house of Israel after those days," declares the LORD, "I will put My law within them and on their heart I will write it; and I will be their God, and they shall be My people. They will not teach again, each man his neighbor and each man his brother, saying, 'Know the LORD,' for they

> will all know Me, from the least of them to the greatest of them," declares the LORD, "for I will forgive their iniquity, and their sin I will remember no more." (Jer. 31:31–34; cf. 32:38)

God's control of history irrefutably evidences His sovereignty. And as surely as He cut off unbelieving Israel from His tree of salvation, He will just as surely graft believing Israel back in—a nation completely restored and completely saved. Just as the fullness of the Gentiles will initiate the salvation of Israel, so the salvation of Israel will initiate the millennial kingdom of Jesus Christ.

As an expert in the Old Testament, Paul was intimately familiar with the promises God had given to Israel. In Romans 3 and 11, the apostle made it abundantly clear that he believed those promises would yet be literally fulfilled in the future.

Did John Reject Futuristic Premillennialism?

Anyone who claims that the apostle John denied a literal, future millennial kingdom must deal first with Revelation 20:1–6. (For more on this passage, see chapters 3 and 6.) The text could not be more clear. Consider the words of John, writing from his exile on Patmos, as he encouraged his readers with their future hope:

> Then I saw an angel coming down from heaven, holding the key of the abyss and a great chain in his hand. And he laid hold of the dragon, the serpent of old, who is the devil and Satan, and bound him for a thousand years; and he threw him into the abyss, and shut it and sealed it over him, so that he would not deceive the nations any longer, until the thousand years were completed; after these things he must be released for a short time. Then I saw thrones, and they sat on them, and judgment was given to them. And I saw the souls of those who had been beheaded because of their testimony of Jesus and because of the word of God, and those who had not worshiped the beast or his

> image, and had not received the mark on their forehead and on their hand; and they came to life and reigned with Christ for a thousand years. The rest of the dead did not come to life until the thousand years were completed. This is the first resurrection. Blessed and holy is the one who has a part in the first resurrection; over these the second death has no power, but they will be priests of God and of Christ and will reign with Him for a thousand years.

The passage unmistakably teaches that Christ's return precedes the millennial kingdom—a scenario incompatible with Postmillennialism and Amillennialism, but exactly what Futuristic Premillennialism teaches. To circumvent the impossible chronology that Revelation poses for their views, Postmillennialists and Amillennialists must deny that chapter 20 follows chapter 19 chronologically.[11] But such a denial ignores the chronological significance of the phrase "and I saw" (vv. 1, 4, 11; cf. Rev. 6:1, 2, 5, 8, 12; 7:2; 8:2, 13; 9:1; 10:1; 13:1, 11; 14:1, 6, 14; 15:1; 16:13; 17:3; 19:11, 17, 19; 21:1), as well as the continuity of the context. Having dealt with Antichrist and the false prophet in chapter 19, Christ deals with their evil master, Satan, in chapter 20. Why reject such an obvious chronology? The main motivation would appear to be an avoidance of Futuristic Premillennial conclusions—given that a compelling biblical justification is lacking.

The length of the period for which Satan will be bound is defined as a thousand years, the first of six precise and important references to the duration of the millennium (cf. Rev. 20:3, 4, 5, 6, 7). Satan's binding poses a serious difficulty for both Postmillennialists and Amillennialists. Amillennialists argue that Satan is already bound, since, as noted previously, they believe we are in the millennium now (though they do not view it as one thousand literal years in length). Many Postmillennialists also believe that Satan is presently bound, because otherwise it is difficult to see how the church could usher in the millennium. Yet the biblical description of Satan's activity in this present age makes it impossible to believe he has already been bound. Satan plants lying hypocrites in the church (Acts 5:3), schemes against believers (2 Cor. 2:11; Eph. 6:11), disguises himself as an angel of light to deceive people (2 Cor. 11:14), attacks believers (2 Cor. 12:7; Eph. 4:27), must be resisted (James 4:7), hinders those in the ministry (1 Thess. 2:18), and leads believers astray (1 Tim. 5:15).

Amillennialists and Postmillennialists generally argue that Satan was bound at the cross, and that his binding simply means that he can no longer deceive the nations and keep them from learning God's truth. But Satan did not keep the Gentile nations from the knowledge of the truth before his alleged binding at the cross. The Egyptians heard about the true God from Joseph, and from the Israelites during the four hundred years they lived in Egypt. The Assyrians of Nineveh not only heard the truth from Jonah, but also repented (Matt. 12:41). The Queen of Sheba heard about the true God from Solomon (1 Kings 10:1–9); the Babylonians from Daniel and his Jewish friends; and the Persians from Esther, Mordecai, and Nehemiah. Further, in what sense is Satan restrained from deceiving the nations in the present age, since he blinds the minds of unbelievers (2 Cor. 4:4), "is now working in the sons of disobedience" (Eph. 2:2), and holds unbelievers captive (2 Tim. 2:26) in his kingdom (Col. 1:13)?

Scripture testifies that Satan is anything but bound in this present age, but will be during the coming earthly kingdom of the Lord Jesus Christ. Only then will he be incarcerated in the abyss, which will be shut and sealed so that he cannot deceive the nations any longer (cf. Is. 24:21–22). His activity in the world will not be merely restricted or restrained, but totally curtailed; he will not be permitted to influence the world in any way.

With Satan, his demon hosts, and all God-rejecting sinners out of the way, the millennial kingdom of peace and righteousness will be established. The supreme ruler in that kingdom will, of course, be the Lord Jesus Christ. He alone is "KING OF KINGS, AND LORD OF LORDS" (Rev. 19:16), and "the Lord God will give Him [alone] the throne of His father David" (Luke 1:32). Yet He has graciously promised that His saints will reign with Him (Rev. 2:26–27). They will rule subordinately over every aspect of life in the kingdom, and being glorified and perfected, they will perfectly carry out His will.

In this vision, John sees the panorama of God's people resurrected, rewarded, and reigning with Christ. He saw thrones, symbolizing both judicial and regal authority, with God's people on them, and judgment was given to them. The glorified saints will both enforce God's will and adjudicate disputes. Politically and socially, the rule of Christ and His saints will be universal (Ps. 2:6–8; Dan. 2:35), absolute (Ps. 2:9; Is. 11:4), and righteous (Is. 11:3–5). Spiritually, their rule will be a time when the unbelieving remnant of Israel is converted (Jer. 30:5–8; Rom. 11:26) and the nation is restored to the land God promised to Abraham (Gen. 13:14–15; 15:18). It will be a time when the Gentile nations also will worship the King (Is. 11:9; Mic. 4:2; Zech. 14:16). The millennial rule of Christ and the saints will be marked by the presence of righteousness and peace (Is. 32:17) and joy (Is. 12:3–4; 61:3, 7). Physically, it will be a time when the curse is lifted (Is. 11:7–9; 30:23–24; 35:1–2, 7), when food will be plentiful (Joel 2:21–27), and when there will be physical health and well-being (Is. 33:24; 35:5–6), leading to long life (Is. 65:20).

Though Amillennialists attempt to dismiss Futuristic Premillennialism as merely an Old Testament teaching, the fact is that the most explicit passage on the millennium is found in the final book of the New Testament. Taken at face value, the meaning of John's words is impossible to miss. As Walvoord observes,

> Revelation, while subject to all types of scholarly abuse and divergent interpretation, if taken in its plain intent yields a simple outline of premillennial truth—first a time of great tribulation, then the second advent, the binding of Satan, the deliverance and blessing of the saints, a righteous government on earth for 1000 years, followed by the final judgments, and the new heaven and new earth.[12]

Putting It All Together

The heart of the millennial debate really lies in the New Testament. Nearly everyone acknowledges that the Old Testament teaches

Futuristic Premillennialism—at least if its promises are interpreted in a literal way. The Jews of ancient and intertestamental times certainly understood those promises to be literal. They expected the messianic kingdom to be an earthly reign—a time of great physical blessing and political peace in the world. The question, then, is whether or not the New Testament writers ever disavow that perspective. And the simple answer is that they do not.

In fact, they do just the opposite. When it fits their purposes to talk about God's dealings with the Jews, they emphasize the fact that He is not finished with the nation. The Old Testament promises are yet unfulfilled, but they will one day be realized—in the same way that biblical prophecy was fulfilled in Christ's first coming. Moreover, the New Testament specifies the length of time, one thousand years, that the millennial kingdom will endure before earth's history ends and the eternal state begins. Armed with the confidence that all of God's promises will truly come to pass, believers can look forward to the glorious future—both in the millennial kingdom and beyond—that awaits all who have put their faith in Jesus Christ.

Notes

1. This chapter is adapted, in part, from a lecture given at the 2007 Shepherds' Conference, Grace Community Church, Sun Valley, California. Sections of the chapter are also adapted from *The MacArthur New Testament Commentary* series, published by Moody.
2. Greg L. Bahnsen, "The Prima Facie Acceptability of Postmillennialism," *The Journal of Reconstruction* III:2 (winter 1976–1977): 71–73.
3. John Walvoord, *The Millennial Kingdom* (Grand Rapids: Zondervan, 1959), 114.
4. Stanley E. Porter, "Millenarian Thought in the First-Century Church," in *Christian Millenarianism*, ed. Stephen Hunt (Bloomington, IN: Indiana University Press, 2001), 63–64.
5. Cf. Walvoord, *Millennial Kingdom*, 116. He writes, "It has been noted that rightly or wrongly it was the universal expectation of the Jews that the kingdom promises would be literally fulfilled."
6. Ibid., 116–17. Walvoord notes, "It should certainly be clear that Mary would consider this revelation a confirmation of the literal interpretation and literal fulfillment of the Davidic Covenant. . . . Did Mary for one moment hold the amillenarian view? Would she spiritualize this passage—the throne of David is God's throne in heaven; the kingdom is a spiritual kingdom; Israel is synonymous with the church? Certainly not! It was totally foreign to her thinking. If the amillenarians are right, Mary was sadly deceived. The prophecy of the angel could

hardly have been better worded to confirm the ordinary Jewish hope as well as the exact essentials of the premillennial position—the literal and earthly fulfillment of the Davidic covenant."

7. In light of the overwhelming testimony of the Old Testament prophets and the universal expectations of the Jews in Jesus' day, the burden of proof is on the Amillennialist or Postmillennialist to show that the New Testament clearly rejects Futuristic Premillennialism.
8. This will be discussed in greater detail in chapter 9.
9. Walvoord, *Millennial Kingdom*, 118–19.
10. Some Amillennialists see John 18:36 as a denial of an earthly millennial kingdom, but such is not the case. As Paul Benware explains, ". . . there is a big difference between being 'of the world' and 'in the world.' Jesus Himself made that distinction one chapter earlier (cf. John 17:11–16). Jesus' kingdom would not be 'of the world,' which means that it will not be of the same nature as the kingdoms of this world [not connected to the present evil world system.] It is a distinctly different order, with such realities as peace, truth, and righteousness reigning supreme. But that is not a denial of Christ's kingdom being present on this earth. As Jesus spoke to Pontius Pilate (in John 18:36), He was simply telling the Roman official that, since His kingdom was different, it would not be established in the ways familiar to him; that is, through insurrections or the military victories of disciplined armies. As described in Revelation 19, the Lord's return does bring a sudden, violent end to the kingdoms of this world. But it is the Lord Himself who executes judgment on mankind. This also is the common testimony of the Old Testament prophets." (*Understanding End Times Prophecy* [Chicago: Moody, 1995], 99–100).
11. As Amillennialist Anthony Hoekema admits, "The premillennial interpretation of these verses understands them as describing a millennial reign of Christ on earth which will follow his Second Coming. And it is true that the Second Coming of Christ has been referred to in the previous chapter (19:11–16). If, then, one thinks of Revelation 20 as setting forth what follows chronologically after what has been described in chapter 19, one would indeed conclude that the millennium of Revelation 20:1–6 will come after the return of Christ" (*The Bible and the Future* [Grand Rapids: Zondervan, 1976], 226). For a further defense of taking Revelation 19 and 20 in chronological order, see "The Chronology of John's Visions" in chapter 6.
12. Walvoord, *Millennial Kingdom*, 118.

Chapter Nine

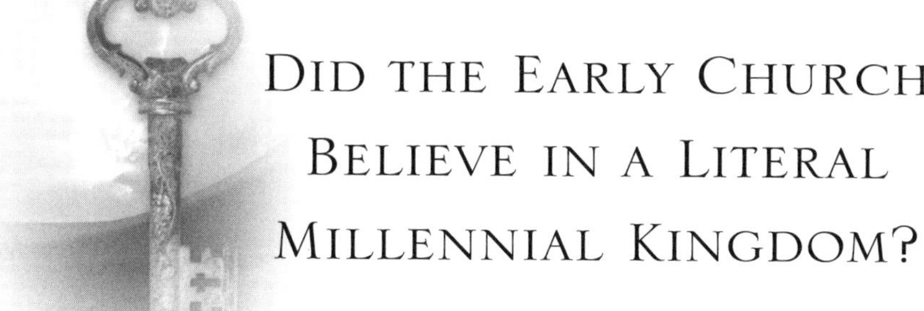

DID THE EARLY CHURCH BELIEVE IN A LITERAL MILLENNIAL KINGDOM?

Nathan Busenitz

The testimony of the church fathers, although not authoritative, is particularly instructive with regard to how the first generations of Christians understood the teachings of the apostles.[1] Their witness is helpful on many theological issues, including eschatology. If, as was suggested in chapter 8, the New Testament upholds a future, earthly millennial kingdom, then we would expect Premillennialism to be the predominant view in the writings of the early church fathers. And that is exactly what we find.

Speaking of the church fathers, the notable nineteenth-century church historian Philip Schaff wrote:

> The most striking point in the eschatology of the ante-Nicene [i.e., prior to AD 325] age is the prominent chiliasm, or millenarianism, that is the belief of a visible reign of Christ in glory on earth with the risen saints for a thousand years, before the general resurrection and judgment. It was indeed not the doctrine of the church embodied in any creed or form of devotion, but a widely current opinion of

> distinguished teachers, such as Barnabas, Papias, Justin Martyr, Irenaeus, Tertullian, Methodius, and Lactantius.[2]

Other scholars, including non-Premillennialists, have acknowledged the prominence of the Premillennial perspective in the early, post-apostolic church.

> **William Alger:** "Almost all the early Fathers believingly looked for a millennium, a reign of Christ on earth with his saints for a thousand years."[3]

> **William Masselink:** "The Chiliastic [Premillennial] conception immediately found acceptance in the Christian church. . . . The Apostolic history shows us that many of the old church fathers were leaning toward this view."[4]

> **Donald K. McKim:** "The eschatology of the early [patristic] theologians regarding the kingdom of God is marked by the development of *chiliasm*, a term that refers to the thousand-year reign of Christ (Rev. 20:1–10) connected with his second coming, the resurrection of the dead, and the final judgment."[5]

> **Stanley Grenz:** "In the vicinity of Ephesus, the location of the seven churches addressed by the book of Revelation (now western Turkey), a millenarian tradition developed that shares certain features with modern premillennialism. This tradition focused on the material blessings that will accompany the future rule of Christ over the renewed physical earth following the resurrection at the end of this age."[6]

> **Roger E. Olson:** "Augustine [in the fourth century] developed what has come to be known as *amillennialism*, whereas most of the earliest church fathers were premillennialists."[7]

> **Christopher Rowland:** "The Book of Revelation offers an example of theology which is at the heart of earliest Christian conviction rather than being marginal to it. Millennial beliefs were still widely held from the second century onward, as is evident in the writings of Justin Martyr, Irenaeus, Hippolytus, Tertullian, and Lactantius."[8]

Summarizing the historical evidence from a Futuristic Premillennial perspective, Leon J. Wood explained:

> There is general agreement among scholars that the view of the early church was premillennial. That is, Christians held that Christ would rule over a literal, earthly kingdom for one thousand years, assisted by raptured saints. No church fathers of the first two centuries are known to have disagreed with this view. The following may be listed as those who favored it: from the first century, Aristio, John the Presbyter, Clement of Rome, Barnabas, Hermas, Ignatius, Polycarp, and Papias; from the second, Pothinus, Justin Martyr, Melito, Hegisippus, Tatian, Irenaeus, Tertullian, and Hippolytus.[9]

In this chapter, the writings of some of these early Christian leaders will be briefly surveyed, allowing them to express their Premillennial views in their own words. Then, the rise of Amillennialism in early church history will be discussed.

Early Premillennial Voices

One of the earliest and most important Premillennialists in the early church was Papias, bishop of Hieropolis (ca. 60–135). Though Papias's writings have been lost, some of his teachings have survived in the writings of Irenaeus (ca. 130–202) and Eusebius (ca. 263–339). In an extended passage, Irenaeus articulated Papias's eschatological position:

> The blessing that is foretold belongs without question to the times of the kingdom, when the righteous will rise from the dead and rule, and the creation that is renewed and set free will bring forth the dew of heaven and the fertility of the soil and abundance of food of all kinds. Thus the elders who saw John, the disciple of the Lord, remembered hearing him say how the Lord used to teach about those times, saying: "The days are coming when vines will come forth, each with ten thousand boughs; and on a single bough will be ten thousand branches. . . . So too the remaining fruits and seeds and vegetation will produce in similar proportions. And all the animals who eat this food drawn from the earth will come to be at peace and harmony with one another, yielding in complete submission to humans." Papias as well, an ancient man—the one who heard John and was a companion of Polycarp—gives a written account of these things in the fourth of his books.[10]

Eusebius, the fourth-century church historian, likewise recorded Papias's Premillennial views. In his *Ecclesiastical History*, Eusebius wrote:

> This Papias, whom we have just been discussing, acknowledges that he received the words of the apostles from those who had been their followers, and he indicates that he himself had listened to Aristion and the elder John. And so he often recalls them by name, and in his books he sets forth the traditions that they passed along. . . . Among these things he says that after the resurrection of the dead there will be a thousand-year period, during which the Kingdom of Christ will exist tangibly here on this very earth.[11]

Papias's testimony is significant, not only because it is so near the time of the apostles but also because it is likely that Papias derived his information directly from the apostle John, or at least from the disciples of John. Moreover, his perspective reflects "the early Christian tradition drawing on its Jewish heritage, as well as the tradition of Jesus' teaching and the Apocalypse of John, as an integral part of its portrayal of the glories to come."[12]

The prominent second-century apologist Justin (ca. 100–165) likewise held a Premillennial perspective. Justin is considered to be "the most important of the Greek apologists of the second century and one of the noblest personalities of early Christian literature."[13] After converting to Christianity, Justin devoted his life to defending the Christian faith. He taught in Ephesus and elsewhere in Asia Minor before moving to Rome where he established a Christian training center.

In his *Dialogue with Trypho the Jew*, Justin emphasized that he interpreted the millennial promises of the Old Testament prophets in a literal way.

> I and others, who are right-minded Christians on all points, are assured that there will be a resurrection of the dead, and a thousand years in Jerusalem, which will then be built, adorned, and enlarged, [as] the prophets Ezekiel and Isaiah and others declare. . . . We have perceived, moreover, that the expression, "The day of the Lord is as a thousand years," is connected with this subject. And further, there was a certain man with us, whose name was John, one of the apostles of Christ, who prophesied, by a revelation that was made to him, that those who believed in our Christ would dwell a thousand years in Jerusalem; and that thereafter the general, and, in short, the eternal resurrection and judgment of all men would likewise take place.[14]

Similar views were held by Irenaeus, bishop of Lyons, who was mentioned earlier in connection with Papias. Born in Asia Minor, Irenaeus was exposed to the teachings of Polycarp (the disciple of John) as a young boy. He later settled in the western part of the Roman Empire, eventually succeeding Pothinus as bishop of Lyons. Known as a true "peacemaker,"[15] Irenaeus helped resolve several inter-Christian disputes during his lifetime—including a controversy over the date of Easter. Yet, he did not allow his love for peace to override his love for truth. For this reason, Irenaeus dedicated himself to the refutation of Gnostic heresies, ultimately producing a five-volume work commonly called *Against Heresies*.

Commenting on Irenaeus's eschatological position, Postmillennialist Keith Mathison has observed:

> The eschatology of Justin received its most developed second-century exposition in the writings of Irenaeus, the bishop of Lyons. According to Ireneaus, the end of the present age will be marked by a three-year reign of the Antichrist, who will desecrate the temple in Jerusalem. His reign will be cut short by the return of Christ, who will cast him into the lake of fire. At this point, Christ will inaugurate the millennial age. When the Millennium is over, there will be a general resurrection, the final judgment, and the inauguration of the eternal state. (*Against Heresies*, 5.30.4)[16]

To quote Ireneaus in his own words:

> But when this Antichrist shall have devastated all things in this world, he will reign for three years and six months, and sit in the temple at Jerusalem; and then the Lord will come from heaven in the clouds, in the glory of the Father, sending this man and those who follow him into the lake of fire; but bringing in for the righteous the times of the kingdom, that is, the rest, the hallowed seventh day; and restoring to Abraham the promised inheritance, in which kingdom the Lord declared, that "many coming from the east and from the west should sit down with Abraham, Isaac, and Jacob."[17]

Elsewhere, after citing a number of millennial prophecies from the Old Testament, Irenaeus concluded:

> For all these and other words were unquestionably spoken in reference to the resurrection of the just, which takes place after the coming of Antichrist, and the destruction of all nations under his rule; in which the righteous shall reign in the earth, waxing stronger by the sight of the Lord.[18]

Like Justin, Ireneaus defended his Premillennial eschatology from both the teachings of the apostles and the prophecies of the Old Testament. For those who would allegorize Old Testament prophecy, Ireneaus simply remarked: "If, however, any shall endeavor to allegorize [prophecies] of this kind, they shall not be found consistent with themselves in all points, and shall be confuted by the teaching of the very expressions [in question]."[19]

Another early Premillennialist is the renowned "Father of Latin Theology," Tertullian (ca. 160–220). Little is known for certain about Tertullian's pre-Christian life, except that he was the son of pagan parents and received an excellent education. He may have been a lawyer in Rome before devoting himself to theology, which would explain the Latin legal terminology that he often Christianizes, thus forming the foundation for theological Latin.

One of Tertullian's clearest statements regarding Premillennial eschatology is found in his treatise denouncing the heretic Marcion. There he wrote,

> But we do confess that a kingdom is promised to us upon the earth, although before heaven, only in another state of existence; inasmuch as it will be after the resurrection for a thousand years in the divinely-built city of Jerusalem, "let down from heaven," which the apostle also calls "our mother from above;" and, while declaring that our [*politeuma*], or citizenship, is in heaven, he predicates of it that it is really a city in heaven. This both Ezekiel had knowledge of and the Apostle John beheld.[20]

Elsewhere, he reiterated his literal interpretation of Revelation 20.

> In the Revelation of John, again, the order of these times is spread out to view, . . . that, after the casting of the devil into the bottomless pit for a while, the blessed prerogative of the first resurrection may be ordained from the thrones; and then again, after the consignment of him [the devil] to the fire, that the judgment of the final and universal resurrection may be determined out of the books.[21]

To Tertullian's testimony we could add, among others, the words of Lactantius (ca. 240–320). In his *Divine Institutes,* which was one of the earliest attempts at a systematic theology in church history, Lactantius wrote:

> But He [Christ], when He shall have destroyed unrighteousness, and executed His great judgment, and shall have recalled to life the righteous, who have lived from the beginning, will be engaged among men a thousand years, and will rule them with most just command. . . . About the same time also the prince of the devils, who is the contriver of all evils, shall be bound with chains, and shall be imprisoned during the thousand years of the heavenly rule in which righteousness shall reign in the world, so that he may contrive no evil against the people of God. After His coming the righteous shall be collected from all the earth, and the judgment being completed, the sacred city shall be planted in the middle of the earth, in which God Himself the builder may dwell together with the righteous, bearing rule in it.[22]

Elsewhere, Lactantius was equally explicit:

> Therefore peace being made, and every evil suppressed, that righteous King and Conqueror will institute a great judgment on the earth respecting the living and the dead, and will deliver all the nations into subjection to the righteous who are alive, and will raise the righteous dead to eternal

> life, and will Himself reign with them on the earth, and will build the holy city, and this kingdom of the righteous shall be for a thousand years.[23]

Lactantius taught that after the thousand years has ended, the devil will be released and will once again organize a rebellion of unbelievers. Once the uprising is crushed, and the enemies of God destroyed, the eternal state will be ushered in and believers "shall always be employed in the sight of the Almighty . . . and serve Him forever."[24]

Though this is only a brief survey of some of the Premillennial church fathers, it should suffice to make the point—namely, that Premillennial eschatology thrived in the earliest generations of the ancient church. Based on their understanding of both Old Testament prophecy and apostolic teaching, these church fathers were convinced that Christ would return victoriously to earth and set up His kingdom in Jerusalem, for a thousand years.

The Rise of Amillennialism

As we saw in chapter 7, Amillennial scholars readily acknowledge that a straightforward reading of the Old Testament prophets leads to Futuristic Premillennial views. Chapter 8 explained that Christ and the apostles never rejected those millennial expectations, but rather affirmed them as right. It is not surprising, then, to find that Premillennialism was the prevailing eschatological view of the early church. It is especially significant to realize that it flourished in Asia Minor—the region where the apostle John had ministered and where the book of Revelation had been written.

But all of this raises an important question. If Premillennialism is taught in the Old Testament, affirmed in the New, and widely embraced in early church history, then how did Amillennialism develop, such that it would become the majority position of the church throughout the Middle Ages?

Scholars have suggested at least four factors that contributed to the rise of Amillennialism—a view that really took shape in the third and fourth centuries. The first two factors—allegorical hermeneutics and Platonic dualism—are connected, and came into the church through the influence of popular Greek philosophy and culture. This influence was particularly strong in Alexandria, Egypt, where it first affected Jewish rabbinical teaching before the time of Christ. As Rick Bowman and Russell L. Penney explain, "This type of allegorical interpretation can be seen in Plato's time when the blatant hedonism of the deities were interpreted symbolically in order to make them acceptable. Unable to reconcile their views with the literal interpretation of Scripture, early Jewish commentators began to allegorize. The rabbis of Alexandria, Egypt, began to teach allegorically in order to counter Gentile criticism of the Old Testament."[25] This rabbinic approach had a major impact on the church. Historian Roger Olson notes the connection: "The Alexandrian pattern had been established in the time of Christ by the Jewish theologian and biblical scholar Philo, who believed that the literal and historical references of the Hebrew Scriptures were of least importance. He sought to discover and explicate the biblical narratives' allegorical or spiritual meaning. . . . Many early Christian thinkers borrowed their hermeneutical strategies from Philo, and that was nowhere truer than in Alexandria itself."[26]

It is not surprising, then, to discover that the initial opposition to Premillennialism came out of Alexandria.[27] "The first prominent opponent [of a literal millennium] was Clement of Alexandria [ca. 150–215], who had been influenced by Platonic idealistic philosophy and had adopted the Greek allegorical method of interpretation of the Scriptures."[28] Clement's pupil, Origen of Alexandria, carried his teacher's opinions even further, popularizing the allegorical hermeneutic. As Paul Benware explains, "Origen (AD 185–254) and other scholars in Alexandria were greatly influenced by Greek philosophy and attempted to integrate that philosophy with Christian theology. Included in Greek philosophy was the idea that those things that were material and physical were inherently evil. Influenced by this thinking, these Alexandrian scholars concluded that an earthly kingdom of Christ with its many physical blessings would be something evil."[29]

Armed with an allegorical hermeneutic, Alexandrian interpreters were able to explain away Old Testament texts that—taken literally—point to an earthly, millennial kingdom. Due to the influence of Greek philosophy (Platonic dualism), they were eager to downplay the material blessings promised by the prophets and reinterpret them as spiritual realities. "According to Gnostic (and on a traditional interpretation) Platonic dualism, the body is inferior to the soul in value, and more generally the material world is inferior to the immaterial world."[30] A spiritual understanding of the millennial kingdom was considered more philosophically acceptable. Accordingly, Premillennial views were rejected, since they were based on a literal interpretation of Old Testament promises. As Amillennialist William Masselink acknowledges, "The Gnostic [dualistic] philosophy of this period and the Alexandrian school with its allegorical interpretations of the scripture were also a great detriment to the progress of Chiliasm."[31]

A third contributor to the development of Amillennialism (or, at least, to the rejection of Premillennialism) was a growing opposition on the part of Christians toward unbelieving Jews. "As Jewish animosity toward Christians continued and it became increasingly clear that the Jews would not believe in Christ, many Christians began to view the Jews as their enemies."[32] This animosity contributed to the decline of Premillennialism, especially when Jewish apologists argued that Jesus could not have been the Messiah since the millennial promises had not yet been literally fulfilled through Him. Thus, Andrew Chester, speaking of the ancient church, observes:

> It is precisely the fact that the glorious transformation of the land has not taken place that makes the Christian messianic claim vulnerable to Jewish attack, while equally the Jewish and Christian sources clearly share the same tradition and scriptural passages, and are in many ways difficult to distinguish from each other. Hence it is the close conjunction between the Jewish and Christian positions that is subjected to polemic by Christian opponents of chiliasm, such as Origen, in order to establish the Christian position as distinctive and rid it of crude materialism.[33]

By spiritualizing the millennial promises, Origen and others attempted to defend Christianity from its Jewish opponents, while further differentiating its eschatology from the teachings of Judaism.[34]

A fourth contributor to the development of Amillennial theology was the significant sociopolitical change that took place in the Roman Empire between the first and fourth centuries. The fall of Jerusalem in AD 70 and the Bar Kochba revolt in 135 seemed to indicate that God no longer had any plans for Israel as a nation. Then, in the fourth century, the beginnings of a Christian kingdom in Rome, under the reign of Constantine, was interpreted by many as the fulfillment of millennial promises. As a result, the Premillennialism that had prevailed in the early church was now completely eclipsed. To quote again from historian Philip Schaff:

> In Alexandria, Origen opposed chiliasm as a Jewish dream and spiritualized the symbolical language of the prophets. . . . But the crushing blow came from the great change in the social condition and prospects of the church in the Nicene age. After Christianity, contrary to all expectations, triumphed in the Roman empire, and was embraced by the Caesars themselves, the millennial reign, instead of being anxiously waited and prayed for, began to be dated either from the first appearance of Christ, or from the conversion of Constantine and the downfall of paganism, and to be regarded as realized in the glory of the dominant imperial state-church.[35]

Thus,

> Attempts to defend the doctrine of a literal millennial reign of Christ were vitiated to a great extent by the conversion of the Emperor Constantine . . . and the cessation of persecution in consequence of the complete change of the official attitude to Christianity. In the enjoyment of imperial patronage, it seemed evident to many that the kingdom had

> arrived and that the millennial blessings foretold by the prophets were to become the possession of God's people here and now. Indeed, Eusebius, the father of church history, specifically stated that the kingdom had already come.[36]

With the Jewish nation gone and a Christian empire established in Rome, many believers no longer found it necessary to look forward to a future messianic kingdom on earth.

Augustine, the Father of Amillennialism

Opposition to Premillennialism had been gaining ground in the third and early fourth centuries, due primarily to the reasons listed above. But, it was Augustine (354–430) who really established Amillennialism as the *de facto* position of the medieval church. Though he had initially leaned toward the Premillennial perspective, the bishop of Hippo ultimately rejected it because he felt it promoted carnality through its emphasis on material blessings in an earthly kingdom. As Keith Mathison notes,

> Early in his Christian life, Augustine had been attracted to millennialism, but he later rejected it. His rejection of it, it seems, was largely due to some of the excessively carnal versions of millennialism that were current in his day. He changed his position and adopted instead a symbolic approach to the twentieth chapter of Revelation. In *The City of God*, Augustine teaches that the first resurrection mentioned in Revelation 20 is a spiritual resurrection, the regeneration of spiritual dead persons (20:6). In contrast to premillennialism, he teaches that the second resurrection occurs at the second coming of Christ, not a thousand years later.[37]

Augustine's theological conclusions were also influenced by the allegorical hermeneutics and Greek philosophy of Alexandria.

> Although Origen and others began to question the premillennial view, it was Augustine who systematized and developed amillennialism as an alternative to premillennialism. Like Origen, Augustine had been educated in Greek philosophy and could not escape its influence, which is probably why he viewed premillennialism with suspicion, seeing it as a view that promoted a time of carnal enjoyment. . . . Augustine's attitude, as well as his theology, has since that time dominated much of the church. Furthermore, he found Origen's allegorical method of interpretation a helpful tool in sidestepping the teachings of certain millennial passages. So Augustine came to reject the premillennial idea of an earthly reign of Christ, which had been held in the church for several centuries.[38]

Augustine states his reasons for rejecting Premillennialism in *The City of God*. There he writes, "This opinion [of a future literal millennium after the resurrection] might be allowed, if it purposed only spiritual delight unto the saints during this space (and we were once of the same opinion ourselves); but seeing the avouchers hereof affirm that the saints after this resurrection shall do nothing but revel in fleshly banquets, where the cheer shall exceed both modesty and measure, this is gross and fit for none but carnal men to believe. But they that are really and truly spiritual do call those of this opinion Chiliasts."[39] From a modern Premillennial perspective, Augustine's reasons for rejecting a literal understanding of millennial prophecy seem trivial.[40] Yet, whatever one might think of the relative merits of Augustine's conclusions, no one questions the influence his change of mind had on church history. Although there were still a few advocates of Premillennialism in the fifth century,[41] "the final defeat of Chiliasm in the West was due to Augustine, who, in his *City of God* identified the millennium with the history of the Church on earth and declared that, for those who belonged to the true Church, the first resurrection was passed already."[42]

Augustine's eschatology became the standard for the medieval church in the West. As Millard Erickson points out, "The first three centuries of the church were probably dominated by what we would today call Premillennialism, but in the fourth century an African Donatist named Tyconius propounded a competitive view. Although Augustine was an arch opponent of the Donatists, he adopted Tyconius' view of the millennium. This interpretation was to dominate eschatological thinking throughout the Middle Ages."[43] In fact, a modified form of Augustine's Amillennial eschatology (one in which the kingdom of God on earth was equated with the Roman Catholic Church)[44] became so dominant that some medieval theologians went to extremes to suppress Premillennialism. "Not only did the nonmillennarian outlook become the standard for orthodoxy; beginning with the Council of Ephesus in the fifth century and throughout the Middle Ages, church leaders sought to suppress millenarianism. They promoted this campaign even to the point of altering the writings of Premillennialists among the early church fathers, such as Irenaeus."[45]

Over a thousand years after Augustine, when the Reformation burst onto the scene, the magisterial Reformers maintained a non-Premillennial eschatology—one they inherited from the medieval church.[46] Though they distanced true Christianity from the institution of the papacy,[47] Luther and Calvin nevertheless rejected Premillennialism outright—seeing it as a dangerous corruption[48] that had long ago been discarded by the church.[49] This rejection is particularly ironic in the case of Calvin, as was discussed in chapter 7, because he adamantly opposed the allegorical hermeneutics of Origen.[50] Yet, it was from that allegorical hermeneutic that Amillennialism initially developed in church history.

The Affirmation of Church History

It is outside the scope of this chapter to discuss the history of eschatology from the Reformation to the present. Our twofold goal was (1) to demonstrate that Premillennialism was the predominant view of the earliest church fathers and (2) to give a plausible explanation for the rise of Amillennialism as it developed in the third and fourth centuries of church history. To reiterate a point made at the beginning: History is not authoritative like Scripture is, but it does affirm the Premillennial position, indicating that the earliest generations of Christians generally interpreted the apostolic witness through a Premillennial lens—one in which a future, thousand-year messianic kingdom was expected on the earth. Premillennialism, then, is not a recent development. Rather, it is the oldest eschatological viewpoint in church history. That reality adds tremendous credibility to the Futuristic Premillennial position.

Notes

1. Larry V. Crutchfield, "Israel and the Church in the Ante-Nicene Fathers," *Bibliotheca Sacra* 575 (July–September 1987): 254–76 and Martin Erdmann, *The Millennial Controversy in the Early Church* (Eugene, OR: Wipf and Stock, 2005) provide exceptionally helpful studies on this subject.
2. Philip Schaff, *History of the Christian Church: Ante-Nicene Christianity* (Edinburgh: T&T Clark, 1884), 614. Schaff also mentions some later (third-century) church fathers who were opposed to Premillennialism. But the earliest church fathers (of the first and second centuries) were predominantly Premillennial.
3. William Alger, *The Destiny of the Soul: A Critical History of the Doctrine of a Future Life* (Boston: Roberts Brothers, 1880), 403.
4. William Masselink, *Why Thousand Years?* (Grand Rapids: Eerdmans, 1930), 26. Cf. J. Daniel Hays, "Many of the early church fathers believed that Christ would return to establish his millennial kingdom prior to the final judgment and establishment of the eternal state." (*The Message of the Prophets* [Grand Rapids: Zondervan, 2010], 88).
5. Donald K. McKim, *Theological Turning Points* (Louisville, KY: John Knox, 1988), 155.
6. Stanley Grenz, *The Millennial Maze* (Downers Grove, IL: IVP, 1992), 38.
7. Roger E. Olson, *The Westminster Handbook to Evangelical Theology* (Louisville, KY: Westminster John Knox, 2004), 171.
8. Christopher Rowland, "The Eschatology of the New Testament Church," in *The Oxford Handbook of Eschatology*, ed. Jerry L. Walls (New York: Oxford University Press, 2008), 68–69.
9. Leon J. Wood, *The Bible and Future Events* (Grand Rapids: Zondervan, 1973), 35. Cf. James Stitzinger, "The Rapture in Twenty Centuries of Biblical Interpretation," *The Master's Seminary Journal* 13/2 (fall 2002): 155. "A cursory examination of the early church fathers reveals that they were predominantly premillennialists or chiliasts. Clear examples in the writings of Barnabas (ca. 100–150), Papias (ca. 60–130), Justin Martyr (110–165), Irenaeus (120–202), Tertullian (145–220), Hippolytus (ca. 185–236), Cyprian (200–250), and Lactantius (260–330) make this understanding impossible to challenge successfully."

10. Irenaeus, *Against Heresies*, 5.33.3–4. Bart D. Ehrman, trans., *The Apostolic Fathers* (Harvard: Loeb Classical Library, 2005), 2:93–95.
11. Eusebius, *Ecclesiastical History*, 3.39.7, 12. Bart D. Ehrman, trans., *The Apostolic Fathers*, 2:101.
12. Andrew Chester, *Messiah and Exaltation* (Tübingen, Germany: Mohr Siebeck, 2007), 425.
13. Johannes Quasten, *Patrology*, 4 vols. (1950; repr., Westminster, MD.: Christian Classics, 1986), 1:196.
14. Justin Martyr, *Dialogue with Trypho*, 80–81. Alexander Roberts and James Donaldson, eds., *Ante-Nicene Fathers* (repr., Grand Rapids: Eerdmans, 1973), I:239–40. Earlier, Justin acknowledged that not all Christians of his day shared his same perspective. "I admitted to you formerly, that I and many others are of this opinion, and [believe] that such will take place, as you assuredly are aware; but, on the other hand, I signified to you that many who belong to the pure and pious faith, and are true Christians, think otherwise." While Amillennialists make much of Justin's comments here, it is important to note that Justin does not specifically articulate the views of these Christians who "think otherwise."
15. Eusebius, *Ecclesiastical History*, 5.24.18.
16. Keith Mathison, *Postmillennialism: An Eschatology of Hope* (Philipsburg, NJ: P&R, 1999), 27.
17. Irenaeus, *Against Heresies*, 5.30.4. Roberts and Donaldson, *ANF*, I:560.
18. Ibid., 5.35.1. Roberts and Donaldson, *ANF*, I:565.
19. Ibid.
20. Tertullian, *Against Marcion*, 3.24. Roberts and Donaldson, *ANF*, III:342.
21. Tertullian, *On the Resurrection of the Flesh*, 25. Roberts and Donaldson, ANF, III:563.
22. Lactantius, *The Divine Institutes*, 7.24. Roberts and Donaldson, ANF, VII:219.
23. Lactantius, *The Epitome of the Divine Institutes*, 72. Alexander and Donaldson, ANF, VII:254.
24. Lactantius, *The Divine Institutes*, 7.26. Roberts and Donaldson, ANF, VII:221.
25. Rick Bowman and Russell L. Penney, "Amillennialism," in *Dictionary of Premillennial Theology*, ed. Mal Couch (Grand Rapids: Kregel, 1996), 37.
26. Roger E. Olsen, *The Story of Christian Theology* (Downers Grove, IL: IVP, 1999), 202.
27. The Epistle of Barnabas (written in the early second century), which also came from Alexandria, has been cited by some as perhaps laying the foundation for later Amillennial interpretations. Though Barnabas asserts certain Premillennial ideas (and is often claimed by Premillennialists), he also purports both an allegorical hermeneutic and replacement theology (cf. D. H. Kromminga, *The Millennium in the Church* [Grand Rapids: Zondervan, 1945], 37–40). In the end, perhaps Keith Mathison's assessment is the safest: "Barnabas's writings on the subject [of the millennium] are not developed enough to place him clearly in any modern eschatological category" (Mathison, *Postmillennialism*, 25).

28. Frederick A. Tatford, *Will There Be a Millennium?* (Eastbourne, England: Prophetic Witness Publishing House, 1969), 24.
29. Paul Benware, *Understanding End Times Prophecy* (Chicago: Moody, 1995), 103.
30. J. P. Moreland and Scott B. Rae, *Body & Soul: Human Nature and the Crisis in Ethics* (Downers Grove, IL: IVP, 2000), 22.
31. Masselink, *Why Thousand Years?*, 27.
32. Michael Vlach, "The Church as a Replacement of Israel: An Analysis of Supersessionism" (Ph.D. diss., Southeastern Baptist Theological Seminary, 2004), 40.
33. Chester, *Messiah and Exaltation*, 433.
34. According to Origen, to reject an allegorical hermeneutic is to reject Christianity altogether. He wrote: "If anyone wishes to hear and understand these words [of the Old Testament] literally he ought to gather with the Jews rather than with the Christians. But if he wishes to be a Christian and a disciple of Paul, let him hear Paul saying that 'the Law is spiritual,' declaring that these words are 'allegorical' when the law speaks of Abraham and his wife and sons" (Origen, *Homilies on Genesis*, 6.1. Ronald E. Hein, trans., *Homilies on Genesis and Exodus* [Washington DC: Catholic University of America, 1982], 121). Later church fathers, like Jerome (ca. 347–420), would further accuse the earlier Premillennialists of adopting views that were too close to Judaism. "In some passages Jerome identifies Jewish hopes with the establishment of a thousand-year reign in Jerusalem (CC 75, 400). The thousand-year reign (millennium) was of course a Christian idea drawn from the book of Revelation, and when Jerome mentions this detail he notes that some Christians held similar views. These Christians he variously calls 'half-Jews,' judaizers, Ebionites, or 'friends of the letter'" (Robert L. Wilken, *The Land Called Holy* [New Haven, CT: Yale University, 1992], 306).
35. Schaff, *History of the Christian Church*, 619.
36. Tatford, *Will There Be a Millennium?*, 24.
37. Mathison, *Postmillennialism*, 30.
38. Benware, *Understanding End Times Prophecy*, 104.
39. Augustine, *The City of God*, 20.7. Cited from Peter Toon, *The Puritans, the Millennium and the Future of Israel* (Cambridge: James Clarke, 1970), 14–15. For a parallel translation, see Philip Schaff, ed., *Nicene and Post-Nicene Fathers*, First Series (repr., Grand Rapids: Eerdmans, 1956), II:426.
40. As John F. Walvoord, *The Millennial Kingdom* (Grand Rapids: Zondervan, 1976), 50, contends: "Thus on trivial grounds Augustine abandons the literal interpretation of Revelation 20. Somehow, for all his genius, he did not see that he could abandon this false teaching without abandoning the doctrine of a literal millennium."
41. Wilken, *The Land Called Holy*, 306.
42. G. E. Post, "Millennium," in *A Dictionary of the Bible*, ed. James Hastings (New York: Scribners & Sons, 1900), 3:373.
43. Millard J. Erickson, *Christian Theology* (Grand Rapids: Baker, 2007), 1213.
44. Mathison, *Postmillennialism*, 33, observes: "The Middle Ages (ca. 1000–1500) were not a time of dramatic eschatological development. A modified Augustinian

eschatology, which closely linked the institutional Roman Catholic Church with the kingdom of God, was the predominant position."

45. Grenz, *The Millennial Maze*, 45–46.
46. Cf. Walvoord, *The Millennial Kingdom*, 54. Walvoord notes, "It is clear that the great Protestant leaders such as Calvin, Luther, and Melanchthon are properly classed as amillennial. As far as millennial teaching was concerned, they were content to follow the Roman Church in a weakened Augustinian viewpoint."
47. Mathison, *Postmillennialism*, 38. The author explains, "Despite his apocalyptic tendencies, Luther agreed with the common Catholic rejection of chiliasm. There were, however, several important developments in Luther's thought which differentiated it from official Catholic doctrine. The most significant of these were: 1. He identified the institution of the papacy as the Antichrist. 2. He interpreted the book of Revelation as a prophecy of the entire history of the church. 3. He believed that the Millennium was fulfilled in the early history of the church and ended either with the rise of the Turks or with the institution of the papacy."
48. Grenz, *The Millennial Maze*, 49. Grenz articulates one of the reasons the Reformers viewed Premillennialism with suspicion: "Officially the churches of the Reformation continued the dominant nonmillennialism of the medieval Roman Catholic church. Wary of the chaos they perceived would arise from the revolutionary ideas of the more radical reformers [e.g., Thomas Münzer and his rebellion of 1534], both Luther and Calvin spurned millenarianism in all forms."
49. Masselink, *Why Thousand Years?*, 28. "The doctrine [of Chiliasm], as we mentioned before, was rejected by both Luther and the other reformers with such absoluteness that it never appeared in any of their confessions. . . . The Augsburg Confession explicitly states that they reject all those who spread the Jewish opinion, that prior to the resurrection of the dead the pious shall receive the administration of the world and then shall bring the ungodly under subjection, (Augsburg Confession, last Art.)."
50. Moreover, based on Calvin's description of ancient Premillennialism, one wonders if he fully understood the view he was rejecting. Calvin seems to suggest that Premillennialists limited the eternal state to only one thousand years. In his *Institutes*, Calvin wrote, "Not long after arose the Millenarians, who limited the reign of Christ to a thousand years. Their fiction is too puerile to require or deserve refutation. Nor does the Revelation, which they quote in favor of their error, afford them any support; for the term of a thousand years, there mentioned, refers not to the eternal blessedness of the Church, but to the various agitations which awaited the Church in its militant state upon earth. But the whole Scripture proclaims that there will be no end of the happiness of the elect, or the punishment of the reprobate. . . . Those who assign the children of God a thousand years to enjoy the inheritance of the future life, little think what dishonor they cast on Christ and his kingdom" (John Calvin, *Institutes of the Christian Religion*, trans. John Allen [repr., Philadelphia: Philip H. Nicklin, 1816], 2:493–94).

Chapter Ten

How Certain Is Futuristic Premillennialism?

John MacArthur

What do Harold Camping, Hal Lindsey, and R. C. Sproul have in common? In spite of their differing positions on the millennium, they each believed that they could be rather specific about the exact time of Christ's second coming in spite of Scripture's warnings not to speculate.

Amillennialist Harold Camping predicted (in 1992) Christ's second coming and the end of this world as we know it for 1994.[1] His latest, updated forecast (in 2005) pointed to May 21, 2011.[2]

Premillennialist Hal Lindsey has also guessed at least twice. First, he predicted 1988.[3] Later, his suggested possible date moved forward to 2007.[4]

Even R. C. Sproul has stepped onto this date-setting stage, albeit in historical retrospect. Being a moderate or partial preterist, he pinpoints Christ's second coming in AD 70. However, to allow for a later general resurrection, he actually proposes a third coming for Christ at an undetermined time in the future.[5]

It seems clear that all three ignored the lessons to be learned from the Old Testament prophets' and the New Testament apostles' unsatisfied curiosity: it is not for human beings to know the precise dates and times at which future prophetic events will occur.

Peter spoke of the Old Testament prophets (1 Pet. 1:10–11):

> As to this salvation, the prophets who prophesied of the grace that would come to you made careful searches and inquiries, seeking to know what person or time the Spirit of Christ within them was indicating as He predicted the sufferings of Christ and the glories to follow.

The New Testament apostles sought Christ's advice on the specific time of His second advent (Matt. 24:3, 36; Mark 13:4, 32).

> As He was sitting on the Mount of Olives, the disciples came to Him privately, saying, "Tell us, when will these things happen, and what will be the sign of Your coming, and of the end of the age?"

> Jesus responded,

> "But of that day and hour no one knows, not even the angels of heaven, nor the Son, but the Father alone."

Also compare Matthew 24:42, 44, 50; 25:13; and Luke 12:39–40, 46, where Christ uses "hour" and "day" in conjunction with parables about His second coming.

Not satisfied with Christ's first answer, approximately seven weeks later on the Mount of Olives, immediately prior to Messiah's departure for heaven, they inquired again (Acts 1:6–7):

> So when they had come together, they were asking Him, saying, "Lord, is it at this time You are restoring the kingdom to Israel?" He said to them, "It is not for you to know times or epochs which the Father has fixed by His own authority; . . ."

Having fielded the earlier question using precise time words, Christ now uses time words of longer duration in a more general sense.

The curiosity factor spread. Paul writes to the Thessalonian church, which apparently had inquired similarly to the Old Testament prophets and New Testament apostles (1 Thess. 5:1–2). He answers,

> Now as to the times and the epochs, brethren, you have no need of anything to be written to you. For you yourselves know full well that the day of the Lord will come just like a thief in the night.

Neither the prophets nor the apostles nor the early church needed to know the times (*chronos*), the seasons (*kaipos*), the day (*hēmera*), or the hour (*hōra*). Whether it be specifics (day/hour) or generalities (times/seasons), both Jesus and Paul taught the futility of such efforts.

So if they couldn't, why do people even try to know or speculate? It will always be because of a woeful ignorance of Scripture, or a shameful misinterpretation of the Bible, or just plain willful disobedience. But the obvious answer from Scripture is that we do not need to know the future with that level of specificity and, therefore, God did not reveal it in His Word.

Does that then mean there is more uncertainty about specifics than certainty? In one way, yes—with respect to a predictable time in the future. But not in regard to the characterization of the coming itself.

Both Christ and Paul make abundantly clear the impossibility of accurately predicting the time of Christ's return. It can't be specifically projected by day and/or hour; nor can it be extrapolated more generally by times and/or seasons. We cannot know and do not need to know the time of Christ's second advent in these precise ways. So let's avoid the impossibility of predicting what only God knows, but has not revealed.

Now, if we cannot know for certain the time (specific or general), then what can we know for sure? What God has disclosed in Scripture!

The following discussion outlines five knowable Futuristic Premillennial certainties regarding Christ's second coming.

The Certainty of Fact[6]

This certainty rests on God's attribute of truthfulness (Is. 65:16) and inability to lie (Titus 1:2). Therefore, whatever God's Word teaches is true. A basic syllogism validates this conclusion: 1) Scripture is the Word of God; 2) the words of God are true; 3) therefore, Scripture is true.

God the Father (Ps. 119:142, 151, 160), God the Son (John 14:6), and God the Spirit (John 14:17; 15:26; 16:13) speak only truth, the whole truth, and nothing but the truth.

Lest anyone doubt that Scripture repeatedly speaks of God's truthful nature, take a moment to digest this short theological statement on God's truthfulness.

> The New Testament emphasis on veracity is most pronounced. It asserts that God is the true God, or the God of truth (John 3:33, 17:3, Rom 3:4, 1 Thess 1:9); that His judgments are veracious and just (Rom 2:2, 3:7, Rev 15:3 and 16:7); that a knowledge of God is a knowledge of the truth (Rom 1:18, 25). It asserts that Christ is the true light (John 1:9), the true bread (John 6:32), and the true vine (John 15:1). Christ bears a true witness (John 8:14, Rev 3:14); His judgments are true (John 8:16); He is a minister of the truth of God (Rom 15:8); He is full of truth (John 1:14); He is personally the truth (John 14:6, Rev 3:7 and 19:11). Further, He speaks the truth of God (John 8:40–47). The Holy Spirit is repeatedly called the Spirit of truth (1 John 5:7, John 14:17, 15:26, and 15:13). His ministry is to guide into truth (John 16:13). The gospel, or Christian faith, is called the word of truth (2 Cor 6:7, Eph 1:13, Col 1:5, 2 Tim 2:15, and James 1:18). It is called the truth of Christ (2 Cor 11:10) and the way of truth (2 Pet 2:2). The Christians are

> said to have found the truth, and the heretic or unbeliever to have missed the truth (1 John 2:27, 2 Thess 2:13, Eph 5:9, and 1 John 3:19). The Church is called the pillar and ground of the truth (1 Tim 3:15).[7]

Now, concerning His future plans, Jesus told the disciples (John 14:3), "I will come again."

The angels told the disciples (Acts 1:11),

> Men of Galilee, why do you stand looking into the sky? This Jesus, who has been taken up from you into heaven, will come in just the same way as you have watched Him go into heaven.

Paul spoke affirmatively to the Thessalonians about Christ's appearing again (1 Thess. 5:23; also 2:19; 3:13; 4:15):

> Now may the God of peace Himself sanctify you entirely; and may your spirit and soul and body be preserved complete, without blame at the coming of our Lord Jesus Christ.

Upon the threefold witness of Christ, the angels, and the apostle Paul in the Word of God, we can rest assured of the certain fact that Jesus will come again. But beyond this point, the various prophetic expectations widely differ. Only Futuristic Premillennialism offers consistent biblical certainties.

The Certainty of Relative Timing

While we cannot know the time of Christ's return in absolute ways, the relative timing—that is, the sequence of events—can be known for certain. Refer to the chart on Futuristic Premillennialism (p. 12) for an illustration of the details in a relative time sequence.

These major certainties include:

- The present church age (Acts 2–Rev. 3)

- That the next major prophetic event is the rapture of the church that precedes Daniel's seventieth week.
- That the seven years of tribulation and God's wrath, which characterize Daniel's seventieth week (Rev. 6–18), follow a pretribulational rapture.
- That at the end of Daniel's seventieth week, Christ comes to earth to set up His kingdom (Rev. 19) according to God's unconditional covenants with and promises to national Israel.
- That Christ then rules over His millennial kingdom (one thousand years in length) promised to Israel, on earth, from Jerusalem, sitting upon the long-ago promised Davidic throne (Rev. 20:4–6).

The Certainty of Satan's Eternal Doom after Christ's One-Thousand Year, Millennial Rule on Earth

Not during the church age but during Christ's kingdom-rule over Israel and the world (Rev. 20:4–6), Satan will be incarcerated (20:1–3). But at the end of the one thousand years, the devil will receive one last opportunity to deceive the world (20:7–8).

The final rebellion against God and His rule will result. All of the anarchists will die in heaven-sent fire (20:9) and Satan ends up in the lake of fire forever and ever (20:10).

The Certainty of All Unbelievers' Eternal Judgment after Christ's One-Thousand Year, Millennial Rule on Earth

Revelation 20:11–15 briefly, but specifically, chronicles the final judgment after Messiah's rule over the world from Jerusalem—the great white throne judgment—where all unbelievers from all of time will be judged guilty of sin as charged by the Righteous Judge and sentenced to an eternal existence in the lake of fire with Satan, the Beast, and the false prophet, away from the presence of God (2 Thess. 1:3–10).

The Certainty of Eternity Future in Which All Believers Will Reside Forever after Christ's One-Thousand Year, Millennial Rule on Earth

What comes after all of this? A new heaven and a new earth (Rev. 21:1). This pictures eternity future in all its glorious splendor (21:2–22:15).

All of these certainties conform to Futuristic Premillennialism, but not completely to Amillennialsm, Historic Premillennialism, nor Postmillennialism. These characteristics have been drawn from Scripture to understand as much as, but no more than, God has revealed in His Word. They have not been imposed on the Scriptures from a preconceived theological system (such as Covenant theology) as occurs in Amillennialism, Historic Premillennialism, and Postmillennialism.

A Final Word

How certain is Futuristic Premillennialism? As certain as the truthfulness and the promises of God in Scripture!

So, the next time someone inquires, "What do you *believe* about the millennium?", you will not have to employ the lame "Promillennial" or "Panmillennial" response spoken of in the preface. Now you can confidently and convincingly answer, "I *believe* in the biblical certainties of Futuristic Premillennialism!"

These prophetic certainties should not only affect your beliefs, but also your *behavior* (2 Pet. 3:13–14, 18).

> But according to His promise we are looking for new heavens and a new earth, in which righteousness dwells. Therefore, beloved, since you look for these things, be diligent to be found by Him in peace, spotless and blameless, . . . grow in the grace and knowledge of our Lord and Savior Jesus Christ. To Him be the glory, both now and to the day of eternity. Amen.

So with the apostle John let us *beseech* Messiah, "Come, Lord Jesus" (Rev. 22:20).

Notes

1. Harold Camping, *1994?* (New York: Vantage Press, 1992), 441–81.
2. Harold Camping, *Time Has an End!* (New York: Vantage Press, 2005), 440–71.
3. Hal Lindsey, *The Late Great Planet Earth* (Grand Rapids: Zondervan, 1970), 53–54.
4. Hal Lindsey, *The Final Battle* (Palos Verdes, CA: Western Front, 1995), 262–63.
5. R. C. Sproul, *The Last Days according to Jesus* (Grand Rapids: Baker, 1998), 170.
6. To be fair about this certainty of fact, all (with rare exception) Futuristic Premillennialists, Historic Premillennialists, Amillennialists, and Postmillennialists, who take the Bible seriously, agree. Over the remaining certainties they disagree.
7. Bernard Ramm, *The Pattern of Religious Authority* (Grand Rapids: Eerdmans, 1959), 22.

Recommended Resources

Futuristic Premillennialism

Benware, Paul N. *Understanding End Times Prophecy.* Rev. ed. Chicago: Moody, 2006.

Eerdman, Martin. *The Millennial Controversy in the Early Church.* Eugene, OR: Wipf and Stock, 2005.

Feinberg, Charles L. *Millennialism: The Two Major Views.* 3rd ed. 1980. Reprint, Winona Lake, IN: BMH, 2009.

MacArthur, John. *Because the Time Is Near.* Chicago: Moody, 2007.

McClain, Alva J. *The Greatness of the Kingdom.* 1959. Reprint, Winona Lake, IN: BMH, 2009.

Thomas, Robert L. *Revelation 1–7: An Exegetical Commentary.* Chicago: Moody, 1992.

____________. *Revelation 8–22: An Exegetical Commentary.* Chicago: Moody, 1995.

Israel

Diprose, Ronald E. *Israel in the Development of Christian Thought.* Rome: Instituto Biblico Evangelico Italiano, 2000.

Fruchtenbaum, Arnold G. *Israelology: The Missing Link in Systematic Theology.* Rev. ed. Tustin, CA: Ariel Ministries, 2001.

Horner, Barry. *Future Israel.* Nashville, TN: B&H, 2007.

House, H. Wayne, ed. *Israel: The Land and the People.* Grand Rapids: Kregel, 1998.

Larson, David. *Jews, Gentiles, and the Church.* Grand Rapids: Discovery House, 1995.

Vlach, Michael. *Has the Church Replaced Israel?* Nashville, TN: B&H, 2010.

Pretribulationism

Ice, Thomas, and Timothy Demy, eds. *When the Trumpet Sounds.* Eugene, OR: Harvest House, 1995.

LaHaye, Tim. *The Rapture.* Eugene, OR: Harvest House, 2002.

____________. *The Return.* Grand Rapids: Kregel, 1999.

Showers, Renald. *MARANATHA–Our Lord, Come!* Bellmawr, NJ: Friends of Israel, 1995.

Glossary

Amillennialism. A fourth-century AD school of prophetic thought that teaches that the church is spiritual Israel, Christ rules a heavenly kingdom (never one on earth), and all end-time events occur almost simultaneously just prior to eternity future commencing.

Antinomianism. Being opposed to God's law and thus living in defiant disobedience to Scripture.

Arminianism. Theology based on the thought of James Arminius (1560–1609) that is opposed to Calvinism, especially on the role of God's sovereignty in salvation.

Calvinism. Theology based on the thought of John Calvin (1509–1564), especially as it relates to Reformed theology.

Church Age. The time period from Pentecost (Acts 2) until the rapture of the church to heaven.

Covenant Theology. A seventeenth-century AD system of theology based on covenants not spoken of directly in Scripture.

Daniel's Seventieth Week. A time spoken of in Daniel 9:24–27 that corresponds to the seven-year period of tribulation following the rapture of the church and just prior to Christ's millennial reign on earth.

Dispensation. Not merely a period of time, but different administrations in the eternal outworking of God's redemptive purpose. However, the way of salvation by God's grace through faith in Jesus Christ remains the same in each dispensation.

Dispensationalism. A nineteenth-century AD school of biblical interpretation that consistently employs normal hermeneutics throughout Scripture.

Dispensational Premillennialism. Another term for Futuristic Premillennialism.

Ecclesiology. Theological study of the church.

Eschatology. Theological study of future things.

Eternity Future. A never-ending era following Christ's millennial reign spoken of in Revelation 21–22.

Exegesis. Drawing the true meaning out of a biblical text by skillful application of hermeneutical principles.

Futuristic Premillennialism. A school of prophetic thought that results from a normal use of hermeneutics and produces a futuristic view of Revelation 6–20, including Christ's one-thousand-year millennial kingdom. This was the predominant view of the early church.

Hermeneutics. Generally accepted principles of interpreting literature, especially the Bible.

Historic (Covenantal) Premillennialism. A prophetic school of thought that believes in a future reign of Christ on earth but interprets Revelation 6–18 as having already been fulfilled, thus the name "historic."

Midtribulationism. Places the rapture at the midpoint of Daniel's seventieth week.

Millennium. A one-thousand-year period of time during which Messiah will rule over the world while seated on the Davidic throne in Jerusalem, described in Revelation 20.

Patristic Era. The second to fifth centuries AD, which encompasses the period of the early church fathers.

Postmillennialism. An eighteenth-century AD prophetic school of thought that anticipates the church triumphing over the world prior to Christ's second coming.

Posttribulationism. Places the rapture at the end of Daniel's seventieth week.

Premillennialism. A second-century AD prophetic school of thought teaching that Christ rules over an earthly kingdom after His second coming.

Preterism. A prophetic school of thought that proposes that Christ's second coming occurred in AD 70.

Pretribulationism. Places the rapture before Daniel's seventieth week.

Rapture. The snatching of the church out of the world by Christ spoken of in 1 Thessalonians 4:13–18.

Reformed Theology. A school of theology that emphasizes God's sovereignty and human sinfulness in relation to salvation.

Replacement Theology. A school of theology that teaches that the church has replaced Israel as the object of God's blessing.

Soteriology. Theological study of salvation.

Supersessionism. The belief that the church has superseded Israel as God's chosen people of blessing.

Tribulation. See "Daniel's Seventieth Week."

Type. A literary device whereby a historical person or event symbolically represents a person or event yet future—the future event or person sometimes being called the "antitype." For example, the Passover lamb of the Old Testament (Ex. 12) is commonly understood to be a *type* of Christ (who in this case is the *antitype* of the Passover lamb). The study of types is known as *typology*. Futuristic Premillennialism denies that Israel is a type of the church in the sense that the church replaces Israel.

Scripture Index

Old Testament

Genesis

2:8 156
2:24 71
3:8–21 81
6 194
6:18 71
9:8–17 71
12 78
12:1 72
12:1–3 72, 107
12:2 72
12:2–3 108
12:3 72
13:14–15 174
13:14–17 11, 72
13:15 72
13:17 72
15:1–21 71, 72
15:6 43
15:7–17 71
15:18 72, 174
17:1–21 72
17:1–22 71
17:2 72
17:4 72
17:4–6 72
17:6 64
17:7 72, 151
17:7–8 72, 74
17:8 72
17:9–14 72
17:13 72
17:14 72
17:19 72
22:15–18 72
22:17 72
22:18 72, 109
26:2–5 71, 72
26:3 72
26:4 72, 109
26:24 72
28:13 72
28:13–14 72
28:13–17 71, 72
28:14 72, 109
28:15 72

35:10–12 72
35:11 72
35:11–12 72
35:12 72
49:10 64

Exodus
2:24 71
6:4 72
8:22 90
9:4 90
9:26 90
10:23 90
11:7 90
19–20 71
19:6 109
19:16 100
24 71
32:13 11

Leviticus
26:42 71, 72
26:43 72
26:44 72

Numbers
23:19 77
25:10–13 71

Deuteronomy
4:31 72
7:6 53
7:9 71
26:19 109
28 80, 81
28–29 110
28:1–14 80
28:15–68 80
28:46 81
30:1–6 110, 111

Joshua
21:45 80
23:14 80
23:15–16 80

1 Samuel
13:3 100
15:29 77

2 Samuel
2:28 100
6:15 100
7:8–16 74
7:8–17 98
7:12 72
7:12–16 71, 72
7:12–17 65
7:13 72
7:14 72
7:15 72
7:16 72
18:16 100
20:1 100
20:22 100
23:5 72, 74

1 Kings
1:34 100
2:3–4 72
8:23 71
8:56 80

2 Kings
9:13 100
13:23 72

1 Chronicles
16:15–17 74
17: 14 72
17:11 72
17:11–14 77
17:12 72
17:13 72
17:14 72

2 Chronicles
6:14 71
13:5 72
20:28 100
21:7 72, 74

Nehemiah
1:5 71
4:20 100
9:32 71

Job
9:3 70
33:23 70

Psalms
2:6–8 174
2:9 174
22 64

47:5 100
50:10 70
67 109
67:1 109
67:2 109
67:7 109
74:20 72
81:3 100
89:3 72
89:3–4 74
89:19–29 74
89:28 72
89:29–37 162
89-30–32 72
89-33–37 72
89:34 72
89:36 72, 74
89:39 72
90:4 70
105:8 72
105:9–10 71
105:10 72
105:11 72
105:14–15 72
106:44–46 72
106:45 72
110:2 72
111:5 72
111:9 72
119:142 200
119:151 200
119:160 200
132:12 72
150:3 100

Ecclesiastes
6:6 70
7:28 70

Isaiah
11:3–5 174
11:4 174
11:6–10 168
11:7–9 174
11:9 174
11:11 81
12:3–4 174
19:24–25 105, 106
24:5 72
24:21–22 173
24:22 140
27:13 100
30:23–24 174
30:25 156
32:17 174
33:24 174
35:1–2 174
35:5–6 174
35:6–7 167, 168
35:7 174
41:8 35
42 150
44:3 168
45:4 150
46:9–11 14
49:3 113
49:3–6 112, 113
49:5 113
49:8 73, 113
54:10 73
55:3 73
55:10–11 17
55:12 132
59:21 73
61 62
61:1–2 101
61:3 174
61:7 174
61:8 73
65:9 150
65:16 200
65:20 90, 174
65:22 150

Jeremiah
6:1 100
23:6 11
24:6–7 74
25:11–12 16
30:1–3 112
30:4–11 162
30:5–8 174
30:7 98
31:12 74
31:15 63
31:25 79
31:31–3 25, 71, 171
31:32 73
31:33 73
31:34 73
31:35 79
31:35–37 79
31:37 79

31:40 75, 78
32:36–44 81
32:38 171
32:40 73
33:19–26 79
33:20 79
33:20–22 72
33:22 79
33:25–26 72
50:5 73

Ezekiel
8–11 81
16:60 72, 73
16:62 73
20:33–38 170
20:37 73
20:39–44 81
28:25–26 81
34:25 73
34:26 167
34:28–29 75
36:22–30 111
37:11–28 98
37:12–14 102
37:15–28 79
37:25 75, 78
37:26 73
37:26–27 73
40:1–48:35 11
44:7 73

Daniel
2 64
2:34–35 83
2:35 174
2:44–45 83
9:1–19 16
9:4 71
9:27 12
11:31 12
12:2 102, 130, 131
12:10 170

Hosea
2:18ff 73
2:19–20 73
11:1 63, 114

Joel
2:1 100
2:15 100
2:21–27 174
2:26 167
2:26–27 75, 78
2:30 168
2:31 168
3:14–16 168
3:18–20 75, 112
3:20 112

Amos
9 144, 145
9:11–15 76
9:13–15 156
9:14–15 11
9:15 78

Micah
4:2 174
5:2 64

Zephaniah
3:8 140
3:14–20 76
3:20 78, 112

Zechariah
1:9 77
2:11 106
6:1–3 156
9:11 73
11:10–11 73
13:8–9 170
14 106
14:1 77
14:5 83
14.9 83
14:9 73, 106
14:9–11 11
14:11 77, 81
14:16 106, 174

Malachi
1:3 73

New Testament

Matthew
1:1 72
2:14–18 63
2:15 63, 114
5:7 53
7:21 140
10:1–9 173
11:12 86
12:22–29 68
12:29 86, 138
12:30 94
12:41 173
13 94
13:19 86, 87, 126
13:24–43 97
13:30 94
13:40 94
13:41–42 90
13:47–50 97
13:48–50 94
19:28 72, 106, 114, 165, 168
20:21 163
21:1–22:14 149
21:35 149
21:36 149
21:41 149
21:43 129, 149
22:31 99
23:37–39 115, 116
23:39 116
24 94
24–25 86, 93, 98
24:3 198
24:8–9 101
24:15 12
24:21 101
24:27 83
24:30 83
24:31 93, 100
24:36 99, 198
24:37 83
24:37–39 97
24:37–41 93
24:37–42 97
24:39 83
24:42 83, 198
24:44 83, 198
24:50 198
25:1–13 88
25:6 97
25:13 198
25:31 72, 83, 90,94
25:31, 34 94
25:31–32 93
25:31–46 12, 93, 97, 140
25:34 93
25:41 90
26:28 73
28:19–20 15

Mark
4:15 126
9:12 168
10:37 163
12:26 99
13:4 198
13:32 99, 198
14:13 97

Luke
1:31–33 163
1:32 114, 173
1:32–33 106
1:33 73
1:72 71
8 126
8:12 126
8:31–32 126
12:39–40 198
12:46 198
13:34–35 115
13:35 116
17:12 97
22:24 163
22:28–30 165
22:29–30 114
22:31 127
24:45 165

John
1:9 200
1:14 200
1:17 43
3:3–5 140
3:33 200
4:21 139
4:23 139
5:25 128, 139

5:28–29 130, 131, 139
6 141
6:15 87
7:34 92
7:42 72
8:14 200
8:16 200
8:40–47 200
8:44 126
10:12 87
10:28 87
10:29 87
12:31 126
14 93
14:1 92
14:1–3 92, 93
14:3 92
14:6 200
14:17 200
14:30 126
15:1 200
15:13 200
15:26 200
16:2 139
16:11 126
16:13 200
17:3 200
17:11–16 176
17:15 95, 96
18:36 176
18:37 72

Acts

1:3 165
1:6 106, 166, 167, 168
1:6–7 116, 198
1:7 116, 166
1:8 166
1:11 201
2 22, 167
2:30 72
2:42 15
3 167, 168
3:6–7 167
3:12 30
3:12–26 167
3:18 167
3:18–21 167
3:20–21 167
3:25 168
4:4 70
4:8 30
4:10 30
5:3 68, 126
5:20 15
5:21 30
5:31 30
5:35 30
7:8 72
8:39 87
12:5 95
13:32–35 16
13:42–44 16
17:26a 105
20:20 14
20:25 14
20:27 14, 15
20:29–30 91
21:28 30
23:10 87
24:15 130, 131
26:18 126
28:15 97

Romans

1:16 32
1:18 200
1:25 200
2:28–29 153, 200
3 171
3:4 200
3:7 200
3:24–26 43
4:3 43
4:9–12 34
4:11 72
4:13 72
4:16 34
4:16–18 72
4:24 43
4:25 43
9 141
9–11 117, 119, 158
9:3–4 30
9:3b–4 117
9:4 71
9:6 35, 82, 152, 153, 169
9:24 32
10:1 30
10:4 49
10:9–10 13

11 171
11:1 117, 121, 153, 169
11:2 158
11:11–12 117
11:11–32 73
11:12 158
11:17 170
11:25 74, 158, 170
11:25–27 25, 118
11:25–29 169
11:26 33, 153, 158, 174
11:26–27 11, 106
11:27 73
11:28 118
11:28–29 150
11:29 74, 151, 158, 162
14:10 12
15:8 200

1 Corinthians 150
1:8 158
1:24 32
3:10–15 12, 91
7:5 126
10:8 70
11:25 73
12:13 32
15 86
15:23 102
15:50–58 93, 102
15:51 88
15:51–52 12, 87, 88
15:51–57 94
15:52 100

2 Corinthians
1:10 95
1:20 77
2:11 126, 173
3:6 73, 156
4:4 68, 126, 127, 173
5:10 12, 91
6:7 200
11:2–3 68
11:3 126
11:10 200
11:13–15 68, 126
11:14 173
12:2 87
12:4 87
12:7 126, 173

Galatians
2:14 32
2:15 32
3:7 34, 38, 72
3:7–9 109
3:8 72
3:16 72
3:17 72
3:21–22 43
3:26–29 72
3:28 32, 105
3:29 34, 35, 38, 109
4:24 71
4:24–31 63
6:16 82, 152, 159

Ephesians
1 141
1:13 200
2 31
2:2 126, 173
2:4–6 128
2:8–10 13
2:11–15 31
2:11–22 105
2:12 71
2:15 31
2:16 31
4:25 91
4:27 126, 173
5:7 91
5:9 201
6:11 173
6:11–17 127

Colossians
1:5 200
1:13 173
2:12–13 128
2:15 138

1 Thessalonians
1:9 200
1:10 95

2:13–14 91
2:18 68, 126, 173
2:19 201
3:5 126
3:13 201
4 86, 91, 92, 99
4:3–8 91
4:9 99
4:13–15 92
4:13–18 12, 16, 91, 92, 93, 98, 99, 140
4:15–16 93, 201
4:15–17 93, 94
4:16 100
4:16–17 87, 88, 93
4:17 92, 93, 96, 100
4:18 16, 92
5 99
5:1 99, 100
5:1–2 199
5:3 140
5:4–8 88
5:6 97, 99
5:6–9 16, 97
5:11 16
5:23 201

2 Thessalonians
1:1 150
1:3–10 202
1:4 91
1:5–10 16
1:6–10 101
2:12 140
2:13 150, 201

1 Timothy
2:9–15 32, 105
3:15 201
5:15 173
5:21 150

2 Timothy
2:15 13, 15, 200
2:26 127, 173
3:16–17 13

Titus
1:2 77, 200
2:11–14 16
2:13 16

Hebrews
2:14–15 138
6:13–18 72, 163
7:22 73
8:6 73
8:8–12 25
8:8–13 25
8:10 73
9:15 73
9:28 88
10:16 73
10:17 73
10:29 73
12:1 91
12:24 73
13:17 32, 105
13:20 73

James
1:18 200
1:27 95
2:14–26 51
4:7 173
5:7–11 16

1 Peter 91
1:4 95
1:10–11 15, 198
2:6 150
5:8 68, 126

2 Peter
1:10–11 101
2:1 91
2:2 200
3:1–13 16
3:8 70, 132
3:11–13 16
3:13–14 203
3:14–15 97, 99
3:14–18 13
3:18 203

1 John
2:18 139
2:27 201
3:2–3 16
3:8 138

3:14 128
3:19 201
4:1–3 91
4:4 126
5:7 200
5:19 96, 126

Jude
4 91
21 95
23 87

Revelation
1 69
1–3 12, 82, 89
1:3 13, 16
1:4 69
2-3 89, 99
2:10 69
2:26–27 173
3:6–18 86
3:7 200
3:7–13 94
3:10 94, 96, 98
3:14 200
3:22 82
4–5 98
4–19 98
4–20 69
6–18 61, 91, 202
6–19 12, 82, 89, 99, 124
6:1–8 101
6:9–11 96
6:17 69
7 89
7:1–8 120, 170
7:4–8 119, 120
7:9 119, 120, 170
7:14 96, 101
9:1–3 126
9:5 69
9:15 69
11:1–2 63
11:2 69
11:2–3 12
11:3 69
11:3–13 170
11:13 70
11:15 73, 100
12 90, 134, 135, 136
12–19 137
12:1 69
12:5 73, 87
12:7–12 134
12:9 127, 135, 137
12:12 136
12:13 90
12:14 12
13–19 140
13:1 69
13:5 12
13:14 127, 137, 140
13:18 69
14 89
14:1–5 170
14:6 170
14:7 69
14:14 101
14:20 69
15:3 200
16:1–21 168
16:7 200
16:13 69
16:14 137, 140
17:9–10 69
18:20 98
18:23 127, 137, 140
19 94, 134, 136, 137, 140, 157, 176, 202
19–20 137
19–22 124
19:6–10 91
19:11 157, 200
19:11–16 83, 97, 101, 124, 176
19:11–21 134
19:15–16 73
19:16 173
19:17–19 140
19:17–21 124
19:18 140
19:19–20 137
19:20 127, 137, 140

20 12, 68, 69, 70, 71, 124, 126, 127, 128, 130, 131, 133, 134, 136, 137, 138, 139, 140, 157, 176, 183, 189
20:1 124, 134, 135, 136
20:1–2 68
20:1–3 124, 125, 202
20:1–6 11, 123, 134, 137, 138, 157, 164, 171, 176
20:1–10 67, 68, 73, 178
20:2 60, 68, 139
20:3 60, 68, 127, 134, 136, 157
20:4 60, 68, 83, 102, 128, 129, 139, 140, 157
20:4–5 102, 128
20:4–6 124, 128, 129, 138, 202
20:5 60, 68, 128, 129, 139
20:5–6 102
20:6 60, 68, 102, 189
20:7 60, 68, 126, 139
20:7–8 68, 202
20:7–9 137
20:7–10 90, 124
20:8 126, 134
20:9 202
20:10 137, 202
20:11–15 12, 124, 128, 202
20:14 1–2
20:37–40 139
21 107
21–22 12, 81, 124
21:1 203
21:2–22:15 203
21:8 102
21:10–14 120
21:12 69, 120
21:14 69, 120
21:24, 26 107
21:24–26 106
22 107
22:3 81
22:7 13, 16
22:16 82, 89
22:20 204

Apocryphal Works

1 Enoch
6–36 163
91–104 163

2 Enoch
33:1 163

4 Ezra
7:28–29 163

Isaac
6–8 163

Jubilee
23:27 163

Pseudipigrapha

Psalm of Solomon
11:1–8 163

Ancient Texts

Irenaeus
Against Heresies
5.30.4 182

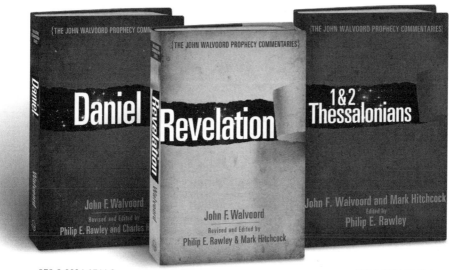

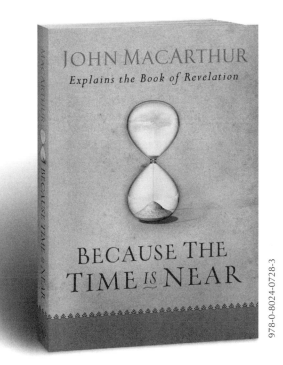